An Introduction to the Gospels and Acts

An Introduction to the Gospels and Acts

Charles B. Puskas *&* David Crump

WILLIAM B. EERDMANS PUBLISHING COMPANY
GRAND RAPIDS, MICHIGAN / CAMBRIDGE, U.K.

© 2008 Wm. B. Eerdmans Publishing Co.

Published 2008 by
Wm. B. Eerdmans Publishing Co.
2140 Oak Industrial Drive N.E., Grand Rapids, Michigan 49505 /
P.O. Box 163, Cambridge CB3 9PU U.K.

Printed in the United States of America

13 12 11 10 09 08   7 6 5 4 3 2 1

Library of Congress Cataloging-in-Publication Data

Puskas, Charles B.
    An introduction to the Gospels and Acts / Charles B. Puskas & David Crump.
       p.   cm.
    Includes bibliographical references and index.
    ISBN 978-0-8028-4557-3 (pbk.: alk. paper)
    1. Bible. N.T. Gospels — Introductions.   2. Bible. N.T. Acts — Introductions.
    I. Crump, David, 1956-   II. Title.

BS2548.P85   2008
226′.061 — dc22

                        2008011993

www.eerdmans.com

Contents

Illustrations

Tables

Preface

This book was born from the collaboration and friendship of two different types of scholars — one mainline, the other more evangelical in orientation. Several years ago, as we visited together in my office, I (David Crump) shared my frustration at failing to discover a single-volume, introductory textbook to both the Gospels and the book of Acts. For, as the reader will soon discover, the Gospel of Luke and the Acts of the Apostles were originally written as a single, two-volume work, so that neither may be properly understood apart from the other. As fortune (or Providence) would have it, Charles Puskas had once tried to fill this void with a book that was still waiting to see the light of day. He generously entrusted his manuscript to me and asked for my input, something he received most graciously as I offered my additions and subtractions to his already excellent work. I am happy to say that our collaboration has resulted in the present text, which not only meets a definite need but does so in a rather distinctive fashion.

Beginning with the Big Picture

Exploring new territory requires taking in the big picture before choosing a particular course for the journey. Similarly, introducing students to New Testament studies should open their eyes to the breadth of opinion throughout the discipline rather than focusing on only one way of thinking. This book attempts to do the former by introducing its readers to the various ways historical and literary evidence can be evaluated depending on one's presuppositions and different methodological perspectives. Since the authors themselves hold different opinions on these issues, we have decided that rather than asserting a certain set of conclusions, whether liberal, conservative, critical, or traditional, we will invite our readers to share in the debate. We believe that this approach will better serve the purposes of education as opposed to indoctrination. It is too easy for students merely to learn the particular views found in selected assigned readings without being introduced to the broader context, conflicting evidence, and alternative ways of reading the same pieces of evidence. Although some may claim that the authors' divergent perspectives produce a degree of incoherence in failing to advance any particular set of critical conclusions, we believe that this restraint actually serves the long-term goals of education more effectively. The reader is asked to think about the evidence and how it relates to the questions under discussion (such as a book's authorship, date of composition, place of origin, and intended audience), then analyze the different conclusions and consider an argument's persuasiveness. This is the process by which we can reach informed opinions.

What You Will Find Inside

This book can be helpful to a wide range of readers: undergraduate students at public, private, secular, and religious (mainline or evangelical) institutions, as well as seminary students, pastors, teachers of religion and Bible courses, and interested laypersons. Chapter 1 is devoted to the historical and cultural contexts, Jewish and Greco-Roman, of the New Testament. This is followed by a chapter on methodology introducing the fields of historical, source, form, and redaction criticism. Case studies are provided for each of these methods in order to illustrate how they are applied and the results a reader can expect from each. Not only is Luke-Acts studied as a literary whole, but the important theological themes unique to each Gospel, as seen through redaction, narrative, and rhetorical analysis, are also explained. Because of their concern for the length of the book and for not overloading the student with too much theory, the authors have decided not to focus on the newer methods of sociological, ideological, and reader-response criticism, although some are cited in the footnotes.

Chapters 1 and 2 are adapted from material in *An Introduction to the*

New Testament (Peabody, Mass.: Hendrickson, 1989). All copyrights in this work have been reassigned by the publisher to Charles Puskas, the author.

Many thanks to Michael Thomson, Linda Bieze, and Craig Noll, on the staff of Eerdmans, for their great help in preparing and producing this book. Even deeper thanks go to our spouses, Susan Puskas and Terry Crump, for their encouragement and support.

Abbreviations

Modern Publications and Series

AB	Anchor Bible
ABD	*Anchor Bible Dictionary*. Edited by D. N. Freedman. 6 vols. New York: Doubleday, 1992
BC	*The Beginnings of Christianity*. Edited by J. F. Foakes Jackson and K. Lake. 5 vols. London: Macmillan, 1920-33
BR	*Biblical Research*
BTB	*Biblical Theology Bulletin*
BZ	*Biblische Zeitschrift*
CBQ	*Catholic Biblical Quarterly*
DB(H)	*Dictionary of the Bible*. Edited by J. Hastings. 5 vols. New York: Charles Scribner's Sons, 1898-1905
EncJud	*Encyclopedia Judaica*. 16 vols. Jerusalem, 1972
ETL	*Ephemerides theologicae lovanienses*
ExpTim	*Expository Times*
GNC	Good News Commentary
HBD	*HarperCollins Bible Dictionary*. Edited by P. J. Achtemeier et al. Rev. ed. San Francisco: HarperSanFrancisco, 1996
HibJ	*Hibbert Journal*
HNTC	Harper's New Testament Commentaries
HUCA	*Hebrew Union College Annual*
IB	*Interpreter's Bible*. Edited by G. A. Buttrick et al. 12 vols. New York: Abingdon-Cokesbury, 1951-57
ICC	International Critical Commentary

IDB	*The Interpreter's Dictionary of the Bible.* Edited by G. A. Buttrick. 4 vols. Nashville: Abingdon, 1962
IDBSupp	*The Interpreter's Dictionary of the Bible, Supplementary Volume.* Edited by K. Crim. Nashville: Abingdon, 1976
JBL	*Journal of Biblical Literature*
JBR	*Journal of Bible and Religion*
JETS	*Journal of the Evangelical Theological Society*
JRS	*Journal of Roman Studies*
JSNT	*Journal for the Study of the New Testament*
JTS	*Journal of Theological Studies*
LB	*Linguistica Biblica*
NAB	New American Bible
NCBC	New Century Bible Commentary
NEB	New English Bible
NIC	New International Commentary
NIV	New International Version
NJB	New Jerusalem Bible
NJBC	New Jerome Bible Commentary
NIDB	*New Interpreter's Dictionary of the Bible.* 5 vols. Nashville: Abingdon, 2006
NIV	New International Version
NovT	*Novum Testamentum*
NRSV	New Revised Standard Version
NTS	*New Testament Studies*
NW	New World Translation
PRSt	*Perspectives in Religious Studies*
RB	*Revue biblique*
RelSRev	*Religious Studies Review*
RSV	Revised Standard Version
SBL	Society of Biblical Literature
SJT	*Scottish Journal of Theology*
TBT	*The Bible Today*
TDNT	*Theological Dictionary of the New Testament.* Edited by G. Kittel and G. Friedrich. Translated by G. W. Bromiley. 10 vols. Grand Rapids: Eerdmans, 1964-76
TZ	*Theologische Zeitschrift*
WBC	Word Biblical Commentary
ZPEB	*Zondervan Pictorial Encyclopedia of the Bible.* Edited by M. C. Tenney. 5 vols. Grand Rapids: Zondervan, 1975

Books of the Bible

Acts	Acts of the Apostles
1–2 Chr	1–2 Chronicles
Col	Colossians
1–2 Cor	1–2 Corinthians
Dan	Daniel
Deut	Deuteronomy
Eccl	Ecclesiastes
Eph	Ephesians
Esth	Esther
Exod	Exodus
Ezek	Ezekiel
Gal	Galatians
Gen	Genesis
Hab	Habakkuk
Hag	Haggai
Heb	Hebrews
Hos	Hosea
Isa	Isaiah
Jas	James
Jer	Jeremiah
Josh	Joshua
Judg	Judges
1–2 Kgs	1–2 Kings
Lam	Lamentations
Lev	Leviticus
Mal	Malachi
Matt	Matthew
Mic	Micah
Nah	Nahum
Neh	Nehemiah
Num	Numbers
Obad	Obadiah
1–2 Pet	1–2 Peter
Phil	Philippians
Phlm	Philemon
Prov	Proverbs
Ps	Psalms

Rev	Revelation
Rom	Romans
1–2 Sam	1–2 Samuel
1–2 Thess	1–2 Thessalonians
1–2 Tim	1–2 Timothy
Zech	Zechariah
Zeph	Zephaniah

Apocrypha and Old Testament Pseudepigrapha

2 Bar.	2 Baruch
1–2 Macc	1–2 Maccabees
Pss. Sol.	Psalms of Solomon
Sir	Sirach/Ecclesiasticus
T. Adam	Testament of Adam

Tractates of the Mishnah and Talmud

m.	Mishnah
b.	Babylonian Talmud
Ber.	Berakot
Ketub.	Ketubbot
Meg.	Megillah
Menah.	Menahot
Mid.	Middot
Pesah.	Pesahim
Roš Haš.	Roš Haššanah
Yad.	Yadayim
Yebam.	Yebamot
Zebah.	Zebahim

Dead Sea Scrolls and Related Texts

CD	Cairo Genizah copy of the Damascus Document
1QpHab	Pesher Habakkuk
1QS	Serek hayahad, or Rule of the Community
1QSa	Rule of the Congregation (Appendix a to 1QS)
4QFlor	Florilegium, or Midrash on Eschatology
4Q254	Commentary on Genesis

Early Writers

Eusebius, *Hist. eccl.*	*Historia ecclesiastica*
Ign. *Eph.*	Ignatius, *To the Ephesians*
Ign. *Magn.*	Ignatius, *To the Magnesians*
Ign. *Pol.*	Ignatius, *To Polycarp*
Ign. *Smyrn.*	Ignatius, *To the Smyrnaeans*
Ign. *Trall.*	Ignatius, *To the Trallians*
Josephus, *Ag. Ap.*	*Against Apion*
Josephus, *Ant.*	*Jewish Antiquities*
Josephus, *Life*	*The Life*
Josephus, *War*	*Jewish War*

General Abbreviations

A.D.	*anno Domini*
B.C.	before Christ
bk(s).	book(s)
C.E.	Common Era
cent.	century
cf.	*confer,* compare
ch(s).	chapter(s)
ed(s).	editor(s); edition; edited by
e.g.	*exempli gratia,* for example
esp.	especially
et al.	*et alii,* and others
i.e.	*id est,* that is
L	material in Luke not found in Matthew or Mark
LXX	Septuagint
M	material in Matthew not found in Mark or Luke
n.	note
n.s.	new series
NT	New Testament
OT	Old Testament
repr.	reprinted
rev.	revised
trans.	translated by
v(v).	verse(s)
vol(s).	volume(s)

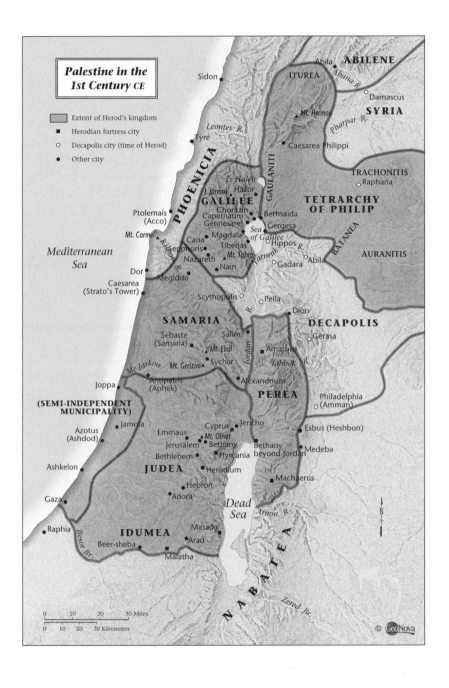

**Palestine in the
1st Century** CE

Extent of Herod's kingdom
■ Herodian fortress city
○ Decapolis city (time of Herod)
● Other city

ABILENE

Abila

ITUREA

Abana R.

Sidon

Damascus

▲ Mt. Hermon

SYRIA

Leontes R.

Pharpar R.

Tyre

Caesarea Philippi

PHOENICIA

GAULANITIS

TRACHONITIS

○ Raphana

Lk. Huleh

J. Jarmuk ▲ Hazor

GALILEE

TETRARCHY
OF PHILIP

Ptolemais
(Acco)

Chorazin
Capernaum ●
Gennesaret ●

Bethsaida
Gergesa

Mt. Carmel

Cana ● Magdala

*Sea
of Galilee*

BATANEA

Kishon R.

Sepphoris ●

Tiberias ●

Hippos ○

R.

AURANITIS

Nazareth ●

▲ Mt. Tabor

Yarmuk

Gadara ○

Abila

*Mediterranean
Sea*

Dor ●

Nain ●

Megiddo ●

● Gadara

Caesarea
(Strato's Tower) ■

Scythopolis ○

● Pella

Dion ○

SAMARIA

DECAPOLIS

Sebaste
(Samaria) ●

Salim?

Jordan R.

○ Gerasa

▲ Mt. Ebal

● Amathus

Me Jarkon

Mt. Gerizim ▲ Sychar

Jabbok R.

Joppa ●

Antipatris
(Aphek) ●

● Alexandrium

PEREA

**(SEMI-INDEPENDENT
MUNICIPALITY)**

Azotus
(Ashdod) ●

Jamnia ●

Emmaus ●

Cyprus ■ Jericho ●

Philadelphia
○ (Amman)

Esbus (Heshbon) ○

▲ Mt. Olivet

Jerusalem ● ● Bethany

Bethany
beyond Jordan

● Medeba

Ashkelon ●

Bethlehem ●

■ Hyrcania

JUDEA

■ Herodium

● Machaerus

Gaza ●

● Hebron

● Adora

*Dead
Sea*

Arnon R.

Raphia ●

Masada ■

IDUMEA

● Arad

Beer-sheba ●

Besor Bk.

▲ Malatha

NABATEA

N

0   10   20   30 Miles

0   10   20   30 Kilometers

Zered Bk.

© GeoNova

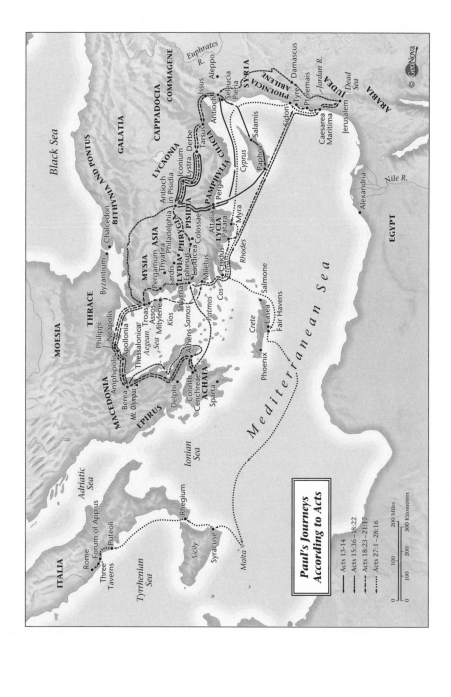

Paul's Journeys According to Acts

Acts 13–14
Acts 15:36 – 18:22
Acts 18:23 – 21:17
Acts 27:1 – 28:16

0   100   200 Miles
0 100 200 300 Kilometers

CHAPTER 1

The Historical Context of the Gospels and Acts

Historical background is as important to NT study as water is to a fish; just as gills and fins make sense only for an animal living in an aquatic environment, so the four gospels and the book of Acts require an accurately reconstructed historical environment before they will properly make sense to today's reader. In fact, understanding historical context is crucial for the serious study of *any* written document (postmodern literary theories notwithstanding). For example, no thoughtful interpreter of the U.S. Constitution can safely ignore the importance of eighteenth-century mercantilism, the prevalence of social-contract theory, and ideas of popular sovereignty. So it is with NT study. If we are to accurately interpret these early Christian writings, historical details such as the widespread influence of Hellenism and Judaism, as well as the provincial policies of first-century Rome, cannot be ignored. So, before looking at the books themselves, we begin with an overview of a millennium of Holy Land history.

The Greco-Roman Context of the New Testament

Hellenization under Alexander the Great

The NT was not written in Aramaic, the native language of Jesus and his disciples, or in Latin, the language of Rome, but in a common Greek dialect of the first century. Why was it written in Greek? The use of this language is chiefly due to the efforts of one extraordinary man: Alexander of Macedon (356-323 B.C.).

Alexander's background is impressive; his achievements are astonishing.[1] As the son of an ambitious Macedonian ruler (Philip II), Alexander studied ethics, geography, and Homer's *Iliad* under the famous Greek philosopher Aristotle; he also received intensive military training from experienced warriors. When he succeeded his father in 336 B.C., young Alexander sought to consolidate his father's power and launch an ambitious campaign eastward. Within ten short years, Alexander and his enormous army of 30,000 infantry and 4,500 cavalry conquered Asia Minor (modern Turkey), Syria, Palestine, Egypt, Babylonia (modern Iraq), Persia (Iran), and northwestern India.[2]

As Alexander marched eastward, he brought his Greek culture with him. Although "Hellenization," or the spread of Greek culture away from its homeland, began centuries earlier with Greek traders and colonists, the process was greatly accelerated by the campaigns of Alexander. As a student of Greek learning, he envisioned a union of East and West through Greek culture.

The type of Greek language disseminated by Alexander and his men was not the classical Attic of Aristotle (although it was dominant) but *koinē* (lit. "common") Greek. Koine was a vernacular Greek, a more simplified form of this classical language. This simplified and adaptable Greek dialect soon supplanted Aramaic, the language of the Persian Empire, becoming the international tongue of the Mediterranean world. Its usefulness as a common language lasted almost a millennium (322 B.C.–A.D. 529, or from the death of Aristotle to Emperor Justinian's closing of Plato's original Academy).

---

1. Primary sources for Alexander and his accomplishments are the works of Diodorus of Sicily (1st cent. B.C.), Quintus of Curtius (1st cent. A.D.), Plutarch of Chaeronea (early 2d cent. A.D.), and Arrian of Bithynia (2d cent. A.D.). Pertinent selections from the above are found in M. M. Austin, *The Hellenistic World from Alexander to the Roman Conquest: A Selection of Ancient Sources in Translation* (2d augmented ed.; Cambridge: Cambridge University Press, 2006), 18-72. Also see N. Hammond, *The Genius of Alexander the Great* (Chapel Hill: University of North Carolina Press, 1997); M. Wood, *In the Footsteps of Alexander the Great* (Berkeley: University of California Press, 1997); and P. Cartledge, *Alexander the Great: The Hunt for a New Past* (New York: Overlook Press, 2004).

2. The above military statistics from Diodorus, *Library of History* 17.7.3-4, are probably not an exaggeration. The geographic extent of Alexander's conquest is most evident (ironically) in the accounts narrating the division of his kingdom (e.g., a fragment of Greek history attributed to Arrian, 156F, in Austin, *Hellenistic World*, 41-43).

Hellenization after Alexander the Great

Although the cultural effects of Alexander's conquests endured beyond his lifetime, the political unity of his empire did not. In 323 B.C., burdened with administration and suffering from a fever, Alexander died at the age of thirty-two with no legal heir. His generals struggled for control of his empire and soon dismantled it into small, petty kingdoms. Ptolemy took Egypt and southern Syria; Antigonus claimed most of northern Syria and portions of Asia Minor; Lysimachus held Thrace and western Asia Minor; and Cassander ruled Macedonia and Greece. For centuries the dynasties established by Seleucus (who eventually added Antigonus's territories to his own) and Ptolemy fought against each other for more territory, with the land of Israel caught between the two.

The Hellenization process begun by Alexander, however, continued under the Seleucids and Ptolemies. Cities like Alexandria of Egypt, Antioch of Syria, and Seleucia on the Tigris River (near modern Baghdad) were model Hellenistic cities. Cultural trends had been set in motion that could not be reversed, despite the splintering of Alexander's empire among his generals and the continued rivalry among their own descendants. After centuries of political conflict, each small kingdom fell in turn to Rome in the first century B.C. By that time, however, a distinctive culture had emerged: a curious blend of Greek and oriental.

A Stable Roman Empire

When Rome became a world empire, it also became the heir to Hellenism.[3] In the second and first centuries B.C., when Rome expanded its borders eastward, it inherited much of the Hellenistic world founded by Alexander.

---

3. Primary sources for the history of Rome are Dio Cassius, *Roman History* (2d cent. A.D.); the works of Livy (1st cent. A.D.); C. Tacitus, *Histories* and *Annals* (1st cent. A.D.); and Suetonius, *Lives of the Caesars* (early 2d cent. A.D.). Excellent summaries of Roman history are found in M. Hadas, *Imperial Rome* (rev. ed.; Alexandria, Va.: Time-Life Books, 1979), 35-44, 57-68; Helmut Koester, *Introduction to the NT* (2 vols.; New York: Walter de Gruyter, 1975), 1:281-322; M. Grant, *The Founders of the Western World: A History of Greece and Rome* (New York: Scribner/Maxwell Macmillan International, 1991); M. Rostovtzeff, *The Social and Economic History of the Roman Empire* (2d ed.; Oxford: Clarendon Press, 1998); and P. Zoch, *Ancient Rome: An Introductory History* (Norman: University of Oklahoma Press, 1998).

Macedonia and Achaia became Roman provinces in 148 B.C., Asia in 133, Syria in 64, and Egypt in 30 B.C. By the first century B.C. the eastern Mediterranean kingdoms linked together by Greek culture were absorbed into the one political entity of Rome.

Augustus Caesar After a half century of bitter power struggles involving Julius Caesar, Pompey, Mark Antony, and Octavian, Rome became an imperial government under Octavian. In 27 B.C. he assumed the title "Augustus," or "revered one." Because the Roman republic was inefficient in handling its vast dominion, the transition to a strong central authority represented a considerable improvement.[4]

The reorganization of the provinces by Augustus is particularly noteworthy. The Senate retained control of the pacified provinces (e.g., Macedonia, Achaia, Crete, Cyprus) without a standing army. Governors such as Sergius Paulus, proconsul (Gk. *anthypatos*) of Cyprus (Acts 13:4, 7), and Gallio, proconsul of Achaia (Acts 18:12-17), were appointed to one-year terms over senatorial provinces. Any provinces requiring legions of troops because they were newly acquired or frontier territories (e.g., Syria, Pamphylia, Galatia) were under the direct control of the emperor, who appointed a "legate" as governor. In some districts (e.g., Egypt, Judea) the emperor ruled through a "prefect" or (after A.D. 41) a "procurator." Thus the Gospel of Luke identifies both the legate of Syria (Quirinius, 2:2) and the prefect of Judea (Pontius Pilate, 3:1).[5] All provinces were ruled by Romans, but certain responsibilities were delegated to local magistrates, especially in the senatorial provinces.[6]

Augustus also created new offices for the construction and repair of public buildings, roads, and aqueducts. The great network of roads built by Augustus and his successors was an impressive accomplishment. Roads extended throughout the empire, making even the remote frontiers accessible. It also was a significant factor in the mission and expansion of Christianity.

---

4. Hadas, *Imperial Rome*, 44, 57-59.

5. Both offices are given the general title "imperial governor" (Gk. *hēgemōn*).

6. For more information on the Roman provincial system, see G. H. Stevenson, *Roman Provincial Administration* (Oxford: Blackwell, 1939); A. H. M. Jones, *Studies in Roman Government and Law* (Oxford: Blackwell, 1960); and A. N. Sherwin-White, *Roman Foreign Policy in the East* (Norman: University of Oklahoma Press, 1983) and *Roman Society and Roman Law in the NT* (Oxford: Clarendon Press, 1963).

The Julio-Claudian Emperors Most of the emperors after Augustus (27 B.C.–A.D. 14) either continued or expanded his provincial policies.[7] The four who followed him are known as the Julio-Claudian emperors because they were descendants of the Julians and Claudians, two families of ancient Roman nobility:

- Tiberius (A.D. 14-37) was the stepson of Augustus.
- Gaius Caligula (37-41) was the great-nephew of Tiberius.
- Claudius (41-54), the uncle of Caligula, proved to be a sensible and competent ruler. Jews were expelled briefly from Rome during his reign (Acts 18:2).
- Nero (54-68), stepson of Claudius, had a successful early reign, but it began to deteriorate when he took full control. He was accused of setting fire to Rome (A.D. 64) but shifted the blame on the Christians. According to tradition, Peter and Paul were executed under Nero.

The Flavian Dynasty The Flavian dynasty, unlike the Julio-Claudians, descended from the middle class of military commanders and merchants.

- T. Flavius Vespasian (A.D. 69-79) was an experienced general who was completing the campaign to end the First Jewish Revolt (66-70) when his supporters proclaimed him emperor, leaving the siege of Jerusalem to his son Titus.
- Titus (79-81) replaced his father, Vespasian, as general overseeing the destruction of Jerusalem in 70 before becoming emperor.
- Domitian (81-96), brother of Titus.

The Emperors of the "Golden Age" The "five good emperors" that followed Domitian saw the "golden age" of the empire.

- Nerva (A.D. 97-98) was a respectable old Roman lawyer who sought to rebuild the state treasury, distribute land to the poor, and encourage building construction.

---

7. Primary sources for the Roman emperors are Suetonius, *The Twelve Caesars;* Tacitus, *Annals* and *Histories of Rome;* and Dio Cassius, *Roman History.* Selections of these and other sources are found in M. P. Charlesworth, ed., *Documents Illustrating the Reigns of Claudius and Nero* (London: Cambridge University Press, 1939); and E. M. Smallwood, *Documents Illustrating the Principates of Nerva, Trajan, and Hadrian* (London: Cambridge University Press, 1966).

- Trajan (98-117) was Nerva's appointed successor. His famous correspondence with Pliny the Younger, governor of Bithynia, provides insights regarding Rome's sometimes hostile treatment of Christians.
- Hadrian (117-38) was Trajan's adopted son and successor. In reaction to Hadrian's attempts to rebuild Jerusalem into a Roman city with a temple dedicated to Jupiter, the Jews revolted under Simon Bar Kochba (or Kosiba, 132-35). The insurrection was suppressed, leading to the expulsion of all Jews from Palestine.
- Antoninus Pius (138-61) enjoyed a reign of peace and prosperity.
- Marcus Aurelius (161-80) was the adopted son of Antoninus. At an early age he gained the favor of Hadrian, who supervised his fine education. Between military campaigns he composed *Meditations,* a work that expresses high Stoic principles.

Despite the sporadic periods of tyranny in the reigns of Caligula, Nero, and Domitian, the emperors of Rome continued and even refined the fair provincial policies of Augustus. They maintained political order and economic stability in an otherwise turbulent Mediterranean world. Early Christianity benefited from such imperial policies. Widespread, official persecution of Christians who refused to pay homage to the emperor did not begin until the reigns of Decius and Valerian (250-60). Such oppression ended with the reign of Constantine (ruled 306-37), who declared Christianity a legal religion of Rome.

An Age of Expanding Diversity

An earlier generation of scholars described the Greco-Roman era as an angst-ridden "age of anxiety" governed by religious dissatisfaction born of polytheistic uncertainties and a pervasive surrender to impersonal Fate.[8] Recently, however, historians have argued for a more balanced perspective, highlighting the many ways in which paganism "worked" for its adherents.[9]

8. See E. R. Dodds, *The Greeks and the Irrational* (Berkeley: University of California Press, 1951), 44, 78, 97, and *Pagan and Christian in an Age of Anxiety* (London: Cambridge University Press, 1965), 3-4, 133; and H. C. Kee and F. W. Young, *Understanding the NT* (Englewood Cliffs, N.J.: Prentice-Hall, 1957), 7-8.

9. "They loved it, trusted it, found fulfillment in it, and so resisted change however eloquently, or ferociously, pressed upon them" (R. MacMullen, *Christianity and Paganism in*

Social, cultural, religious, and technological developments, however, certainly introduced new complexities into Greco-Roman life. Even positive developments could have unexpected consequences. Improved travel not only enhanced communication and trade but also increased the spread of diseases, causing illness, death, or the fear of disease.[10] Improved trade not only stimulated the accumulation of wealth for some but caused the exploitation and displacement of people from their homelands to serve as slaves for a new prosperous merchant class.[11] Pervasive Hellenism in the East resulted in the emergence of oriental thought in Greek dress. Such a transformation brought new life to both oriental religions and Greek philosophy, but it could also engender pessimism about the old traditions and an obsession with fate, sometimes leading to a sense of helplessness.[12]

Belief in fatalism strongly influenced Hellenistic thought. Human life was predetermined by higher powers (e.g., Stoicism, apocalypticism),

---

the Fourth to Eighth Centuries [New Haven: Yale University Press, 1997], 69; see 54-73; also see MacMullen's section "The Vitality of Paganism," in *Paganism in the Roman Empire* [New Haven: Yale University Press, 1981], 62-73, esp. 64).

10. The movement of goods and people was easy and cheap in the empire; for examples, note the travels of the apostle Paul, Aquila, and Priscilla in Acts and the accounts of traveling merchants cited in M. P. Charlesworth, *Roman Empire* (London: Oxford University Press, 1967), 86-87. The spread of disease was also unprecedented; during the reigns of both Titus and Marcus Aurelius, for example, terrible plagues swept across the empire. Note also the diverse list of diseases in *Asclepius: Testimonies* (ed. E. J. Edelstein and L. Edelstein; Baltimore: Johns Hopkins University Press, 1945).

11. The correspondence of Zeno, steward of a large estate in Fayum, Egypt, addressed to Apollonius, the finance minister under Ptolemy II (282-246 B.C.), and the king's extensive "revenue laws" indicate the vast amounts of trade in which money-making Egypt was engaged (Austin, *Hellenistic World,* 395-411). On prosperous Roman trading, see Charlesworth, *Roman Empire,* 81-91. The importance of slaves in labor and commerce cannot be underestimated. In the first cent. B.C., one-third of Rome's population were slaves, most acquired through military conquest. For example, the Jewish historian Josephus stated that Rome took 97,000 prisoners from Palestine during the Jewish revolt of A.D. 66-70 (*War* 6.420). See T. Wiedemann, *Greek and Roman Slavery* (Baltimore: Johns Hopkins University Press, 1981); A. Kirschenbaum, *Sons, Slaves, and Freedmen in Roman Commerce* (Jerusalem: Magnes Press; Washington, D.C.: Catholic University of America Press, 1987); and F. Thompson, *The Archaeology of Greek and Roman Slavery* (London: Duckworth, 2003).

12. See the concern for deliverance from fate in Apuleius, *Golden Ass* 11.6, 15, and in Corpus Hermetica 12.9. For the view of the revival of Eastern religions in Greek language and thought-forms, see Hans Jonas, *The Gnostic Religion: The Message of the Alien God and the Beginnings of Christianity* (3d ed.; Boston: Beacon Press, 2001), 3-27.

which were often identified as fate (Gk. *heimarmenē* or *ananke*, Lat. *fatum*). Fate, sometimes personified, determined the outcome of nations, individuals, and events, with little or no human control.[13]

Astrology The preoccupation with fate was influenced by astrology.[14] Together with magic and divination, astrology afforded the opportunity to circumvent one's fate. If the order of the stars determines one's destiny, then knowledge of one's fate could be known, and perhaps influenced, by a study of the stars. These beliefs explain the wide use of personal horoscopes in such diverse places as the imperial household and Jewish Qumran. Astrology affected every aspect of society: religion, war, politics, trade, and personal matters. In fact, horoscopes became so prevalent in the early Roman Empire that Augustus sought to standardize them by publishing his own. There were voices of dissent. Seneca the Elder (father of the philosopher and statesman Seneca the Younger) insisted that all horoscopes were false, the fanciful inventions of "wily astrologers."[15]

Magic and Divination Closely associated with astrology was the practice of magic. It was an attempt to gain mastery over both the good and the evil powers that determine one's fate. The Great Magical Papyri from Egypt (3d cent. A.D.) contain various prescriptions and rituals to command and control the good and bad spirits (*daimōn*, a neutral word not yet associated

13. Examples of fatalism in Stoicism are Zeno, *Fragments* 175-76; and Chrysippus, *Fragment* 625 (both in C. K. Barrett, *The NT Background: Selected Documents* [rev. ed.; San Francisco: Harper & Row, 1989; henceforth *NTB*], 61-64); Seneca, *On Providence* 5.7-9 and *To Marcia* 18.5-6; see also Pliny, *Natural History* 2.22, and the histories of Suetonius and Tacitus. The following are examples of the apocalyptic view that the events preceding the end are predetermined: Dan 9:24; *1 Enoch* 92:2; *4 Ezra* 4:36-37; 6:1-6; *2 Bar.* 25; see also Jewish Wisdom: Eccl 3:2-8; Sir 23:20; 39:25-31.

14. See the following examples of Hellenistic astrology: Papyri Tebtunis 276 (late 2d cent. A.D.) and Chrysippus, *Fragment* 625 (both in Barrett, *NTB*, 35-36, 61-62); Philo, *On the Migration of Abraham* 179 (early 1st cent. A.D.); 4Q186 and 4QMess (Qumran Scrolls). Note statues and reliefs of Greek gods and zodiac in J. Godwin, *Mystery Religions in the Ancient World* (San Francisco: Harper & Row, 1981), plates 2 (Jupiter in zodiac), 8 (zodiac and intermediate deities), and 142 (Orphic deity and zodiac); see also plates 50 (Jewish zodiac, 6th cent. A.D.) and 75 (Asian goddess Cybele and zodiac).

15. Seneca the Elder, *Suasoriae* 4.2-3. See the full quotation and discussion in H.-J. Klauck, *The Religious Context of Early Christianity: A Guide to Graeco-Roman Religions* (trans. B. McNeil; Minneapolis: Fortress, 2003), 237.

only with evil) that affect one's destiny.[16] Prophetic oracles were also consulted at places like the shrine of Apollo at Delphi, Greece, and divination (the reading of animal entrails, dream interpretation, observing the weather and the flight of birds) was practiced to discern the future.[17]

The Mystery Religions The so-called mystery religions sought to deal with the problem of fate and the fears of the age with promises of immortality and personal communion with a deity.[18] Most of these mystery cults included both the recital and the reenactment of a myth celebrating the death and resurrection of a deity. The "mysteries," comprising secret knowledge gained in secret ceremonies, also promised their initiates immortality, personal communion with a deity, and membership in a close-knit organization of fellow adherents. Because they were close-knit associations attempting to overcome fate and promising immortality and intimate communion with a deity, the mystery religions spread throughout the Roman world. Hellenization and syncretism (or "mixing of religions") contributed to their wide influence. In many cities of the empire, the Romans probably viewed early Christians as devotees of a new mys-

16. Both Jewish and pagan magical texts are found in these Egyptian papyri, now preserved in the National Library of Paris. The texts are reproduced, translated, and discussed in A. Deissmann, *Light from the Ancient East* (New York: George H. Doran, 1927), 254-64; H. Betz, ed., *The Greek Magical Papyri in Translation, Including the Demotic Spells* (2d ed.; Chicago: University of Chicago Press, 1992); and M. Meyer and R. Smith, eds., *Ancient Christian Magic: Coptic Texts of Ritual Power* (Princeton: Princeton University Press, 1994).

17. Prophetic women, called sibyls, originally resided at places like the temple of Delphi and gave ecstatic predictions. Later, prophecies ascribed to these sibyls were published in books, called the Sibylline Oracles. See translations and critical discussion of the vast corpus of the Sibylline Oracles (from the 2d cent. B.C. to the 7th cent. A.D.) by J. J. Collins, in *The OT Pseudepigrapha* (ed. J. H. Charlesworth; 2 vols.; New York: Doubleday, 1983; henceforth *OTP*), 1:317-472. Underscoring their popularity in the Roman world, the emperors also consulted oracles and participated in divination (e.g., Suetonius, *Julius Caesar* 81; *Vespasian* 5; Tacitus, *Histories* 5.13); see Klauck, *The Religious Context of Early Christianity*, 177-249.

18. Primary sources for the mystery religions are a variety of Greek and Latin authors and inscriptions. Selections are found in F. C. Grant, *Ancient Roman Religion* (Indianapolis: Bobbs-Merrill, 1957); J. Ferguson, *Greek and Roman Religion: A Source Book* (Park Ridge, N.J.: Noyes Press, 1980); and W. Burkert, *Ancient Mystery Cults* (Cambridge, Mass.: Harvard University Press, 1987). Informative illustrations of ancient artifacts and excavated sites are also found in J. Ferguson, *The Religions of the Roman Empire* (Ithaca, N.Y.: Cornell University Press, 1970); Godwin, *Mystery Religions;* and *The New Larousse Encyclopedia of Mythology* (new ed.; London: Hamlyn Publishing, 1968).

tery cult (e.g., this was the opinion of Tacitus, Suetonius, and Pliny the Younger).

Gnosticism Competing with the mystery cults was a spiritual phenomenon called Gnosticism, a widespread collection of amorphous religious and philosophical movements of the first three centuries A.D.[19] Like the mystery cults, Gnosticism was the product of Hellenistic syncretism, the mingling of Greek and oriental ideas, which then mixed with Jewish and Christian influences. Although there was no uniform Gnostic system, four myths and motifs were dominant.

The first major concept was *gnōsis* (Gk. "knowledge"), a secret knowledge revealed to initiates that had liberating and redeeming effects. Possessing such knowledge freed the individual from ignorance and bondage in the world.

A second characteristic was a central myth: the presence of a divine "spark" in humans that proceeded from the divine realm and fell into our world. The earth is the tragic result of a downward movement from the divine realm. Redemption involves the recovery of this divine spark.

A third concept is radical dualism ("two opposite realms") interwoven with a monistic view of deity ("supreme unknown God").

The fourth was a myth of the creation of the world (i.e., a cosmogony) explaining humanity's present dilemma: remoteness from God. Most

---

19. Primary sources for Gnosticism are found in J. M. Robinson, ed., *The Nag Hammadi Library in English* (3d ed.; San Francisco: Harper & Row, 1988); W. Foerster, *Gnosis: A Selection of Gnostic Texts* (2 vols.; London: Oxford University Press, 1972-74); R. M. Grant, *Gnosticism* (New York: Collins, 1961); and E. Hennecke, *NT Apocrypha* (ed. W. Schneemelcher; 2 vols.; Philadelphia: Westminster Press, 1963-66); selections of Mandean, Manichean, and other Gnostic texts are found in W. Barnstone, ed., *The Other Bible* (San Francisco: Harper & Row, 1984). For a comprehensive survey and critical discussion of sources, see K. Rudolph, *Gnosis* (trans. R. M. Wilson; San Francisco: Harper & Row, 1983). For a brief survey, see *Nag Hammadi, Gnosticism, and Early Christianity* (ed. C. W. Hedrick and R. Hodgson; Peabody, Mass.: Hendrickson, 1986), 1-11; P. Perkins, *Gnosticism and the NT* (Minneapolis: Fortress, 1993); E. Yamauchi, *Pre-Christian Gnosticism: A Survey of the Proposed Evidences* (Grand Rapids: Baker, 1993); A. Logan, *Gnostic Truth and Christian Heresy: A Study in the History of Gnosticism* (Peabody, Mass.: Hendrickson, 1996); R. Roukema, *Gnosis and Faith in Early Christianity: An Introduction to Gnosticism* (trans. J. Bowden; Harrisburg, Pa.: Trinity International Press, 1999); K. King, *What Is Gnosticism?* (Cambridge, Mass.: Harvard University Press, Belknap Press, 2003); Klauck, *The Religious Context of Early Christianity*, 429-503; and B. Pearson, *Gnosticism and Christianity in Roman and Coptic Egypt* (New York: T&T Clark, 2003).

Gnostic mythologies are influenced by the Genesis creation story and consist of the downward fall of a heavenly being (e.g., Sophia). Like diamonds in mud, a divine spark is hidden within human inhabitants of this dark and ignorant world.

The origins of Gnosticism are difficult to ascertain, since our earliest sources are from the second and third centuries A.D. Evidence from church fathers like Justin Martyr and Irenaeus makes it clear that there were Christian Gnostics in conflict with early catholic Christians at that time. Some scholars suggest that the concept of a Gnostic Redeemer influenced the way some early Christians portrayed Jesus (e.g., Phil 2; John 1). There is no consensus on this view, however, and skeptics point out that Gnosticism gave no importance to a unique appearance of the Redeemer *in history*.[20]

Gods and Divinized Heroes The Greco-Roman world, as we have seen, had many gods and goddesses. Some were mythical deities who dwelt in the heavens or on some mythical mountain; others were associated with the cycles of the seasons. Some of these immortal gods descended from heaven to earth or were sent to fulfill an important mission on behalf of humanity.

There were also "divinely endowed" human figures in both history and legend who performed miraculous deeds, though it is important to recall that Hellenistic religion recognized various "shades" of divinity. A divinized *(theios* or *theotēs)* human being, such as Hercules or a Roman emperor, did not possess the same divine status as an Olympian god *(theos)*.[21] Nevertheless, some heroes were believed to be the offspring of gods and humans, characterized by wisdom and special powers. Usually they were considered to be great benefactors of humanity. This category included divinized rulers, military leaders, politicians, philosophers, physicians, and healers. The idea of emperor worship, for example, was an adaptation of Eastern beliefs about the divinity of the king or pharaoh. But

---

20. Klauck, *The Religious Context of Early Christianity*, 47-74.

21. A selection of primary sources and comments on gods and divinized heroes is found in D. R. Cartlidge and D. L. Dungan, eds., *Documents for the Study of the Gospels* (rev. ed.; Minneapolis: Fortress, 1994); F. C. Grant, *Ancient Roman Religion* (Indianapolis: Bobbs-Merrill, 1957), 169-243; M. Hadas and M. Smith, *Heroes and Gods* (New York: Harper & Row, 1965); J. Campbell, *The Hero with a Thousand Faces* (2d ed.; Princeton: Princeton University Press, 1968), 49-254, 315-64; and Klauck, *The Religious Context of Early Christianity*, 250-65.

Western conquerors also fostered such ideas on their marches eastward; for example, in the eastern provinces the Roman emperor was often believed to be divine. The emperor was commonly called "Lord" and "Savior of the world"; messages about their military victories were announced as "good news," or "gospel." At home, Greeks and Romans tolerated such views for political unity, but some were disillusioned with them. It was customary, however, to pay homage to emperors as gods *after* they died.

Especially widespread was the notion of a hero or philosopher who was revered for his ability to perform miracles or impart great wisdom. These great abilities were believed to be a manifestation of deity, and some of these heroes, such as the legendary Hercules, were granted immortality after death. Another example was the itinerant Pythagorean philosopher Apollonius of Tyana (Asia Minor), who had a miraculous birth, gathered followers, taught, healed, and appeared to his followers after death. He lived in the first Christian century. Shortly after A.D. 217 Philostratus wrote *A Life of Apollonius,* which some compare to a Synoptic gospel.

Hellenistic Philosophies Like the mystery religions and Gnosticism, Hellenistic philosophies also promised deliverance from the fears and uncertainties of life.[22] Unlike most religious cults, these philosophical schools offered a comprehensive picture of the origin and structure of the universe, explaining a person's place and destiny in the universe and how that person might best conduct his or her life. Consequently, the idea of "conversion" as one's entrance into a newfound life of personal and ethical transformation is characteristic of Hellenistic philosophy, though not of Greco-Roman religion.[23]

---

22. For the pragmatic focus in Greco-Roman philosophies, see E. Bevan, "Hellenistic Popular Philosophy," in *The Hellenistic Age* (ed. J. B. Bury et al.; London: Cambridge University Press, 1925), 79-107. For primary sources and comments, see Barrett, *NTB,* 54-79; G. H. Clark, *Selections from Hellenistic Philosophy* (New York: Appleton-Century-Crofts, 1940); Ferguson, *Greek and Roman Religion,* 90-117; Grant, *Ancient Roman Religion,* 59-156; and Klauck, *The Religious Context of Early Christianity,* 331-428.

23. See the classic work by A. N. Nock, *Conversion: The Old and the New in Religion, from Alexander the Great to Augustine of Hippo* (London: Oxford University Press, 1933), ch. 11, "Conversion to Philosophy." Klauck emphasizes, "If one speaks of a conversion experience in the classical period outside the Jewish/Christian sphere, what is meant is the adoption of one particular philosophical world-view with all of its consequences and existential praxis. No one needed to 'convert' in this sense to a belief in the gods or to a mystery cult" (*The Religious Context of Early Christianity,* p. 334).

The ideas of Plato (d. 347 B.C.) were most influential.[24] Platonists followed the three characteristic aspects of Plato's dualism: (1) a distinction between two levels of reality — the imperfect, temporal, changing, material world of particulars over against the perfect, eternal, unchanging, spiritual world of Forms; (2) true knowledge of the Forms as attained only by reason, not by sense experience; and (3) the immortal soul as imprisoned by the mortal body (which is also a Pythagorean idea).

Platonism influenced Alexandrian Jews like Philo (a Jewish scholar who sought to blend OT religion with Greek philosophy), the Gnostic movement, and early Christianity. For example, Philo stated that an invisible plan of Ideas was conceived by God before he created the world (*Creation* 4). He also used biblical stories, like Abraham's migration to Canaan, to illustrate the soul's migration from physical bondage. Gnosticism regarded the soul ("inner spirit") as needing liberation from the body, made extensive use of intermediate beings, and went beyond Platonic dualism in viewing the earthly world and divine realm as irreconcilable opposites. Both early Western Christians, like Justin Martyr, and Eastern Christians, like Clement and Origen, were especially indebted to Middle Platonism for their development of a theology of divine attributes like omniscience, impassibility, and simplicity as expressions of God's unchangeable nature.

Stoicism was probably the most popular Hellenistic philosophy.[25] Its name was derived from the *Stoa Poikile* (lit. "painted porch"), a public hall in Athens where its founder, Zeno (336-263 B.C.), taught.

Zeno and his students sought to develop a complete philosophical system of physics, ethics, and logic. He saw the world ordered by divine reason, or Logos, which he identified with the primal element of fire, from

24. Sources for Plato and Middle Platonism include Plato's dialogues *Republic, Symposium, Timaeus,* and *Parmenides;* Diogenes Laertius, *Lives,* bk. 3; Albinus of Smyrna (A.D. 150); and Plutarch, *Platonic Essays* (A.D. 120). Helpful secondary sources are J. Dillon, *The Middle Platonists, 80 B.C. to A.D. 220* (Ithaca, N.Y.: Cornell University Press, 1977); P. Merlan, *From Platonism to Neoplatonism* (2d ed.; Hague: Nijhoff, 1960); and P. Shorey, *Platonism, Ancient and Modern* (Berkeley: University of California Press, 1938).

25. The lives and teachings of Heraclitus, Zeno, and his students are found in D. Laertius, *Lives* 7; 9.1-17. The works of Epictetus and Seneca are found in the Loeb Classical Library. Collections of Stoic writings are found in H. von Arnim, *Stoicorum Veterum Fragmenta* (4 vols.; Leipzig: B. G. Teubner, 1921-24); G. H. Clark, *Selections from Hellenistic Philosophy* (New York: F. S. Crofts, 1940), 50-105; and Barrett, *NTB,* 61-71. For discussion, see R. D. Hicks, *Stoic and Epicurean* (New York: Russell & Russell, 1962); and J. M. Rist, *Stoic Philosophy* (Cambridge: Cambridge University Press, 1969).

which everything came and to which all would return. The Logos was also identified with Zeus, the supreme (but impersonal) governor of the universe. Conformity with the natural laws of divine reason was imperative. One conforms to divine reason by pursuing the good (virtue) and avoiding evil (vice). Since all adversities are predetermined by fate, they should be endured with self-control and composure. Destiny is overcome by not allowing oneself to become swayed emotionally by life's circumstances. The Stoic commitment to determinism had some influence on early Christian ideas of God's providence.

Hellenistic Judaism In competition with the religious and philosophical aspirations of the Greco-Roman world was Hellenistic Judaism, especially the Diaspora Jews, who lived outside of Palestine.[26] Despite its distinctive adherence to the "law of Moses," Judaism had become a strongly Hellenized religion.[27] By the third century B.C., most Jews of the Diaspora and Palestine had learned to speak Greek. Shortly afterward, a Greek translation of the Hebrew Bible, the Septuagint (commonly abbreviated "LXX"), was begun in Alexandria.[28] Jewish philosophers like Philo of Alexandria (wrote A.D. 20-50) interpreted the Jewish Scriptures figuratively or allegorically to underscore biblical agreement with Hellenistic philosophy.[29] Philo even sought to present Judaism as a type of mystery cult (*On Cherubim* 48-50), although he was not favorably disposed to the pagan mysteries (*On Special Laws* 1.319-321). Jews such as Josephus wrote histories of their people to show that their cultural heritage was as good as that

---

26. See the mention of Diaspora in Josephus, *Ant.* 14.110-118; and Philo, *Against Flaccus* 73-77. See also J. Bartlett, *Jews in the Hellenistic World* (Cambridge: Cambridge University Press, 1985); E. Schürer, *The History of the Jewish People in the Age of Jesus Christ* (ed. G. Vermes and F. Millar; 3 vols.; Edinburgh: T&T Clark, 1973-87), 3:1-176; and J. Collins and G. Sterling, eds., *Hellenism in the Land of Israel* (Notre Dame, Ind.: University of Notre Dame Press, 2001). For further discussion, see the section "The Jewish Context of the New Testament" below in this chapter.

27. P. Schäfer, *The History of the Jews in Antiquity: The Jews of Palestine from Alexander the Great to the Arab Conquest* (trans. D. Chowcat; Luxembourg: Harwood Academic Publishers, 1995); J. Brown, *Ancient Israel and Ancient Greece: Religion, Politics, and Culture* (Minneapolis: Fortress, 2003).

28. *Letter of Aristeas* 1-12, 28-51, 301-11 (2d cent. B.C.); Philo, *On the Life of Moses* 2.26-42 (1st cent. A.D.).

29. Examples of Philo's allegorical exegesis can be found in his *On the Migration of Abraham* 89-93 and *On the Posterity and Exile of Cain* 1-11.

of the Greeks (e.g., *Ag. Ap.* 2.164-171). Archaeological excavations have shown that synagogues, serving as gathering places for worship and instruction, were located throughout the Mediterranean world and were often decorated with Hellenistic artwork.

The distinctives of the Jewish faith offered an appealing alternative to the fears and problems connected with Hellenistic fatalism. The Jews maintained a belief in only one God (monotheism), who created the world and controls its future. Philo devoted his treatise *De Providentia* to the refutation of horoscopes and impersonal fate.[30] For those who live according to the will of God as expressed in the Jewish law (Torah), there is everlasting life; for the disobedient there is everlasting judgment (e.g., Dan 12:2-3; *1 Enoch;* 1QS 4.6-14; *m. 'Abot* 5:19). As a result, Judaism attracted converts and admirers, sometimes called God-fearers (e.g., Acts 2:5-13; 13:43, 50; 17:4, 17). Some Jews may even have been engaged in missionary activity (Matt 23:15; *Numbers Rabbah* 8:3; *b. Yebam.* 47a, b). Converts became sons of Abraham and adopted partners in a covenant relationship with the God of Israel. But Judaism's greatest influence was upon early Christianity, which began as an apocalyptic (i.e., end-time oriented) Jewish sect.[31] It drew upon the Septuagint, rather than the Hebrew Bible, as its primary source of OT authority for NT writings.

Summary

A common language in a world of many dialects, improved travel, and political stability under a world power, combined with the hopes, fears, and aspirations of an age in rapid transition — these are major characteristics of the NT Greco-Roman world. It was an age when vernacular Greek was spoken by diverse peoples of the East and West, when Greek culture penetrated every major city of the Mediterranean world. It was a Roman age when political peace and economic stability were long-awaited realities in a war-torn and politically fragmented world. Roman resourcefulness and efficiency improved travel and trade in an unprecedented manner. Despite the irrational actions of a few despots, most Roman emperors and provincial rulers were fair and tolerant to those willing to live peaceably under

---

30. See Klauck, *The Religious Context of Early Christianity,* 249.

31. See the section "Apocalyptic Eschatology," under "The Persistent Faith of Judaism."

their rule. It was a time of rapid change through improved communication and increased mobility.

Christianity was born and developed in this environment of cultural exchange, increased mobility, political stability, philosophical pursuits, and religious diversity. Just as Freudian psychologists remind us that the behavioral development of a child cannot be determined solely by his or her environment but must include the genetic relationship to the parents, so also we must examine carefully the parent religion that gave birth to Christianity: Judaism. Although we have briefly surveyed the phenomenon of Hellenistic Judaism, we must now examine the ancient development of Judaism and its beliefs more closely, especially in the context of its homeland, Palestine.

The Jewish Context of the New Testament

The Tragic History of Judaism

From the sixth century B.C. to the second century A.D., the history of Israel is a story of foreign dominance, with a brief interlude of independence.[32] This "tragic history" of Israel can be outlined in five series of events: the Babylonian exile, resettlement under Persia, Greco-Syrian oppression, a disappointing interlude of independence, and conflicts with Rome.

The Babylonian Exile The Babylonian exile (beginning in 587 B.C.) marked the end of a great period of Israelite independence under such notable kings as David, Solomon, Hezekiah, and Josiah. Although the northern kingdom had seceded from unified Israel in 922 B.C. and had fallen to the Assyrians in 722, the southern kingdom of Judah (west of the Dead Sea and including Jerusalem) had a relatively stable government and economy

---

32. The provocative title of this subsection is based primarily on the history of Israel as one of domination by foreign oppressors (e.g., Assyrians, Babylonians, Egyptians, Syrian Greeks, and Romans). A secondary consideration is Israel's interpretation of its own history as one of disobedience to the words of Yahweh (e.g., see Isa 6:9-10; 8:17; Jer 5:20-31; Third Isa 64:5-7; Ezek 2–3; Deut 32; 1 Kgs 22; Neh 9; Damascus Document of Qumran [CD]). See also the early Christian interpretations of Israel (Acts 7; 28:24-28; Rom 9–11). The titles "Tragic History" and "Persistent Faith" have also been applied to Judaism in R. A. Spivey and D. M. Smith, *Anatomy of the NT* (New York: Macmillan, 1969), chs. 7, 13.

before the fateful years leading to its conquest by the Neobabylonians under Nebuchadnezzar II.[33]

The Babylonian exile meant the loss of a king, land, and temple for the people of Judah.[34] The city of Jerusalem lay in ruins, and the magnificent temple built by Solomon had been destroyed. This terrible series of events, as indicated by the sources, produced negative responses of fear, loneliness, anger, despair, and the loss of both cultural and religious identity among the southern kingdom.[35]

But these fifty years of Babylonian exile were also a time of reorganization and growth for Judaism.[36] Many old traditions were written down and collected as sacred literature. Circumcision and Sabbath-day observance acquired special binding force. The Jewish belief in only one God reached its classic definition. The synagogue, a meeting place for prayer and study of the law of Moses, also emerged. Finally, in the course of fifty years, many of the Jews who were dispersed throughout the Near East as slaves soon earned their freedom and entered trade and commerce. This dispersement of the Jews is the beginning of the Diaspora, or the "scattering" of Jews throughout the world. During the Greco-Roman period, the Diaspora is almost synonymous with Hellenistic Judaism.[37]

---

33. The rise and fall of the Israelite monarchy is narrated in the Hebrew Bible (1–2 Sam; 1–2 Kgs; 1–2 Chr) and also by Josephus (*Ant.* bks. 7–9). See the following modern studies: J. Bright, *A History of Israel* (4th ed.; Louisville, Ky.: Westminster John Knox, 2000), 183-339; J. H. Hayes and J. M. Miller, eds., *Israelite and Judean History* (Philadelphia: Westminster, 1977); S. Herrmann, *A History of Israel in OT Times* (trans. J. Bowden; Philadelphia: Fortress, 1975); L. Grabbe, *A History of the Jews and Judaism in the Second Temple Period* (London: T&T Clark, 2004); and J. Miller, *A History of Ancient Israel and Judah* (Louisville, Ky.: Westminster John Knox, 2006).

34. For biblical accounts of the fall of Judah, see 2 Kgs 24–25; 2 Chr 36; Jer 52; Lam. See also Josephus, *Ant.* 10.74-185. For modern studies, see P. R. Ackroyd, *Exile and Restoration* (Philadelphia: Westminster, 1968); Bright, *History of Israel,* 343-59; Herrmann, *History of Israel,* 289-97; and R. W. Klein, *Israel in Exile* (Philadelphia: Fortress, 1979).

35. See, for example, Lam; Pss 44; 74; 79; 102; 137.

36. See the exilic and postexilic writings of the so-called Deuteronomistic historian (Deut to 2 Kgs), the Priestly writer (Lev and related cultic legislation of the Pentateuch), Second and Third Isa (40–66), and Ezek. See also the following studies: Ackroyd, *Exile and Restoration;* Bright, *History of Israel,* 347-51; and Klein, *Israel in Exile.*

37. Josephus, *Ant.* 10.186-187; 14.110-118; *War* 7.43; Philo, *Against Flaccus* 73-75. See also the discussion in S. Safrai and M. Stern, eds., *The Jewish People in the First Century* (2 vols.; Assen: Van Gorcum, 1974-76), 1:117-215; J. A. Sanders, "Dispersion," *IDB* 1:854-56; T. Rajak, *The Jewish Dialogue with Greece and Rome* (Leiden: Brill, 2001); J. Bartlett, ed., *Jews in the*

The Resettlement under Persia Even though the conquest of Babylon by the Persians and the edict of Cyrus in 538 B.C. permitted the Jews to return home, there were many problems involved in the resettlement.[38] First, not many exiled Jews wished to return to their homeland. Most of them were descendants of the exiles, who were comfortably settled in Babylon and elsewhere. Second, there was much work to be done if Palestine was to be reestablished as a Jewish nation. Jerusalem lay in ruins, and there was no temple to unify the Jews in worship. Third, the exiles that arrived in Palestine were not welcomed by the current inhabitants. There was conflict with the scattered Jewish communities that were not deported in 587 B.C., who were now practicing a form of Judaism less structured than that of the exiles. There also was opposition from the Samaritans, a Torah-observant people who claimed to be the descendants of the northern kingdom, although this area had been resettled by Assyrian colonists after the fall of the north in 722. Finally, there was also armed conflict with Arab tribes of surrounding nations (e.g., Edomites).

Despite many problems, groups of exiles returned to Palestine from 536 to 444 B.C. A modest temple was constructed around 515, lending the religion of this era its common name: "second temple Judaism." The walls of Jerusalem were then rebuilt under Nehemiah (437 B.C.). About this time, Ezra, "a scribe skilled in the law of Moses" (Ezra 7:6), arrived to instruct the people of Judah in the sacred Torah, which contained laws for the life and faith of the people. By this time, few Jews remained conversant in Hebrew. Aramaic, the international language of commerce in the western Persian Empire, had become the language of Palestine. By the time of Jesus, many Jews, in both Palestine and the Diaspora, were bilingual, speaking both their local languages and Koine Greek.

The Greco-Syrian Oppression Palestine entered a turbulent period under the Seleucid ruler Antiochus IV (175-163 B.C.).[39] The situation reached a crisis in 168 B.C., when Antiochus plundered the temple treasury of Jerusalem. Conservative Jewish factions revolted in response. The humiliated

---

Hellenistic and Roman Cities (London: Routledge, 2002); and E. Gruen, *Diaspora: Jews amidst Greeks and Romans* (Cambridge, Mass.: Harvard University Press, 2002).

38. See Ackroyd, *Exile and Restoration*, 138-231; and Bright, *History of Israel*, 360-402.

39. For further discussion of Alexander and his successors, see "The Greco-Roman Context of the NT," in this chapter.

Seleucid king returned to Jerusalem intent on subduing this rebellion.[40] He captured Jerusalem, killed or expelled its Jewish inhabitants, and repopulated the city with Syrian Greeks. As a result, the Jewish temple was devoted to the worship of Zeus, the Jewish religion was outlawed in Judea, and pious Jews were persecuted.[41]

The Interval of Jewish Independence   In response to these tragic events, the Maccabean revolt of 167 B.C. erupted. Many Jews who defied the laws of Antiochus IV fled to the hills of Judea and joined the guerrilla forces of Judas, called Maccabeus ("the Hammer").[42] This resistance was actively supported by the Hasidim (lit. "pious ones"), who advocated traditional Jewish values and discouraged Hellenistic reform. Judas waged effective guerrilla warfare against the Syrian Greeks. In 164 he and his forces captured Jerusalem and reestablished Jewish worship in the temple.[43] Judaism has commemorated this event in the Feast of Dedication, or Lights, also called Hanukkah.[44]

The Maccabean revolt restored freedom of worship to Judea, but there was no independence until the ruling house of Simon was established, also called the Hasmonean dynasty.[45] Through the efforts of Simon and his

---

40. See 1 Macc 1; 2 Macc 4–5; Josephus, *Ant.* 12.242-264. See also E. Bickerman, *The God of the Maccabees: Studies on the Meaning and Origin of the Maccabean Revolt* (Leiden: Brill, 1979); Koester, *Introduction*, 1:210-15; H. Jagersma, *A History of Israel from Alexander the Great to Bar Kochba* (trans. J. Bowden; Philadelphia: Fortress, 1986), 44-67; J. Efron, *Studies on the Hasmonean Period* (Leiden: Brill 1987); D. J. Harrington, *The Maccabean Revolt: Anatomy of a Biblical Revolution* (Wilmington, Del.: Michael Glazier, 1988); and J. Sievers, *The Hasmoneans and Their Supporters: From Mattathias to the Death of John Hyrcanus* (Atlanta: Scholars Press, 1990).

41. Because of his anti-Jewish legislation, the figure of Antiochus IV has been portrayed as the archetypal villain in Jewish apocalyptic and historical writings: e.g., Dan 11:20-39; 1 Macc 1; 4 Macc 4:15–5:38; Josephus, *Ant.* 12.242-286; *T. Adam* 4:6-7.

42. Judas appears to have been the founder of the resistance movement in 2 Macc 5:27; 8:1, whereas in 1 Macc 2–3 it seems to be Mattathias of Modein, the father of Judas. The discrepancy may be explained by the fact that 1 Macc was composed by a Hasmonean court historian. The Hasmonean dynasty was founded by Simon, who was also a son of Mattathias.

43. Jerusalem's temple was officially returned to traditional Jewish worship by Antiochus (probably Antiochus V, 2 Macc 11:22-26). The other letters in 2 Macc 11:16-38 presuppose a lengthy period of negotiation, probably 164-162 B.C.

44. See 1 Macc 4:36-59; 2 Macc 10:5-8; Josephus, *Ant.* 12.323-326.

45. Simon was the brother of Judas and son of Mattathias of Modein. Josephus calls Si-

brother Jonathan, the Syrian garrison was expelled from Jerusalem (142 B.C.). Shortly afterward, in 140, Simon was heralded by the Jewish people as both ruler and high priest.[46] During the reign of his son, John Hyrcanus (134-104), Syrian interference in the Jewish state finally ended.[47]

The dynasty established by Simon had the appearance of Hellenistic royalty.[48] Simon and his descendants had full military and political power. As high priests, they were in charge of the sanctuary and its priests. Although the establishment of the dynasty was a welcomed alternative to foreign rule, certain priests regarded the Hasmonean office of high priest as illegitimate because of their questionable descent from Zadok.[49] Others considered their claims to kingship equally illegitimate because they were Levites, not from the tribe of Judah. It was probably at this time that the Essenes, a faction of Hasidim whose leader was a Zadokite priest (the "Teacher of Righteousness"), left Jerusalem to establish their own community of Qumran, near the Dead Sea.[50] Another faction of the Hasidim, the Pharisees, were also persecuted under a later Hasmonean, Alexander Jannaeus (104-78 B.C.).[51]

Under the reigns of John Hyrcanus and his son Alexander Jannaeus, most of Palestine became a Jewish state through conquest. Although they were practicing Hellenists, the Hasmoneans compelled the inhabitants of the Greek cities to emigrate or convert to Judaism.[52]

---

mon's family the "Asamoneans," probably the name of one of Simon's ancestors (*Ant.* 16.187; 20.190, 238).

46. 1 Macc 14:41-49.

47. Josephus, *Ant.* 13.254-300.

48. 1 Macc 14:41-49 and Josephus, *Ant.* 13.213-217.

49. In the Chronicler's history, Zadok was a descendant of Aaron (1 Chr 6:50-53) and was appointed high priest by King David (16:39-40; 29:22). Ezekiel underscores the case that only descendants of Zadok could serve as high priests (Ezek 40:46; 48:11). For evidence that the Hasmoneans may well have been Zadokites, see J. VanderKam, *From Joshua to Caiaphas: High Priests after the Exile* (Minneapolis: Fortress, 2004), 270n.90.

50. Some of the writings of this Qumran community, called the Dead Sea Scrolls, underscore both the preeminence of the Zadokite priesthood (CD 3.18–4.4; 1QS 5.1-3) and the corruption of the Jerusalem (Hasmonean) priests (1QpHab 9.4-5; 12.7-9). See A. Dupont-Sommer, *The Essene Writings from Qumran* (trans. G. Vermes; Oxford: Blackwell, 1961) and F. García Martínez and E. J. C. Tigchelaar, *The Dead Sea Scrolls: Study Edition*, 2 vols. (Grand Rapids: Eerdmans, 2000).

51. Josephus, *Ant.* 13.372-376. Pharisees were probably among the thousands of Jewish rioters punished by Alexander Jannaeus, since they were outspoken critics of Hyrcanus, his father. See *Ant.* 13.288-292.

52. For the conquests of Hyrcanus, see Josephus, *Ant.* 13.230-300.

After the reigns of Jannaeus and his widow, Alexandra (76-67 B.C.), the Hasmonean dynasty came to a close with the intrigues and fighting of two sons. In the year 65 there was such a struggle for power between Aristobulus II and Hyrcanus II that the latter requested Rome to intervene. Rome happily obliged, thereby ending Jewish independence.[53]

The Roman Occupation When the Roman general Pompey ended the dispute between the two Hasmoneans in 64 B.C., Palestine came under Roman control. Eventually, Augustus made it a part of the imperial province of Syria (27 B.C.).[54] Pontius Pilate served as prefect of these regions in A.D. 26-36. His chief responsibilities were to maintain order and collect taxes, while the Jewish leaders of Jerusalem were allowed a modicum of self-rule by the emperor.

The Roman provincial system also used the services of local magistrates. In the case of Palestine, the Idumeans Antipater and his son Herod, eventually known as "the Great," became powerful vassal kings of Rome.[55] Herod (ruled 37-4 B.C.) was a crafty politician, a magnificent builder, a ruthless tyrant, and a passionate Hellenizer. He surrounded himself with Greek scholars and undertook many building projects: an impressive fortified palace, the magnificent Jerusalem temple, the fortress of Masada (35 miles south of Jerusalem), and numerous Greek cities with theaters, baths, and amphitheaters.[56] Numerous acts of cruelty, combined with the fact that he was an Idumean convert to Judaism, ensured that Herod was never greatly liked by the Jews. Before he died, Jesus of Nazareth was born.[57]

---

53. Josephus, *Ant.* 14.1-79.

54. For more discussion of the Augustan provincial policies, see the subsection "A Stable Roman Empire," under the section "The Greco-Roman Context of the NT." All of the prefects and procurators of Palestine are mentioned in Josephus, *Ant.* 18.1-108; 19.360-365; 20.1-53, 148-223; *War* 2.117-183, 204-249, 271-404. Pilate is also mentioned in Philo, *On the Embassy to Gaius* 38. See also G. W. Stevenson, *Roman Provincial Administration* (2d ed.; Oxford: Blackwell, 1959).

55. N. Kokkinos, *The Herodian Dynasty: Origins, Role in Society, and Eclipse* (Sheffield: Sheffield Academic Press, 1998); P. Richardson, *Herod: King of the Jews and Friend of the Romans* (Minneapolis: Fortress, 1999).

56. D. Roller, *The Building Program of Herod the Great* (Berkeley: University of California Press, 1998).

57. For extensive material on Herod the Great, see Josephus, *Ant.*, bks. 14–17; and *War* 1.195-673. See also M. Grant, *Herod the Great* (New York: American Heritage, 1971); and S. Perowne, *The Life and Times of Herod the Great* (London: Hodder & Stoughton, 1956).

After Herod's death, his kingdom was divided among his three sons. Philip became tetrarch of the largely non-Jewish areas northeast of the Sea of Galilee (4 B.C.–A.D. 34). Herod Antipas was named tetrarch of Galilee and Perea across the Jordan River (4 B.C.–A.D. 39).[58] Herod Antipas had John the Baptist executed (Mark 6:14-29) and later had an unsatisfying interview with Jesus (Luke 23:6-12); he was eventually exiled by Emperor Caligula (A.D. 39). Archelaus, the third son, was given Samaria and Judea. Because his rule was challenged both by his subjects and by Antipas, and because there was general unrest brewing in Galilee, Archelaus was dismissed by Rome and banished to Gaul in A.D. 6. Except for the short reign of Herod Agrippa I over all Palestine (41-44; Acts 12:1, 19-23), the entire region was under Roman procurators after A.D. 44.[59]

According to ancient Jewish sources, life under Rome was difficult. By A.D. 44, national discontent was stirring Jewish revolutionaries, who sought to rekindle the spirit of the Maccabean revolt. Self-styled prophets and messiahs appeared, as well as the Sicarii, a radical group of assassins.[60] The procurators Felix (A.D. 52-60) and Festus (60-62) spent a great deal of time putting down Jewish revolts (both men are mentioned in Acts 23–24).

Conflict finally erupted in A.D. 66, when the procurator Gessius Florus (A.D. 64-66) embezzled funds from the temple treasury. While the people of Jerusalem protested, Florus had his troops plunder the city. In retaliation, the temple sacrifices for Rome and the emperor were stopped, and the fortress of Masada was captured by Jewish rebels. The First Jewish Revolt against Rome had begun, giving birth to a Jewish resistance party called the Zealots.[61]

---

58. Galilee was not a predominantly Gentile area, as has traditionally been claimed, but was mostly Jewish by this time. See M. Chancey, *The Myth of a Gentile Galilee* (Cambridge: Cambridge University Press, 2002).

59. For information on the later Herods, see Josephus, *Ant.,* bks. 17–19; *War,* bks. 1–2. See also H. Hoehner, *Herod Antipas* (Cambridge: Cambridge University Press, 1972); A. H. M. Jones, *The Herods of Judea* (2d ed.; Oxford: Clarendon Press, 1967); and S. Perowne, *The Later Herods* (New York: Abingdon, 1959).

60. For example, see Judas the Galilean, who inspired the Zealot sect (Josephus, *Ant.* 17.271-272; 18.1-10; *War* 2.117-118), as well as Theudas the false prophet (*Ant.* 20.97-99), the Egyptian prophet (*Ant.* 20.167-172), and other false prophets (*War* 6.285-287). For data on the Sicarii and Zealots, see *War* 7.252-274, 407-419. See also D. M. Rhoads, *Israel in Revolution, 6-74 C.E.* (Philadelphia: Fortress, 1976).

61. Josephus, *War* 2.405-456. Although many resistance groups existed before A.D. 66, a case can be made for the emergence of a specific "Zealot" party only after this date. See *War*

After some successful attacks by the rebels, Nero dispatched his able general Vespasian to quell the revolt that was spreading throughout Palestine. With the aid of his son, Titus, who commanded the forces of Egypt, Vespasian made a successful assault upon Galilee with a massive army.[62] Jerusalem at this time was caught in a bitter civil war between moderate and radical Jewish rebels. The experienced Vespasian subdued the surrounding areas and waited for the Jews to exhaust themselves in Jerusalem. But before Vespasian could end the revolt in Jerusalem, his actions were delayed by the death of Nero. In 69 Vespasian left his command post to his son Titus and went to Rome to become its ninth emperor.[63]

In the spring of 70, Titus began his siege of Jerusalem.[64] Hunger and thirst took their toll; the city was gradually taken and then left in ruins. The great temple was destroyed by fire in the midst of the battle.[65] Titus returned to Rome, exhibiting hundreds of prisoners in the victory parade through the city. But Titus would have two additional memorials: the Arch of Titus, standing in the Roman Forum today; and the Coliseum, financed by plunder looted from the Jerusalem temple.[66]

The destruction of Jerusalem and the second temple was a terrible blow to Judaism. What survived was a reorganized religion under the Pharisees, the only group of Palestinian religious leaders to survive the war, who gathered at the coastal town of Jamnia (Heb. Jabneh).[67] They began to devise a form of Judaism without a temple or priests that became

---

2.441-448, 564; 4.158-161; 7.268-270; Rhoads, *Israel in Revolution*, 52-58, 97-110; M. Borg, "The Currency of the Term 'Zealot,'" *JTS*, n.s., 22 (1971): 504-12; M. Goodman, *The Ruling Class of Judea: The Origins of the Jewish Revolt against Rome* (Cambridge: Cambridge University Press, 1987); and M. Hengel, *The Zealots: Investigations into the Jewish Freedmen Movement in the Period from Herod I until 70 A.D.* (trans. David Smith; Edinburgh: T&T Clark, 1989).

62. Josephus, *War* 3.1–4.120.

63. Josephus, *War* 4.486-502, 545-555, 588-663; Suetonius, *Vespasian* 4-6.

64. Josephus, *War* 5.1-20, 39-46.

65. Josephus, *War* 6.1-8, 15-53.

66. Titus's triumph over the Jews is described in Josephus, *War* 7.116-162; and Suetonius, *Titus* 4-5.

67. The Hebrew name "Jabneh" is mentioned in 2 Chr 26:6; the Greek name "Jamnia," in 1 Macc 4:15; 5:58; 2 Macc 12:8-9; Josephus, *War* 2.335. The Jewish Mishnah (ca. A.D. 220) mentions the transfer of the court ("Beth-Din") or college ("Yeshiva") of seventy-two elders from Jerusalem to Jabneh in the following tractates: *Roš Haš.* 4:1-2; *Zebaḥ.* 1:3; *Ketub.* 4:6. Jabneh was the center of Judaism from A.D. 70 to the early second century. See J. P. Lewis, "What Do We Mean by Jabneh?" *JBR* 32 (1964): 125-32; and S. Cohen, "The Significance of Yavneh: Pharisees, Rabbis, and the End of Jewish Sectarianism," *HUCA* 55 (1984): 27-53.

known as rabbinic Judaism.[68] Palestinian Judaism lingered until the Judean uprising led in 132-35 by Simon Bar Kochba ("Son of the Star," a messianic title from Num 24:17).[69] This Second Jewish Revolt was in reaction to Emperor Hadrian's attempt to rebuild Jerusalem as a Greco-Roman city with a temple for Jupiter. Hadrian crushed the revolt and carried out his plans, banishing all Jews from the city. From that time on, until the establishment of a Jewish state in 1948, Judaism was primarily a religion of the Diaspora.[70]

The Persistent Faith of Judaism

Although Judaism's history was characterized by foreign dominance, its traditions and beliefs persisted for centuries. Unlike the diverse religions of their foreign conquerors, the Jews retained their belief in only one God, offered sacrifices at only one temple, observed feasts that repeated their history as a people, sought to follow laws of God written in sacred books, worshipped God and studied the laws in meetinghouses called synagogues, and maintained confidence in their destiny as the people of God. Even though foreign thought-forms (e.g., Babylonian, Persian, and Greek) influenced Jewish beliefs and practices, their appropriation into a complete system of monotheism, law, and religious history made Judaism a distinct religious phenomenon. We now look more closely at these Jewish beliefs and practices.

---

68. Third-century rabbinic sources containing earlier traditions are the Mishnah, or legal interpretations of the Torah; the early Midrashim, or commentaries on the Hebrew Bible; and the Tosefta, additions to the Mishnah. See also J. Neusner, *Early Rabbinic Judaism* (Leiden: Brill, 1975) and *Method and Meaning in Ancient Judaism* (Missoula, Mont.: Scholars Press, 1979); L. Schiffman, *From Text to Tradition: A History of Second Temple and Rabbinic Judaism* (Hoboken, N.J.: Ktav Publications, 1991); H. Strack and G. Stemburger, *Introduction to the Talmud and Midrash* (trans. M. Bockmuehl; Edinburgh: T&T Clark, 1991); and J. Neusner, *Rabbinic Judaism: The Documentary History of Its Formative Age, 70-600 C.E.* (Bethesda, Md.: CDL Press, 1994).

69. Spartianus, *Hadrian* 4; Dio Cassius, *Roman History* 69.12-15; Eusebius, *Hist. eccl.* 4.6.1-4; 8.4. See recently discovered letter from Simon Bar Kochba in Y. Yadin, *Bar Kochba* (New York: Random House, 1971).

70. See A. Ebban, *My People: The Story of the Jews* (new ed.; New York: Random House, 1984), a popular history that underscores this point.

The One God   Allegiance to only one God, or practical/ethical monotheism, came to its fullest expression in Judaism during the exile, when the sovereignty of other gods was decisively and uniformly rejected.[71] However, stress on the oneness of God and the need for exclusive obedience to God occurred before the exile, when Israel's classic expression of faith was framed: "Hear, O Israel: The LORD is our God, the Lord is one" (Deut 6:4 NIV; see also 4:35, 39). The Jews viewed their God as the creator distinct from his creation, who was active in the world as provider and savior. During the Greco-Roman period, the Jews were often accused of atheism by the Gentiles (i.e., the non-Jews) because they refused to recognize the sovereignty of any other deity except their own.[72]

Connected with the belief in only one God was the idea of a covenant that bound Israel with their God.[73] These OT covenants, or binding agreements with God, usually included (1) a list of gracious acts that God had performed on Israel's behalf, such as delivering it from bondage in Egypt (Exod 19:4-6), and (2) stipulations that Israel was expected to carry out in response to God's acts of favor (20:1–23:19). The circumcision of every male child was also required as a sign of the covenant (Gen 17:10-14). This covenant with God gave the people of Israel both a special status as God's elect and a sacred responsibility to carry out God's statutes and laws.

The Sacrificial System   Although attempts were made to construct rival temples,[74] the temple of Jerusalem remained the exclusive place of sacrificial

---

71. Second Isa 43:10-11; 44:8; 45:5-6, 21-22; 46:8-9. See also B. W. Anderson, "God, OT View of," *IDB* 2:427-28; and M. Smith, *The Early History of God: Yahweh and the Other Deities in Ancient Israel* (San Francisco: Harper & Row, 1990), 145-60.

72. For Roman suspicions of Judaism, see Seneca, *Epistulae morales* 95.57; and Tacitus, *Histories* 5.2-13. For Jewish opposition to emperor worship, see Josephus, *Ant.* 18.257-268; and Philo, *On the Embassy to Gaius* (concerning the deification of Emperors Caligula and Augustus).

73. Many of the covenant formulations found in the Jewish Scriptures were based on secular treaties of the ancient Near East that were instituted by kings on behalf of their vassal subjects; for discussion, with primary sources, see D. J. McCarthy, *Treaty and Covenant* (new ed.; Rome: Biblical Institute Press, 1978) and *OT Covenant* (Atlanta: John Knox, 1972); G. E. Mendenhall, "Covenant Forms in Israelite Tradition," in *The Biblical Archaeologist Reader* (3 vols.; ed. D. N. Freedman and G. E. Wright; Garden City, N.Y.: Anchor Books, 1961-70), 3:25-53; and S. Porter and J. de Roo, eds., *The Concept of Covenant in the Second Temple Period* (Leiden: Brill, 2003).

74. W. F. Stinespring, "Temple, Jerusalem," *IDB* 4:534-60; M. Ben-Dov, "Temple of Herod," *IDBSupp* 870-72; M. Haran, "Priests and Priesthood," *EncJud* 13:1069-88.

worship for almost all Jews.[75] The first temple, built by Solomon one thousand years before the Christian era, was destroyed by the Neobabylonians in 587 B.C. A modest temple was built by the returning exiles in 515 B.C. and rebuilt on a much grander scale in the Herodian period. This temple was begun under Herod the Great in 20 B.C. but was not completed until A.D. 60, ten years before its destruction.[76] The guardians of the temple and its worship were the priests. When temple worship was restored in 515 B.C., they regained much of the influence they had lost during the exile, especially the high priest, who now had both civil and religious authority. Under the Seleucid Greeks, the high priesthood became a political position sought after by competing priestly families. In the Herodian period high priests were appointed from priestly families of the Diaspora. They presided over both the temple worship and the Great Sanhedrin, the high court of Judaism.[77] The power of the priesthood ended with the destruction of Jerusalem in A.D. 70.

The major religious function of the priests was to maintain national purity through the sacrificial system at the temple.[78] In ancient Israel a whole system of sacrifices had arisen to set sinful people right with the one, holy God. Such sacrifices were offered on an altar at least twice daily.

The architectural design of the Herodian temple reflected the various degrees of holiness.[79] Only the outermost part of the temple was accessible to Gentiles. Moving toward the central buildings (for Jews) came the Court of Women, the Court of Israel (men), the Court of Priests, where daily sacrifices took place, the Holy Place, where the priests regularly burned incense, and the Holy of Holies, into which the high priest entered only once a year on the Day of Atonement.

Even though the temple was a holy center where the priest interceded for the people, it was also the center of commercial activity. It housed the

75. When the Jerusalem temple was captured by Antiochus IV, the high priest, Onias IV, built a similar but inferior temple in Heliopolis, Egypt; see Josephus, *Ant.* 13.62-68.

76. The earliest descriptions of the Herodian temple and priesthood are Josephus, *Ant.* 15.380-425; 20.224-251 (high priests); *War* 5.184-247; Mishnah *Mid.* ("Measurements" of the temple) 1–5; see T. C. Eskenazi and K. H. Richards, eds., *Temple and Community in the Persian Period* (vol. 2 of *Second Temple Studies;* Sheffield: JSOT Press, 1994).

77. For an excellent survey, see H. Mantel, "Sanhedrin," *IDBSupp* 784-86.

78. Lev 1–10; 16; 21–23; 27; Ezek 44–46. See also L. H. Schiffman, "Priests," *HBD* 821-23; J. Neyrey, "Clean/Unclean, Pure/Polluted and Holy/Profane," in *The Social Sciences and NT Interpretation,* ed. R. Rohrbaugh (Peabody, Mass.: Hendrickson, 1996), 80-104.

79. Josephus, *Ant.* 15.380-425; *War* 5.184-247; Mishnah *Mid.* 1–5.

national treasury, the monies of which came from an annual temple tax, which every Jew was expected to pay. The priests were also responsible for the collection and allocation of these funds.

The Feasts Closely related to the temple worship were the religious festivals and holy days of the Jews.[80] The Jewish civil year began in September/October, whereas the religious year began in March/April. Regulations for the feasts are prescribed in the books of the law (Exod; Lev; Deut), with the exception of Hanukkah and Purim, which were instituted later. Pilgrims from outside Jerusalem and Palestine thronged to the holy city for the three main festivals: Passover–Unleavened Bread (March/April, celebrating the barley harvest and the exodus from Egypt), Pentecost/Weeks (May/June, celebrating the wheat harvest and the giving of the law), and Booths (September/October, celebrating God's care during the wilderness wandering).

The Law After the exile, Judaism gave new focus to the obedience of God's will in its collection of sacred writings.[81] The Deuteronomic History (Deut through 2 Kgs) had been finalized and added to the Pentateuch (Gen, Exod, Lev, and Num) to serve as Israel's primary history. Several prophetic books were also added: Isaiah 1–39, Jeremiah, Ezekiel, and some so-called minor prophets (e.g., Amos, Hos, Mic). Supplements to Isaiah (chs. 40–66) and additional minor prophets were added shortly afterward. This collection of the Law (Gen–Deut) and the Prophets (Josh–2 Kgs, Isa–Ezek, and 12 Minor Prophets) was closed by the second century B.C. (see Sir, prologue), but a third undefined group of "other books" (Writings) remained open. This third general category included such books as the Psalms, Proverbs, Esther, and Daniel.[82]

---

80. Early sources outside the Bible are Josephus, *Ant.* 3.237-257; 11.109-113; 12.323-326; *War* 2.42-44; 6.423-427; Mishnah *Mo'ed* ("Set Feasts"), second major division. For a listing of some Mishnaic texts with comments, see Barrett, *NTB*, 153-62.

81. H. Mantel, "The Development of the Oral Law during the Second Temple Period," in *Society and Religion in the Second Temple Period* (vol. 8 of *World History of the Jewish People*; ed. M. Avi-Yonah and Z. Baras; Jerusalem: Massada, 1977), 41-64, 325-37; "Torah Scholarship" and "Life and Law," in Schürer, *History,* 2:314-80 and 464-87; H. L. Strack, *Introduction to the Talmud and Midrash* (Philadelphia: Jewish Publication Society, 1931).

82. D. N. Freedman, "Canon of the OT," 130-36, and J. A. Sanders, "Torah," 909-11, in *IDBSupp*; A. C. Sundberg, "'The OT': A Christian Canon," *CBQ* 30 (1968): 143-55; S. Z. Leiman, *The Canonization of the Hebrew Scriptures: The Talmudic and Mishnaic Evidence* (Hamden, Conn.: Archon Books, 1976).

Obedience to the Torah ("instruction"), particularly the legal material of the Law collection (Exod–Deut), was of primary importance in Judaism. To know the law was to know the will of God. To study and to do the law was the greatest blessing. By the Hasmonean period, different attitudes to the Torah had evolved. The Pharisees were concerned with interpreting and applying the law in a manner applicable to contemporary problems. They held that God had given Moses two laws — a written one (Law, Prophets, and Writings) and an oral one to interpret the written.[83] The Sadducees rejected the concept of oral law and did not regard the prophetic books or the Writings as binding. The Essenes, like the Pharisees, devoted themselves to the study of the Law, Prophets, and Writings but focused on ascetic practices and prophetic predictions in their communities outside of Jerusalem.[84] After A.D. 70 the position of the Pharisees was assumed by rabbinic Judaism. The practice of the Pharisees and their descendants — to expand the written word by oral tradition in order to apply it to new conditions — is documented in the Mishnah and the Talmud. It consisted of restatement and revision through discussion and debate. By the first century there were already differing schools of interpretation within the Pharisees (e.g., Hillel and Shammai). Debate and discussion were necessary to make a hedge for the Torah — that is, to keep it from being transgressed. For instance, to preserve the Sabbath commandment (Exod 20:8-11), one should not work. But what is work? Oral tradition, transcribed into the Mishnah by A.D. 220, set out to define precisely what activities constitute "work." So important was the Torah to the Jews that all aspects of life and thought were to be inspired and guided by it.[85]

---

83. On Pharisees and oral law, see Josephus, *Ant.* 13.297. For an example of oral traditions codified in writing, see Mishnah *'Abot* ("Fathers"), selections of maxims in praise of the law, handed down in the names of sixty teachers of the law who lived between 300 B.C. and A.D. 200.

84. Josephus, *Ant.* 18.18-22; *War* 2.119-161; the Dead Sea Scrolls of the Qumran community (an Essene sect).

85. English translations of major rabbinic works include H. Danby, *The Mishnah* (London: Oxford University Press, 1933); I. Epstein, ed., *The Babylonian Talmud* (35 vols.; London: Soncino Press, 1935-52); H. Freedman and M. Simon, *Midrash Rabbah* (10 vols.; London: Soncino Press, 1951); J. Neusner, *Tosefta* (New York: Ktav, 1977), *The Mishnah: A New Translation* (New Haven: Yale University Press, 1988), and *The Talmud of Babylonia* (36 vols.; Chico, Calif., and Atlanta: Scholars Press, 1984-90); H. W. Guggenheimer, *The Jerusalem Talmud* (Berlin: Walter de Gruyter, 2000). The Mishnah and Talmud contain halakah (exposition of law) and haggadah (stories and maxims). The Midrash is primarily haggadah.

The Synagogue The synagogue ("gathering place") played an important part in the growth and persistence of Judaism.[86] In the Roman period, synagogues existed in most regions of the empire.[87] Although the Talmud mentions their origins during the exile,[88] the earliest archaeological evidence is from the Christian era.[89] The synagogue was a meeting place for prayer and an educational center for the study of the law. No sacrifices were offered there. The synagogue services probably consisted of a recitation of the Shema (Deut 6:4), Scripture readings, expositions, blessings, and prayers.[90]

The Final Destiny Judaism was concerned not only with remembering the past and living faithfully in the present but also with understanding its future destiny.[91] In reaction to the tragic events of Jewish history (e.g., the Babylonian exile, Syrian oppression, and the disappointing Hasmonean rule), two alternative lines of thought developed regarding the future. First, Judaism could repeat the lofty nationalistic hopes of the ancient prophets (e.g., Isa 11; Mic 4) and leave to God the time and circumstances under which these glorious promises would be fulfilled. Second, it could assess the national tragedies as the work of a demonic power opposed to God and shift the sphere of God's final triumph from a future time in plain history to the cosmic realms of heaven and earth at the end of time.

86. "The Synagogue," in Safrai and Stern, *Jewish People*, 2:908-44; "Synagogue," in Schürer, *History*, 2:423-63; H. Kee and L. Cohick, eds., *Evolution of the Synagogue: Problems and Progress* (Harrisburg, Pa.: Trinity Press International, 1999); L. Levine, *The Ancient Synagogue: The First Thousand Years* (New Haven: Yale University Press, 2000).

87. Allusions to these synagogues can be found in the four gospels, Acts, Josephus, Philo, and rabbinic sources.

88. Palestinian Talmud, *Meg.* 3.73d; Babylonian Talmud, *Meg.* 29d, alluding to Ezek 11:16, a "sanctuary" *(mikdash)* for the Diaspora.

89. See archaeological illustrations, with comments about synagogues in Palestine, Babylon, Egypt, Asia, Greece, and Italy, in I. Sonne, "Synagogue," *IDB* 4:480-84; and E. Meyers, "Synagogue, Architecture," *IDBSupp* 842-44.

90. For the two versions of the Eighteen Benedictions *(Amidah* or *Shemoneh 'Esreh)* used in early synagogue worship, see Schürer, *History*, 2:455-63; for other prayers, with some Christian interpolations, see D. R. Darnell and D. A. Fiensy, "Hellenistic Synagogal Prayers (Second to Third Century A.D.)," in Charlesworth, *OTP* 2:671-97; and R. Langer and S. Fine, eds., *Liturgy in the Life of the Synagogue* (Winona Lake, Ind.: Eisenbrauns, 2005).

91. For primary sources, see Charlesworth, *OTP*, vol. 1; G. Vermes, *The Complete Dead Sea Scrolls in English* (New York: Penguin Press, 1997); and H. S. Ryle and M. R. James, *Psalmoi Solomontos: Psalms of the Pharisees* (Cambridge: Cambridge University Press, 1891).

Nationalistic Hopes By the first century B.C. most Jews assumed the first alternative — namely, that of repeating the nationalistic hopes of the earlier prophets. Documentation for this outlook is found in the *Psalms of Solomon*.[92] The unknown author of this work was a Jew who longed for the establishment of a Davidic ruler as God's vice-regent over Israel (17:4-5, 32) and saw the Hasmonean Sadducees as the opponents of the devout (8:12, 22; 17:5-8, 22, 45). His teaching of divine providence (5:3-4) and final retribution (2:34-35; 15:12-13) reflects a Pharisaic or Essene viewpoint.[93]

Like the Essenes, Pharisees, and Zealots, most Jews hoped for a coming Messiah (lit. "anointed one"), probably from the dynasty of King David.[94] In contrast to the early Christians, the popular Jewish hope concerned a political ruler who would defeat the foreign oppressors and reestablish Israel as a political kingdom. Unlike the revolutionary Zealots (who attracted many Pharisees and Essenes in A.D. 66), this would come about not through violent resistance to Rome but through the hand of God. In distinction from the Essenes and other esoteric groups of end-time orientation, this nationalistic hope would take place in the real politics of plain history, sometime in the future.

Apocalyptic Eschatology The Essenes, certain early Christians, and other related messianic or prophetic groups assumed the second alternative of

---

92. Here we follow "Psalms of Solomon," trans. R. B. Wright, in Charlesworth, *OTP* 2:639-70.

93. The *Pss. Sol.* contain no predictions about the "trials of the faithful" before the Messiah's coming or any cryptic clues as to when the event will occur. God will establish the rule of the Davidic Messiah at a time determined by him (17:21). For more information, see H. C. Kee, *The NT in Context: Sources and Documents* (Englewood Cliffs, N.J.: Prentice-Hall, 1984), 85-87; Ryle and James, *Psalmoi Solomontos*.

94. Jer 23:4-5; 33:14-22; Zech 6:12-13; 9:9-10; *Pss. Sol.* 17; Philo, *On Rewards and Punishments* 16.95-97 (conquering Messiah); Josephus, *War* 6.288-315 (6.312, on messianic oracles); Qumran scrolls on Davidic Messiah: 1QSa 2.11-27; 4Q254 on Gen. 49:10 1-8; 4QFlor 1.11-13; also, J. Charlesworth, H. Lichtenberger, and G. Oegema, eds., *Qumran Messianism: Studies in the Messianic Expectations in the Dead Sea Scrolls* (Tübingen: Mohr Siebeck, 1998); early Christian accounts of Jewish messianism: Mark 8:11-12; 12:35-37; 15:43; Luke 23:2-3; John 1:41, 49; 6:15; Mishnah *Ber.* 1:5 and *Soṭah* 9:15 (approaching age of the Messiah); and *Midrash Rabbah* on Ps 60:9-10, where Rabbi Akiba hails Simon Bar Kosiba (Kochba) as Messiah in A.D. 132-35. Some scholars now question the importance of Davidic descent for the Messiah; see K. Pomykala, *The Davidic Dynasty Tradition in Early Judaism: Its History and Significance for Messianism* (Atlanta: Scholars Press, 1995)

"apocalyptic eschatology."[95] They taught that God had revealed to them the secret schedule of his plan by which the evil powers of this world would be overcome and God's eternal rule established. They did not expect the restoration of all Israel or the world but, rather, the vindication of a small faithful remnant, usually identical with the sect that propagated the teaching. The type of literature produced by these groups was highly symbolic and esoteric in style. It was filled with veiled references to historical events structured in a certain time frame that led to a final conflict followed by a new age of salvation. All was predetermined by God, and only those within the group could decipher the revelations ("apocalypses") and discern the movement of the divine purpose. Ultimate deliverance would come from God through a messianic figure: a Davidic king, a prophet like Moses, an ideal priest, a leader of eschatological (end-time) war, or a heavenly Son of Man.

Unlike the Pharisaic hope of national deliverance, these disclosures of the end time were no longer translated in terms of plain history, real politics, and human instrumentality. They were portrayed as cosmic battles between heaven and earth, angels and demons, with ultimate salvation coming from God alone. Examples of apocalyptic literature are Daniel, *1 Enoch, 2 Baruch, Testament of Moses, 4 Ezra*, Mark 13, Revelation, and many of the Dead Sea Scrolls from Qumran. Most of the books listed here are written in the name of famous individuals, like Daniel, Moses, and Enoch. Although the real authors are unknown, this procedure (called pseudonymity) was a feature of apocalyptic books designed to lend the writing a certain authority.

---

95. For a convenient collection of the literature, see Charlesworth, *OTP.* For studies, see W. Schmithals, *The Apocalyptic Movement* (trans. J. E. Steely; Nashville: Abingdon, 1975); "Special Issue on Apocalyptic Literature," *CBQ* 39 (1977): 307-409; P. D. Hanson, "Apocalypse, Genre" and "Apocalypticism," *IDBSupp* 27-34; Hanson, "Jewish Apocalyptic against Its Near Eastern Environment," *RB* 78 (1971): 31-58; P. D. Hanson, *The Dawn of Apocalyptic: The Historical and Sociological Roots of Jewish Apocalyptic Eschatology* (rev. ed.; Philadelphia: Fortress, 1979); K. Koch, *The Rediscovery of the Apocalyptic* (London: SCM Press, 1972); S. Cook, *Prophecy and Apocalypticism: The Post-Exilic Setting* (Minneapolis: Fortress, 1995); D. Russell, *Divine Disclosure: An Introduction to Jewish Apocalyptic* (Minneapolis: Fortress, 1992); and J. Collins, *The Apocalyptic Imagination: An Introduction to Jewish Apocalyptic Literature* (Grand Rapids: Eerdmans, 1998).

The Competing Parties within Judaism

By the time of Jesus, second temple Judaism had become a religion of competing parties. Although there was basic agreement on such points as monotheism, Torah, Sabbath, and the feasts, there was much diversity regarding how to interpret and implement them. Since we have already discussed Hellenistic Judaism of the Diaspora, we limit our discussion here to the four major parties of Palestinian Judaism: the Sadducees, Pharisees, Essenes, and Zealots.[96]

The Sadducees The Sadducees,[97] whose name was probably derived from Zadok, a high priest of Solomon's time (1 Kgs 2:35, approx. 950 b.c.), were the party of priestly, urban aristocrats who were favorably disposed to Hellenistic culture but conservative in politics and religion. They had supported the policies of the Hasmoneans and later sought to secure the favor of the Herods and the Romans. As priests, they officiated at the sacrificial offerings in the temple, and from their ranks the high priest was appointed. Their members dominated the Jewish high court of the Sanhe-

---

96. See the following studies: M. Simon, *Jewish Sects at the Time of Jesus* (trans. J. H. Farley; Philadelphia: Fortress, 1967); Schürer, *History*, 2:381-414, 562-90, 598-606; M. Avi-Yonah and Z. Baras, eds., *Society and Religion in the Second Temple Period* (vol. 8 of *World History of the Jewish People*; Jerusalem: Massada, 1977), 99-152, 263-302; G. W. E. Nickelsburg and M. E. Stone, *Faith and Piety in Early Judaism* (Philadelphia: Fortress, 1983), 24-40; J. Neusner, ed., *The Pharisees and Other Sects* (2 vols.; New York: Garland Publications, 1990); A. Baumgarten, *The Flourishing of Jewish Sects in the Maccabean Era: An Interpretation* (Leiden: Brill, 1997); and M. Weinfeld, *Normative and Sectarian Judaism in the Second Temple Period* (London: T&T Clark, 2005).

97. For primary sources, see Josephus *Ant.* 13.171-173 (their denial of fate), 13.293-298 (adhere only to written law, not oral traditions of the fathers, 297); 18.16-17 (deny immortality of the soul); *War* 2.162-166 (concerned only with human free will and deny final rewards and punishments, 164-165); Mark 12:18; Acts 23:8 (they deny there is a resurrection from the dead); Mishnah *Ber.* 9:5 (classified with "heretics" for denying a world to come?); *Parah* 3:3, 7 (scrupulous in temple sacrifices); *Yad.* 4:6-8 (disagreements with Pharisees on legal issues); *Menaḥ.* 10:3; Babylonian Talmud *Pesaḥ.* 57a (identified with the house of Boethus, from Alexandria, 23 b.c.; Josephus, *Ant.* 15.320); and J. Goldin, *The Fathers according to Rabbi Nathan* (New Haven: Yale University Press, 1955), 5 (supposed split of Boethusian and Sadducean parties over doctrine of final reward). For discussion, see A. Saldarini, *Pharisees, Scribes, and Sadducees in Palestinian Society* (Wilmington, Del.: Michael Glazier, 1988); and G. Stemberger, *Jewish Contemporaries of Jesus: Pharisees, Sadducees, Essenes* (trans. A. Mahnke; Minneapolis: Fortress, 1995).

drin. In both politics and religion they came in conflict with the popular Pharisee party, whose members were generally more antagonistic to Roman rule and tended to associate themselves with the synagogue and its particular emphases. The Sadducees regarded only the five books of Moses as binding, whereas the Pharisees appealed also to oral tradition in seeking to apply the Torah to all aspects of life. The Sadducees, in contrast, limited the scope of the Torah by a more literal interpretation, without employing oral tradition as an authoritative guide. Whereas the Pharisees held to the belief of angels and a resurrection of the dead, the Sadducees rejected these beliefs as later formulations not derived from the authoritative books of Moses. After the destruction of the temple in A.D. 70, the priestly group of the Sadducees lost its power and eventually disappeared.

The Pharisees The Pharisees were probably the most influential and significant Jewish group of the Greco-Roman times.[98] Their name is probably derived from Hebrew *perushim,* meaning "the separated ones," although it may have been a pejorative nickname signifying "Persian" (Aram. *Parsāy*) because they shared certain Persian beliefs (e.g., in resurrection, angels vs. demons). Their intense devotion to the law makes them the spiritual descendants of the Hasidim, who joined the Maccabean revolt to oppose religious persecution under the Syrian Greeks (1 Macc 2:42).

Most Pharisees were lay scholars responsible for the development and preservation of the oral legal tradition. They were therefore connected with the synagogue, known for pious living (including prayer, fasting, almsgiving, and tithing) and precise interpretations of the law, especially

---

98. For primary sources, see Josephus, *Ant.* 13.288-298, 408-415; 17.32-45 (their politics, popularity, and adherence to the traditions of the fathers); 13.171-173 (fate is balanced with human freedom); 18.11-15 (their lifestyle of moderation; belief in immortality of the soul, final rewards, and punishments); *War* 1.110-112 (their piety, precise interpretation of the law, and political influence); *Life* 189-194 (their accurate knowledge of Jewish law); and Matt 23 (a Christian critique of their religious zeal and legalism). Much of the teaching of the Mishnah and Talmud, which can be traced back to the so-called Tannaitic period (200 B.C.–A.D. 200), is from Pharisaic schools. See L. Finkelstein, *The Pharisees* (2 vols., 3d ed.; Philadelphia: Jewish Publication Society, 1963); W. D. Davies, *Introduction to the Pharisees* (Philadelphia: Fortress, 1967); J. Neusner, *The Rabbinic Traditions about the Pharisees before 70* (3 vols.; Leiden: Brill, 1971) and *The Pharisees: Rabbinic Perspectives* (Hoboken, N.J.: Ktav Publications, 1973); R. Meyer and H. F. Weiss, "Φαρισαῖος," *TDNT* 9:11-48; J. Kampen, *The Hasideans and the Origin of Pharisaism* (Atlanta: Scholars Press, 1988); and S. Mason, *Flavius Josephus on the Pharisees* (Leiden: Brill, 1991).

in the areas of food purity, crops, Sabbath observance, festivals, and family affairs. In contrast to the Sadducees, the Pharisees accepted the larger body of Scripture (Law, Prophets, and Writings), as well as "new doctrines" about angels, demons, and the resurrection of the dead. The Pharisees also divided into various schools of interpretation, for example, the schools of Hillel and Shammai in the first century A.D. The Pharisees survived the war with Rome and reorganized Judaism along Pharisaic lines at the coastal town of Jabneh (Jamnia), becoming the ancestors of rabbinic Judaism.

The Essenes The Essenes were an ascetic group who maintained a strict adherence to the law.[99] Those who resided at Qumran near the Dead Sea were a strict monastic community with an eschatological perspective of the world.[100] Their name may have been derived from the Aramaic *Hasayyah,* or "pious ones," reflecting their close associations with the Hasidim of the Maccabean revolt. Both Philo and Josephus mentioned that thousands of Essenes lived in towns and villages of Judea. The discovery of the Dead Sea Scrolls at Khirbet Qumran in 1947 revealed a monastic end-time-oriented wilderness community that most believe was probably a major Essene center. The location confirmed the reports of the Roman

---

99. Primary sources: Josephus, *Ant.* 13.171-173 (fate governs everything); 15.373-379 (foreknowledge of the future and knowledge of divine revelations ascribed to Menahem the Essene); 17.345-348 (interpretation of dreams ascribed to Simon the Essene); 18.18-22 (their belief in immortality and resurrection, strict ascetic and communal lifestyle, refusal to worship in the Jerusalem temple); *War* 2.119-136 (ascetic practices, abstinence from marriage, communal living in towns of Judea, study of ancient writings); Philo, *That Every Good Person Is Free* 12.75-91 (they do not offer sacrifices; their living in villages, ethical concerns, synagogues, sharing of goods and monies); and Pliny, *Natural History* 5.15.73 (their community near the Dead Sea, celibacy, recruitment of members). The Dead Sea Scrolls and community discovered at Khirbet Qumran (1947) are from an Essene group. For English texts, see Dupont-Sommer, *Essene Writings;* T. H. Gaster, *The Dead Sea Scriptures* (rev. ed.; Garden City, N.Y.: Anchor, 1976); M. Wise, M. Abegg, and E. Cook, eds., *The Dead Sea Scrolls: A New Translation* (San Francisco: HarperSanFrancisco, 1996); and Vermes, *The Complete Dead Sea Scrolls.* See also F. M. Cross, *The Ancient Library of Qumran and Modern Biblical Study* (rev. ed.; Grand Rapids: Baker, 1980); T. Beall, *Josephus' Description of the Essenes, Illustrated by the Dead Sea Scrolls* (Cambridge: Cambridge University Press, 1988); and G. Vermes and M. Goodman, eds., *The Essenes according to the Classical Sources* (Sheffield: JSOT Press, 1989).

100. Although a minority of scholars question this association, see L. Consdale, *Qumran and the Essenes: A Re-evaluation of the Evidence* (Tübingen: Mohr Siebeck, 1997).

scholar Pliny the Elder in A.D. 70. The founder of the Qumran community was a Zadokite priest called the Teacher of Righteousness, who opposed the (non-Zadokite) Hasmonean priesthood and left Jerusalem with a sizable group of followers. Probably in fulfillment of the prophetic utterance "in the wilderness prepare the way of the LORD" (Isa 40:3), the group founded a center in the wilderness of Judea near the Dead Sea.[101]

The Zealots The Zealots were a Jewish resistance group that sought to revive the spirit of the Maccabeans in their revolt against Rome (A.D. 67-70).[102] Their name is probably derived from Phinehas, who was "zealous for his God" (Num 25:13), or from statements like "a zealot for the laws" (2 Macc 4:2). Like the Pharisees, they envisioned Israel's national deliverance under a messiah. Unlike (most of) the Pharisees, the Zealots sought to bring this about through armed resistance.

Even though the Zealot movement probably began in Jerusalem during the First Jewish Revolt, it was influenced by many rebels and resistance movements that preceded it. For example, in A.D. 6 Judas the Galilean rebelled against the Roman legate of Syria because of a provincial census (Acts 5:37).[103] In reaction to the Hellenizing policies of Emperor Hadrian, the spirit of the Zealot resistance revived in the Second Jewish Revolt (A.D.

---

101. Although some Essenes in outlying towns ("camps") married and reared children (CD 7.6-8; 12.1, 2, 19; Josephus, *War* 2.160-161) and the bones of a few women and children were found on the periphery of the Qumran graveyard (where only adult male skeletons have been uncovered), the Qumran sect was primarily a male celibate community. See 1QS 1.6; 11.21; Josephus, *War* 2.120-121; Philo; Pliny; Vermes, *Complete Dead Sea Scrolls* (1997), 34, 44, 47-48, 83; Cross, *Ancient Library*, 97-99.

102. Most of our information is from Josephus; see *War* 2.647-651 (their conflicts with the high priest, 651); 4.158-161 (they profess to be zealous for a good cause, 160-161); 4.300-304 (Zealot raids on Jerusalem); 4.556-576 (fighting against other Jewish factions); 5.1-10 (their seizure of the temple); 5.98-105 (more fighting in the temple); 5.248-257 (uniting with other factions to fight the Romans); and 7.252-274 (their violent activities summarized). See also Rhoads, *Israel in Revolution*, 94-181; M. Stern, "Zealots," *EncJud Yearbook*, no. 1 (1973), 135-52; M. Hengel, *Was Jesus a Revolutionist?* (Philadelphia: Fortress, 1971); and R. Horsley, *Jesus and the Spiral of Violence: Popular Jewish Resistance in Roman Palestine* (San Francisco: Harper & Row, 1987).

103. Josephus, *Ant.* 18.4-10 (author of the fourth sect of the Jews); 20.97-104 (concerning the rebel Theudas and the sons of Judas the Galilean, 98, 102); *War* 2.117-118 (the revolt against Roman taxation, 118); Acts 5:36-37 (Theudas and Judas); 21:38 (the Egyptian and Assassins). See also W. R. Farmer, *Maccabees, Zealots, and Josephus* (New York: Columbia University Press, 1956).

132-35), under Simon Bar Kochba. Mention is also made of rebels in the NT (Mark 15:7; Acts 5:36-37; 21:38). Even one of Jesus' disciples was thought to have been a Zealot ("Simon the Zealot," Acts 1:13; also Luke 6:15).

Summary

A tragic history of foreign dominance could not stifle the persistent faith of Judaism in the earliest Christian era. Through such tragedies as the Babylonian exile, the struggles in resettlement of Palestine, Syrian oppression, a disappointing interval of independence, and revolts against Rome, Judaism revived, readjusted, and reorganized as a monotheistic faith devoted to the law, the Sabbath, circumcision, and the feasts. This unifying faith of Judaism also persisted in a diversity of expressions, as we have seen in the parties of the Sadducees, Pharisees, Essenes, and Zealots. Despite this diversity, after A.D. 90 a new consolidation of beliefs and practices was begun by the surviving Pharisaic party, a trajectory that led to the complex legal systems of rabbinic Judaism.

This was the environment in which the Gospels and Acts emerged: a Greco-Roman society of pervasive Hellenism, under a stable Roman government, in an eclectic age of searching and aspiration, conceived and mothered by Judaism, its parent religion.

CHAPTER 2

The Historical Methods of Criticism

Why does a "popular" collection of writings require such careful interpretation to be understood properly? This or a similar question might be raised by the reader after noting the technical title of this chapter. But this predicament of interpreting popular writings is not restricted to the NT. It also applies to the U.S. Constitution. Both the NT collection and the Constitution were written for the benefit of "common people," and both require careful interpretation to be understood properly.

The reasons for the predicament in interpretation are analogous for the two documents. First, both are a diverse collection of documents. The NT contains twenty-seven books; the Constitution contains seven articles and twenty-seven amendments. Second, both are products of a lengthy historical process. The NT includes over a century of tradition and composition (A.D. 30-140); the Constitution and its Amendments represent almost two centuries of tradition (1789 to the present). Third, both contain technical language belonging to specific communities: the religious communities that produced the NT, and the legislative bodies that produced the Constitution.

The above reasons also substantiate two key points: (1) both the NT and the U.S. Constitution are difficult documents to read, and (2) a proper understanding of them necessitates the assistance of specialists. Despite the above difficulties and necessities, there are some positive aspects of the analogy: both sets of writings were compiled for the benefit of nonspecialists, who are encouraged to be familiar with their contents. We should not forget that, though each requires careful interpretation, these documents of the common people were intended to be understood by common people.

Two Presuppositions

The NT methods that concern us presuppose two kinds of historical distance: (a) that which exists between the modern reader and the ancient texts, and (b) that which exists between the time of writing and the events narrated.

Modern Reader and Ancient Texts

The first type of distance concerns the great span of about 2,000 years that exists between us and the NT. On the one hand, we live in a modern industrial age of computer technology and space exploration. On the other hand, the NT was written in a pre-industrial, agricultural age of primitive machinery and slow travel. Clearly, these are two different worlds, separated historically by almost two millennia. The methods that we are about to discuss presuppose this historical distance, which must be acknowledged in all objective historical study that seeks to interpret ancient texts. Once the historical gap is recognized, steps can be taken to establish a common ground of understanding between the modern reader and ancient documents. For example, in order to become acquainted with a foreign culture, one must be able to understand the differences between one's own and the foreign culture. This understanding of historical and cultural differences is presupposed in the historical methods of literary criticism. With this historical premise in view, we approach the NT in a manner different from that of reading the daily newspaper.

The Writings and the Events

Another type of distance that these literary methods presuppose is that between the time of writing (A.D. 65-95) and the time of the events narrated (e.g., the life of Jesus and the apostles, 30-62). This is especially the case between the time when the four gospels were written (65-95) and the date of the ministry of Jesus (30-33).[1]

---

1. See chart 2.1; the dating of each gospel will be discussed individually in the chapters that follow.

Why would historical distance imply a change in viewpoint from the time of Jesus to the time of the Evangelists? Did not the ancient person have a greater propensity to preserve and transmit old traditions than we do today? Were not some of the words and deeds of Jesus committed to writing during his lifetime? The historical gap of thirty-five to sixty-five years includes many social, cultural, and political changes. For example, the destruction of both the city of Jerusalem and its temple by the Romans in A.D. 70 is only one event that produced diverse changes in Palestinian Judaism, Diaspora Judaism, and early Christianity.

In reply to the second question, people of the ancient world did devote themselves to preserving and transmitting old traditions, but subtle and sometimes substantial changes took place in the process. Some changes took place to assist in memorization (i.e., mnemonics). The transmitters of the traditions would also adapt the materials for their respective audiences or revise them when combined with other traditions. As a result, different versions of the same tradition appeared. An idea of the complexity of the editorial history between A.D. 30 and 90 is suggested in chart 2.1 on page 40 (the various terms in which are discussed below).

Several responses can be given to the third question, concerning whether there were early written documents about Jesus that would minimize any different perspectives between Jesus and the Evangelists. First, we have no evidence that material about Jesus was committed to writing during his lifetime. It is clear from the Gospels that Jesus did not lecture in a classroom with students taking class notes. He taught where the common people of the Jews worked and gathered (e.g., marketplace, synagogue). Although many of Jesus' disciples were probably literate, it is uncertain if any were skilled in writing documents for use in their communities (see Acts 4:13). Most of Jesus' disciples worked in manual trades, like fishing.

Second, immediately after Jesus' death, his followers devoted themselves, not to writing his "memoirs," but to preaching the gospel. Evangelization was undertaken with a special sense of urgency because they believed that Jesus would soon return as a conquering Messiah and divine judge.

Third, the writing down of oral traditions about Jesus became a great necessity only after the death of most of the eyewitnesses. In fact, there is some indication that the earliest generations valued oral reminiscence

CHART 2.1. THE DEVELOPMENT OF THE GOSPELS

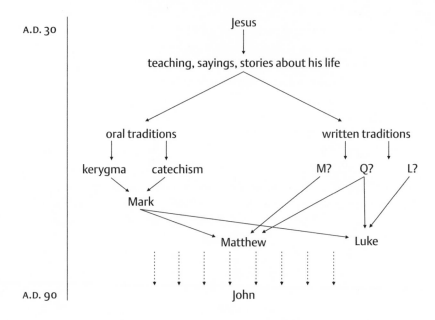

above written records.[2] Second- and third-generation Christians, who were probably confronted by diverse teachings, concerned about their heritage, and convinced that the return of Jesus would be delayed, were the ones who devoted themselves to the task of writing for posterity. These later compilers and writers had conceptions and perceptions that differed from their predecessors because of the new concerns and circumstances accompanying a later time period. Ancient documents that evidence a similar distance between the historical person and its author include the dialogues of Plato, which eulogize the life and teachings of Socrates, and the laudatory accounts of Apollonius of Tyana by Philostratus, a later disciple. Both documents are attempts by students to maximize the positive

2. Eusebius quotes Papias (late first to early second century) as saying, "If I met with anyone who had been a follower of the elders anywhere, I made it a point to inquire what were the sayings of the elders . . . for I do not think that I derived as much benefit from books as from the living voice of those that are still alive" (*Hist. eccl.* 3.39.4). See also B. Gerhardsson, *Memory and Manuscript: Oral Tradition and Written Transmission in Rabbinic Judaism and Early Christianity with Tradition and Transmission in Early Christianity* (Grand Rapids: Eerdmans, 1998).

and minimize the negative perceptions others may have had of their teachers. Socrates and Apollonius probably would have told their own stories differently. For such reasons the writings of the gospel tradition were relatively late and reflect the special concerns of later generations.

The problem of historical distance between (a) us and the ancient text and (b) the time of writing and the events narrated is a working presupposition of the historical methods of literary criticism. Similarly, the science of textual criticism presupposes the historical distance between our Greek copies of the NT (written between the 2d and 4th centuries) and the autographs (1st cent.). Awareness of these historical gaps should underscore the importance of carefully considering the differences between the two time periods before drawing conclusions about the common features.

Common Objectives and Conclusions

The historical methods of literary criticism trace and define the long process involved in the collection and composition of the NT writings. It is their common objective to investigate the three periods of (1) oral transmission, (2) the transcription of oral traditions, and (3) their incorporation into complete narrative books. Although these methods concentrate on the four gospels and Acts, they also apply to the study of the remaining NT books. These historical methods seek to reveal the historical dynamics at work in the production of ancient texts.

The historical methods of criticism enable us to view the NT books as intricate works with ingenious literary patterns and highly developed interpretations.[3] This modern perception of the NT has some early precedent. For instance, Papias of Asia Minor (born during the period of the apostles) described the author of Mark's gospel as the apostle Peter's "interpreter/translator,"[4] admitting that Mark did not know, and seemingly was unconcerned, about the actual chronology of Jesus' words or deeds.

---

3. Old and new perceptions of the NT are from D. Via, in his foreword to E. McKnight, *What Is Form Criticism?* (Philadelphia: Fortress, 1969), v.

4. The Greek word is *hermēneutēs,* from which we derive the English word "hermeneutics"; see Eusebius, *Hist. eccl.* 3.39.15. Whether or not one accepts the connection between Peter and Mark as historical, the important issue here is Papias's sensitivity to the author's method of composition. See R. Bauckham, *Jesus and the Eyewitnesses: The Gospels as Eyewitness Testimony* (Grand Rapids: Eerdmans, 2006), 202-39.

His method of composition was directed by other apologetic interests. Unfortunately, such insights have not always been appreciated; the Gospels have frequently been read as if they were simple recollections of events merely set together and told in a very straightforward manner. The story of Jesus, for example, has been viewed as a verbatim report of the busy itinerary of Jesus narrated in a precise chronological order. The specific problems with this view will be discussed below in the sections on form and redaction criticism. Learning to (re)appreciate the literary achievement of the gospel writers is one of the important insights gained in the past two centuries of modern NT research.

Modern research draws certain historical conclusions about the NT books. First, they are not merely a collection of factual reports but reflect various sociological and religious concerns, different contexts, and different literary purposes. Second, the religious topics discussed in the text are not necessarily precise images of reality but reflect the faith and life of early communities and their authors. Third, all historical reconstructions of modern research are subject to refinement and revision. Because every age has its biases, limited knowledge, and perspectives, one should avoid all cultural chauvinism. Uncritical loyalty either to our own modern age or to the ancient culture of the NT hinders the interpretive process.[5]

Three Methods of Criticism

The three methods of criticism to be examined in this chapter are source, form, and redaction criticism. *Source criticism* seeks to detect the primary documents used in a book. In the nineteenth century it became a well-defined method. *Form criticism* attempts to determine the original setting and function of the traditional oral forms reproduced in a book. It was applied to the Bible in the first decades of the twentieth century. *Redaction criticism* underscores the final writers' editing of traditional materials for their own readers. Shortly after World War II, it began to be employed in NT research. Prior to their use in interpreting Scripture, these critical tools were employed in the study of classical Greek and early Western literature.

---

5. These three points on modern biblical research are derived from J. H. Hayes and C. R. Holladay, *Biblical Exegesis: A Beginner's Handbook* (3d ed.; Louisville: Westminster John Knox, 2007), 193-94.

Although they are technical approaches to the ancient texts, they can be understood and employed by nonspecialists.

Before approaching a text with the historical methods, it is important to be familiar with the literary and historical context of the passage to be studied. First, consult and use modern English translations that are based on the most reliable Greek manuscripts (e.g., RSV, NRSV, NAB, NEB, NIV, NJB). Second, read the passage carefully. Be alert to the literary relationship of the passage to its immediate context (e.g., paragraph, chapter, section) and the book in which it occurs. Familiarity with the general outline of the book is helpful. Third, get acquainted with the names, places, and concepts in the passage. This can be done by consulting a current Bible encyclopedia, such as *ABD, HBD, IDB, IDBSupp, NIDB*, or *ZPEB*. Fourth, outline the passage to discover and highlight the major points (i.e., do a grammatical analysis). Fifth, check your research by consulting a Bible commentary on the NT passage, for example, AB, Hermeneia, HNTC, NCBC, NIC, NJBC, or WBC.[6] This process of understanding the text need not be followed in the exact order listed above, nor does it have to be a long, time-consuming project, since you will learn more as you utilize the historical methods of literary criticism.

Source Criticism

The method of source criticism seeks to determine (1) the presence and significance of sources in a written document and (2) the author's use of these sources.[7]

---

6. For specific books on tools for NT study, see D. M. Scholer, *A Basic Bibliographic Guide for NT Exegesis* (2d ed.; Grand Rapids: Eerdmans, 1973); J. A. Fitzmyer, *An Introductory Bibliography for the Study of Scripture* (rev. ed.; Rome: Biblical Institute Press, 1981); Hayes and Holladay, *Biblical Exegesis;* and R. P. Martin, *NT Books for Pastor and Teacher* (Philadelphia: Westminster, 1984). On the practice of NT interpretation, or exegesis (Gk. *exēgēsis*, from the related verb meaning "explain, interpret"), see O. Kaiser and W. G. Kümmel, *Exegetical Method: A Student's Handbook* (rev. ed.; New York: Seabury, 1981); J. B. Green, S. McKnight, and I. H. Marshall, *Dictionary of Jesus and the Gospels* (Downers Grove, Ill.: InterVarsity Press, 1992); S. E. Porter, ed., *Handbook to the Exegesis of the NT* (Leiden: Brill, 1997); S. McKnight, *Synoptic Gospels: An Annotated Bibliography* (Grand Rapids: Baker, 2000); G. D. Fee, *NT Exegesis: A Handbook for Students and Pastors* (3d ed.; Louisville, Ky.: Westminster John Knox, 2002); M. J. Gorman, *Elements of Biblical Exegesis: A Basic Guide for Students and Ministers* (Peabody, Mass.: Hendrickson, 2001); and S. McKnight and G. R. Osborne, *The Face of NT Studies: A Survey of Recent Research* (Grand Rapids: Baker, 2004).

7. For introductions to source criticism, see D. J. Harrington, *Interpreting the NT: A*

The Importance of Detecting Sources Knowing sources is especially important if one encounters startling information or conflicting accounts. Consider the following scenario. You are driving home from school and suddenly hear on the radio that the United States has invaded Iran. Certainly you would want to know the source of information for such startling news — especially if you are of a draftable age! When you arrive home to view the evening news on television, you hear that the United States has *not* invaded Iran. Rather, a democratic revolution has successfully taken place within that nation! Certainly you would be interested in knowing the sources behind these two conflicting reports. You would want to learn more about the event or would weigh carefully the credibility of the sources used (e.g., foreign correspondents, Pentagon officials). The presence of startling information and conflicting reports are at least two reasons why it is important to have access to primary sources.

The above scenario is similar to the situation often faced in NT studies. For example, in the narrative of Matt 8:28-34, there are *two* demoniacs from *Gadara,* but in Mark 5:1-20 there is only *one* demoniac from *Gerasa* mentioned. Do the two accounts presuppose two different sources? Or are we dealing with two variations of the same source? The issues raised by these two passages are part of the concern of source criticism.

The Basic Assumptions Source criticism assumes that the NT authors used written as well as oral traditions in the production of their works.[8] In the Gospels, the gap of thirty-five to sixty-five years from the time of the events to the time of their written narration lends good support to

---

Practical Guide (Wilmington, Del.: Michael Glazier, 1979; henceforth *IntNT*), 56-57; and D. Wenham, "Source Criticism," in *NT Interpretation: Essays on Principles and Methods* (ed. I. H. Marshall; Grand Rapids: Eerdmans, 1977; henceforth *NTI*), 139-52.

8. For background on the history of source-critical research, note the following scholars, with dates of major works reflecting this concern. Source criticism (mainly of the Pentateuch) had a long history, originating in the late seventeenth century with R. Simon and later developed by, for example, A. Kuenen (1860), K. H. Graf (1860), and J. Wellhausen (1870). Scholars of early European history also employed the method, including B. G. Niebuhr (1811) and L. von Ranke (1824). NT source criticism focused on the Synoptic Gospels, beginning with, for example, J. J. Griesbach (1776), J. G. Eichhorn (1795), and K. Lachmann (1835) and developed further by H. J. Holtzmann (1863), B. H. Streeter (1924), W. R. Farmer (1964), and others. For more discussion, see W. G. Kümmel, *The NT: The History of the Investigation of Its Problems* (trans. S. M. Gilmour and H. C. Kee; Nashville: Abingdon, 1972), 74-88, 144-61, 325-41.

this assumption. Because of this presupposition, source criticism excludes from its approach two extreme positions. First is the view that the events narrated in the NT are complete literary fabrications of the author. Many of them correspond too closely to what we know from archaeology and other ancient literature to support this view. Second is the view that the NT writers were merely "stenographers for God," who wrote at his dictation. Such an extreme confessional position would require a much greater degree of uniformity in content, style, and purpose than exists in the NT. Source criticism presupposes that the NT was primarily the product of a human process of collecting oral and written traditions and committing them to writing. This assumption is not incompatible with faith in the divine inspiration of the NT, however.

The NT writers made use of written traditions. This is evident, first of all, by the explicit use of passages from the Jewish Scriptures, especially the Septuagint. There are approximately 1,600 citations in the NT of over 1,200 different passages from the Jewish Scriptures, as well as several thousand allusions. Second, the so-called Triple Tradition, or those places where Matthew and Luke follow the Gospel of Mark, provides additional evidence.[9] Furthermore, the author of Luke-Acts explicitly mentions written accounts of Jesus (Luke 1:1-4), which he probably utilized in his own work. Unfortunately, he does not tell us when he is relying on these written Jesus traditions.

How to Detect Sources How does one detect the presence of sources in the NT writings? Sometimes explicit reference is made of a source before it is cited. This is especially the case with citations of the Jewish Scriptures. They are often preceded by such formulas as "it is written" (Rom 1:17) or "as Isaiah predicted" (Rom 9:29). There are over 200 instances of OT citations introduced by these formulas.[10] Another example of the explicit use of a written document is stated by the apostle Paul in his first letter to the Corinthian church: "Now concerning the matters about which you wrote . . ." (1 Cor 7:1). A final example is a source introduced with a stereotyped phrase designating it as traditional material: "For I handed on to

---

9. See the discussion below in "The Synoptic Problem."

10. H. M. Shires, *Finding the Old Testament in the New* (Philadelphia: Westminster, 1974), 15. See esp. indexes of quotations, allusions, and parallels in K. Aland et al., *The Greek NT* (4th rev. ed.; New York and Stuttgart: United Bible Societies, 1994), 897-911.

you . . . what I in turn had received" (1 Cor 15:3). It is unclear in this last instance whether the author is using an oral or a written source.

When the use of sources is not mentioned, the task becomes more difficult. Source criticism suggests possible internal criteria for detecting them, although it is worth remembering that this process is as much an art as it is a science. The criteria include (1) the displacement or discontinuity of thought and literary style and (2) the use of unusual vocabulary that is uncharacteristic of the rest of the book. Other criteria will be introduced in our comparisons of Matthew, Mark, and Luke.

A passage in 2 Corinthians well illustrates these issues. If one carefully reads 2 Cor 6:1–7:4, it will be noted that the contents of 6:14–7:1 seem to interrupt the thought pattern. The topic of 6:1-13 (an appeal for openness) abruptly changes at v. 14 and does not resume until 7:2. The vocabulary and style of 6:14–7:1 are also different from the rest of 2 Corinthians specifically, and from the rest of Paul's other letters generally. This difference has led some commentators to observe similarities between this seemingly displaced passage and certain teachings found in the Dead Sea Scrolls of Qumran; a few even go so far as to speculate that it was an Essene document revised by Christians. As we have seen, displacement of thought and the presence of unusual vocabulary are two internal criteria for detecting possible sources, especially when the writer of a work does not identify them. The observable comparisons between Matthew, Mark, and Luke, however, offer more opportunities for identifying sources than in Paul's letters. Other significant examples will be given to better understand the methodology of source criticism.

A Case Study from Mark   Let us apply these principles of source criticism to a passage in the Gospel of Mark (the second gospel):

> The beginning of the good news of Jesus Christ, the Son of God. As it is written in the prophet Isaiah, "See, I am sending my messenger ahead of you, who will prepare your way; the voice of one crying out in the wilderness: 'Prepare the way of the Lord, make his paths straight.'" (1:1-3)

The source used by Mark in this passage is clearly introduced by the stereotypical formula "as it is written in the prophet Isaiah." Most modern translations indent the quotation. A difficulty arises, however, in attempting to identify precisely what source or sources are used. The passage

cited in Mark is from Isa 40:3, probably in a Greek translation of the Hebrew Bible.[11]

> The voice of one crying out in the wilderness: "Prepare the way of the
> Lord, make *our God's* path straight."

With only one modification (italicized) Mark makes use of the passage of
Isa 40:3 in a Greek translation similar to the one from which we have translated (i.e., the Septuagint). But the Isa 40 passage accounts for only the second part of the quotation. Nowhere in Isa 40 or in the entire book of Isaiah
(chs. 1–66) is there found the first part of Mark's quote attributed to Isaiah!
It is, however, found in Mal 3:1 and follows closely a Hebrew text similar to
the one from which our OT is translated.[12]

> See, I am sending my messenger before *my face* to prepare the way.

Some of the wording in Mark's quote may have been influenced by a Greek
translation of Exod 23:20, since part of it agrees verbatim with Mark: "See,
I am sending my messenger before your face."[13] But the quote in Mark 1:2,
ascribed to Isaiah, is clearly referring to the passage in Mal 3. As odd as this
may appear to us, Mark provides an example of a common Jewish practice
of biblical citation and interpretation called *conflation*. By splicing together pieces of two, or probably three, similarly worded OT passages,
Mark identifies "the beginning of the good news" with not one but three
crucial moments in Israel's history of salvation: the exodus from Egypt
(Exod 23:20), the return from Babylonian exile (Isa 40:3), and the yet-to-
be-fulfilled expectation of a deliverer (Mal 3:1).[14]

The Synoptic Problem Now compare Mark with the Gospels of Matthew
and Luke.[15] All three gospels are called the Synoptics (from two Greek

---

11. Our translation of the LXX is based on A. Rahlfs, ed., *Septuaginta* (1935 ed.; rev. ed.;
R. Hanhart; Stuttgart, 2006), 619.

12. Our translation of the Hebrew Bible is based on K. Elliger and W. Rudolph, eds.,
Biblia Hebraica Stuttgartensia (Stuttgart: Deutsche Bibelstiftung, 1967), 1084.

13. Translation based on Rahlfs, ed., *Septuaginta*.

14. For a more detailed discussion, see R. A. Guelich, *Mark 1–8:26* (WBC 34A; Dallas:
Word Books, 1989), 10-12.

15. In our comparison we have used B. H. Throckmorton Jr., ed., *Gospel Parallels: A
Comparison of the Synoptic Gospels; with Alternative Readings from the Manuscripts and
Noncanonical Parallels* (5th ed.; Nashville: Thomas Nelson, 1992); and K. Aland, ed., *Synopsis

words meaning "see" and "together") because they share a "common vision" of the life of Jesus. Note that all three accounts deal with John the Baptist, and both Matthew and Luke cite the passage from Isa 40 found in Mark: "The voice of one crying out in the wilderness." (See table 2.1 on p. 49.) But what happened to that problematic Malachi passage found in Mark 1:2? It is omitted in the accounts of both Matthew and Luke. These two gospels use the Malachi passage in another context, perhaps influenced by another source (Matt 11:10 / Luke 7:27). Could it be that both Matthew and Luke eliminated Mark's Jewish practice of conflation (involving Isa and Mal) because it would have been problematic for their Gentile audiences? We can only surmise here.

In these three selections we should also note how Matthew and Luke employ the Isa 40 quote differently from Mark, observing what precedes and follows in all three gospel accounts. First, neither Matthew nor Luke employs Mark's superscription, "The beginning of the good news." The basic reason for this omission is that Matthew and Luke begin their gospels (or "good news announcements") not with the account of John (as does Mark) but with the birth and infancy narratives. Second, Luke begins his account of John with a chronological notation (Luke 3:1-2), endeavoring to link his narrative with secular history, a distinctive concern of Luke. Third, both Matthew and Luke feel it necessary to first acquaint their readers with the message of John's preaching before the Isaiah quote, whereas Mark introduces John after the quotation (Mark 1:4). Fourth, although Luke retains Mark's phrasing of John's message, "proclaiming a baptism of repentance for the forgiveness of sins," Matthew changes it to "Repent, for the kingdom of heaven has come near," which is a special emphasis in his gospel (e.g., Matt 3:11; 4:17). Fifth, only Luke expands upon the Isaiah quote, citing 40:3-5 (LXX, with two words and a phrase omitted from 40:4-5). This was done especially to highlight the statement "all flesh shall see the salvation of God," which is another distinctive emphasis of the author of Luke-Acts (e.g., see Luke 2:30; Acts 28:28). The above five points show how differently the Isa 40 passage in Mark is employed by Matthew and Luke.

It also appears from our comparison that Matthew and Luke are dependent on Mark, a phenomenon called the Markan priority. Several factors offer support to this idea, and problems are raised by resisting it. First, we

---

of the Four Gospels (10th ed.; Stuttgart: German Bible Society, 2001); see also R. J. Swanson, *The Horizontal Line Synopsis of the Gospels* (Dillsboro: Western North Carolina Press, 1975).

TABLE 2.1. MATTHEW, MARK, AND LUKE: JOHN THE BAPTIST (1)

Matt 3:1-3	Mark 1:1-3	Luke 3:1-6
	1The beginning of the good news of Jesus Christ, the Son of God.	
1In those days		1In the fifteenth year of the reign of Emperor Tiberius, when Pontius Pilate was governor of Judea, and Herod was ruler of Galilee, and his brother Philip ruler of the region of Ituraea and Trachonitis, and Lysanias ruler of Abilene, 2during the high priesthood of Annas and Caiaphas, the word of God came to John son of Zechariah in the wilderness. 3He went into all the region around the Jordan, proclaiming a baptism of repentance for the forgiveness of sins,
John the Baptist appeared in the wilderness of Judea, proclaiming,		
2"Repent, for the kingdom of heaven has come near." 3This is the one of whom the prophet Isaiah spoke when he said,	2As it is written in the prophet Isaiah, "See, I am sending my messenger ahead of you, who will prepare your way; 3the voice of one crying out in the wilderness: 'Prepare the way of the Lord, make his paths straight.'"	4as it is written in the book of the words of the prophet Isaiah,
"The voice of one crying out in the wilderness: 'Prepare the way of the Lord, make his paths straight.'"		"The voice of one crying out in the wilderness: 'Prepare the way of the Lord, make his paths straight. 5Every valley shall be filled, and every mountain and hill shall be made low, and the crooked shall be made straight, and the rough ways made smooth; 6and all flesh shall see the salvation of God.'"

saw that both Matthew and Luke, possibly influenced by a common source, omit the problematic Malachi passage that Mark had ascribed to Isaiah (Mark 1:2). Second, Matthew and Luke either arranged in different order or revised material they seem to have gotten from Mark (e.g., the content of John's preaching). Third, there is an example of one gospel apparently expanding upon the quotation originally cited in Mark (i.e., Luke's expansion of the Isa 40 quote in Mark). The theory of Markan priority — the idea that Mark's gospel was written first and then used as the primary source for both Matthew and Luke — appears to provide the best explanation of the evidence, as we have shown by the three observations listed above.

Resisting the conclusion of Markan priority raises several problematic questions.[16] First, why would anyone want to abbreviate or conflate Matthew and Luke to produce a gospel like Mark? Second, why would Mark have omitted so much material from Matthew and Luke? For example, why would Mark have ignored the infancy stories and postresurrection appearances? Third, what kind of author and religious teacher would Mark have been if he really had copies of Matthew and Luke but omitted so much from them? The above problems are raised to support the view that Mark was the first gospel and that Matthew and Luke used Mark independently. For a majority of scholars, this hypothesis best explains the so-

---

16. The three points concerning Markan priority are from Harrington, *IntNT*, 61-62. For further arguments, see J. A. Fitzmyer, "The Priority of Mark and the 'Q' Source in Luke," in *To Advance the Gospel: NT Studies* (2d ed.; Grand Rapids: Eerdmans, 1998), 3-40; W. G. Kümmel, *Introduction to the NT* (trans. H. C. Kee; rev. ed.; Nashville: Abingdon, 1975), 35-63; B. H. Streeter, *The Four Gospels: A Study of Origins* (London: Macmillan, 1924); G. M. Styler, "The Priority of Mark," in *The Birth of the NT* (ed. C. F. D. Moule; New York: Harper & Row, 1962), 223-32; D. J. Neville, *Arguments from Order in Synoptic Source Criticism: A History and Critique* (Macon, Ga.: Mercer University Press, 1994); D. A. Black and D. R. Beck, eds., *Rethinking the Synoptic Problem* (Grand Rapids: Baker, 2001); and C. A. Evans, *Mark 8:27–16:20* (WBC 34B; Nashville: Thomas Nelson, 2001), xliii-lviii. Note, however, the following works, which favor Matthean priority (i.e., the Griesbach hypothesis) and argue for Markan dependency on Matthew and Luke: D. L. Dungan, "Mark — the Abridgement of Matthew and Luke," in *Jesus and Man's Hope*, ed. Miller, 1:51-97; W. R. Farmer, *The Synoptic Problem: A Critical Analysis* (Dillsboro: Western North Carolina Press, 1976) and "Modern Developments of Griesbach's Hypothesis," *NTS* 23 (1976-77): 275-95; T. R. Longstaff, *Evidence of Conflation in Mark?* (Missoula, Mont.: Scholars Press, 1977); and J. Wenham, *Redating Matthew, Mark, and Luke: A Fresh Assault on the Synoptic Problem* (Downers Grove, Ill.: InterVarsity Press, 1992). For other views including the importances of oral tradition, see B. Reicke, *The Roots of the Synoptic Gospels* (Philadelphia: Fortress, 1986) and R. L. Thomas, ed., *Three Views on the Origins of the Synoptic Gospels* (Grand Rapids: Kregel, 2002).

called Synoptic Problem — that is, the phenomena of similarities and differences between Matthew, Mark, and Luke.

We encounter a second problem in the Synoptic Gospels, which concerns the close similarities between Matthew and Luke that are not found in Mark. Let us look again at our Synoptic comparison. After following Mark's account of John the Baptist and his ministry, both Matthew and Luke add an account that it is not found in Mark. (See table 2.2 below.)

TABLE 2.2. MATTHEW AND LUKE: JOHN THE BAPTIST

Matt 3:7-10	Luke 3:7-9
7But when he saw many Pharisees and Sadducees coming for baptism, he said to them, "You brood of vipers! Who warned you to flee from the wrath to come? 8Bear fruit worthy of repentance. 9Do not presume to say to yourselves, 'We have Abraham as our ancestor'; for I tell you, God is able from these stones to raise up children to Abraham. 10Even now the ax is lying at the root of the trees; every tree therefore that does not bear good fruit is cut down and thrown into the fire."	7John said to the crowds that came out to be baptized by him, "You brood of vipers! Who warned you to flee from the wrath to come? 8Bear fruits worthy of repentance. Do not begin to say to yourselves, 'We have Abraham as our ancestor'; for I tell you, God is able from these stones to raise up children to Abraham. 9Even now the ax is lying at the root of the trees; every tree therefore that does not bear good fruit is cut down and thrown into the fire."

Despite the differences between Matt 3:7 and Luke 3:7 in the opening sentence, the rest of the two passages are verbatim in the Greek, with the exception of one word (Gk. *doxēte* vs. *arxēsthe*) and one noun phrase differing in number (*karpon axion* vs. *karpous axious;* Luke also in one place adds a *kai*, "and"). These two passages show such close verbal similarities that it is quite likely that a common written source is used here. This parallel is only one of many (e.g., Matt 6:24 / Luke 16:13; Matt 23:37-39 / Luke 13:34-35). Often this common non-Markan material is arranged in different places by Matthew and Luke, indicating that each one utilized this source independently. This common written source, not found in Mark, is often called Q, from the German *Quelle*, meaning "source." It is also called the Synoptic Sayings Source, because it contains mostly sayings of Jesus, rather than stories about him.[17] (See table 2.3 on pp. 52-53.)

17. See B. W. Bacon, "The Nature and Design of Q, the Second Synoptic Source," *HibJ*

TABLE 2.3. CONTENTS OF HYPOTHETICAL Q

1. The Preparation
   A. John's preaching of repentance (Luke 3:7-9; Matt 3:7-10)
   B. The temptation of Jesus (Luke 4:1-13; Matt 4:1-11)
2. Sayings
   A. Beatitudes (Luke 6:20-23; Matt 5:3-4, 6, 11-12)
   B. Love to one's enemies (Luke 6:27-36; Matt 5:39-42, 44-48; 7:12)
   C. Judging (Luke 6:37-42; Matt 7:1-5; 10:24; 15:14)
   D. Hearers and doers of the Word (Luke 6:47-49; Matt 7:24-27)
3. Narrative
   A. The centurion's servant (Luke 7:1-10; Matt 7:28a; 8:5-10, 13)
   B. The Baptist's question (Luke 7:18-20; Matt 11:2-3)
   C. Christ's answer (Luke 7:22-35; Matt 11:4-19)
4. Discipleship
   A. On the cost of discipleship (Luke 9:57-60; Matt 8:19-22)
   B. The mission charge (Luke 10:2-16; Matt 9:37-38; 10:9-15; 11:21-23)
   C. Christ's thanksgiving to the Father (Luke 10:21-24; Matt 11:25-27; 13:16-17)
5. Various Sayings
   A. The pattern prayer (Luke 11:2-4; Matt 6:9-13)
   B. An answer to prayer (Luke 11:9-13; Matt 7:7-11)
   C. The Beelzebub discussion and its sequel (Luke 11:14-23; Matt 12:22-30)
   D. The sign of the prophet Jonah (Luke 11:29-32; Matt 12:38-42)
   E. About light (Luke 11:33-36; Matt 5:15; 6:22-23)

The theory that Matthew and Luke used both Mark and Q as sources is called the Two Document Hypothesis. In addition to these two written documents, two oral (or written) sources have been postulated to explain the presence of distinctive Matthean and Lukan material. "M" refers to

---

22 (1923/24): 674-88; R. A. Edwards, *A Concordance to Q* (Missoula, Mont.: Scholars Press, 1975) and *A Theology of Q* (Philadelphia: Fortress, 1976); J. M. Robinson and H. Koester, *Trajectories through Early Christianity* (Philadelphia: Fortress, 1971), 71-113, 158-204; V. Taylor, "The Order of Q," *JTS*, n.s., 4 (1953): 27-31; N. Turner, "Q in Recent Thought," *ExpTim* 80 (1968-69): 324-28; and J. S. Kloppenborg, *Q Parallels: Synopsis, Critical Notes, and Concordance* (Sonoma, Calif.: Polebridge, 1988).

6. Discourse against the Pharisees (Luke 11:37–12:1; Matt 23)
7. Sayings
    A. About fearless confession (Luke 12:2-12; Matt 10:19, 26-33; 12:32)
    B. On cares about earthly things (Luke 12:22-34; Matt 6:19-21, 25-33)
    C. On faithfulness (Luke 12:39-46; Matt 24:43-51)
    D. On signs for this age (Luke 12:51-56; Matt 10:34-36; 16:2-3)
    E. On agreeing with one's adversaries (Luke 12:57-59; Matt 5:25-26)
8. Parables of the mustard seed and leaven (Luke 13:18-21; Matt 13:31-33)
9. Other Sayings
    A. Condemnation of Israel (Luke 13:23-30; Matt 7:13-14, 22-23; 8:11-12)
    B. Lament over Jerusalem (Luke 13:34-35; Matt 23:37-39)
    C. Cost of discipleship (Luke 14:26-35; Matt 10:37-38; 5:13).
    D. On serving two masters (Luke 16:13; Matt 6:24)
    E. On law and divorce (Luke 16:16-18; Matt 11:12-13; 5:18, 32)
    F. On offenses, forgiveness, and faith (Luke 17:1-6; Matt 18:6-7, 15, 20-22)
    G. The day of the Son of Man (Luke 17:23-27, 33-37; Matt 24:17-18, 26-28, 37-41)

Note: Scholars vary as to the contents of Q.

Adapted from Ralph Martin, *NT Foundations: A Guide for Christian Students* (vol. 1; Grand Rapids: Eerdmans, 1975) and *Chronological and Background Charts of the NT,* by H. Wayne House (Grand Rapids: Zondervan, 1981)

---

the material found only in Matthew, such as the coming of the Magi, the slaughter of children by Herod, and the flight and return of Jesus and his family from Egypt. "L" refers to the material only found in Luke, such as the birth of John the Baptist, Mary's Magnificat, the visit of the shepherds, and the presentation of the infant Jesus in the temple. This expanded version of the theory, postulating that M and L included additional written sources, is sometimes called the Four Document Hypothesis.[18] (See chart 2.2 on p. 54.) Unlike Mark and Q, however, it is

18. Streeter, *The Four Gospels*, 223-70.

CHART 2.2. THE TWO DOCUMENT / FOUR DOCUMENT HYPOTHESIS

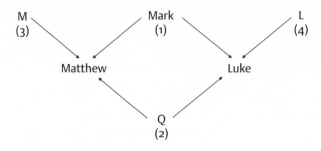

difficult to determine if M and L are (1) oral or written sources or (2) the literary creations of the authors.

The documentary hypothesis outlined here has been followed by a majority of biblical scholars since the beginning of the twentieth century. Regarding Q, it should be noted also that a minority of scholars continue to dispute the necessity of a Q document, arguing that the same results would be produced by either Matthew or Luke copying from the other.[19]

One problem raised by the Two Document Hypothesis concerns the minor agreements of Matthew and Luke against Mark.[20] If they used Mark independently, they really should not agree in their modifications of it. Four responses to this problem can be given. First, on certain topics, Q and Mark may have overlapped, and here Matthew and Luke may have relied on Q instead of Mark. Second, Matthew and Luke may have had access to a

19. For example, M. Goodacre defends the order Mark-Matthew-Luke in *The Synoptic Problem: A Way through the Maze* (London: Sheffield Academic Press, 2001) and *The Case against Q: Studies in Markan Priority and the Synoptic Problem* (Harrisburg, Pa.: Trinity Press International, 2002). Others defend the order Mark-Luke-Matthew; see R. V. Huggins, "Matthean Posteriority: A Preliminary Proposal," in *The Synoptic Problem and Q* (ed. D. E. Orton; Leiden: Brill, 1999), 204-25; and M. Hengel, *The Four Gospels and the One Gospel of Jesus Christ: An Investigation of the Collection and Origin of the Canonical Gospels* (trans. J. Bowden; Harrisburg, Pa.: Trinity Press International, 2000), 169-207. A very few even argue for no literary relationship whatsoever among the Synoptics; e.g., see E. Linnemann, *Is There a Synoptic Problem? Rethinking the Literary Dependence of the First Three Gospels* (trans. R. W. Yarbrough; Grand Rapids: Baker, 1992).

20. F. Neirynck, *Minor Agreements of Matthew and Luke against Mark, with a Cumulative List* (Gembloux: Duculot, 1974); R. T. Simpson, "The Major Agreements of Matthew and Luke against Mark," *NTS* 12 (1965-66): 273-84. For problems and responses to this position, see Harrington, *IntNT,* 63.

slightly different edition of Mark from what we have. Third, those who copied the early Greek manuscripts may have harmonized the Matthean and Lukan texts. Fourth, just as two competent teachers independently reading a student's paper will naturally introduce many of the same corrections, so Matthew and Luke may have independently yet harmoniously corrected Mark's rough Greek style. The Two Document explanation of the Synoptic Problem is only a hypothesis, although it is a plausible explanation of the facts and explains more evidence than any alternate theories.

Source Criticism: Conclusions Source criticism attempts to do three things: (1) detect the presence of a source, (2) determine the contents of the source, and (3) understand how the source was used. Source criticism seeks to deal seriously with the NT as a historical document. Its importance is obvious to anyone who is confronted with startling or conflicting information. When the reader of the NT encounters a problem passage or two conflicting accounts of one event, the quest for sources can often help clarify or explain the problem. Although most of our examples for source criticism have been taken from the Synoptic Gospels, this method is used throughout the NT. The relationship of 2 Peter and Jude, for example, has raised several source-critical questions not unlike those of the Synoptic Problem. The usefulness of source criticism is augmented by the historical methods of form criticism and redaction criticism.

Form Criticism

Form criticism concentrates on the traditional units that originated in an oral or preliterary setting. It attempts to get behind the written sources to the oral period before the literary forms were put into writing. Before discussing form criticism, the nature and significance of literary forms will be examined.

Literary forms are various modes of communication available to a writer for his or her readers.[21] There are numerous assortments of literary

---

21. The NT literary forms relevant to the Synoptic Gospels are classified as *sayings* (or direct discourse; e.g., proverbs and parables) and *stories* (or indirect discourse; e.g., miracle accounts and legends). See R. Bultmann, *The History of the Synoptic Tradition* (trans. J. Marsh; New York: Harper & Row, 1963; trans. of *Die Geschichte der synoptischen Tradition* [4th ed.; Göttingen: Vandenhoeck & Ruprecht, 1958]), vii-viii, 11.

forms in every culture, ancient and modern. In our culture literary forms include a personal letter, an obituary notice in the newspaper, a school drama script, and the love poem on a greeting card. All of these widely diverse examples are modes of communication used by writers for various audiences. As we can easily recognize, literary forms are an important and pervasive phenomenon in human culture.

Basic Features of Literary Forms At least five basic characteristics of literary forms in culture can be reflected in form criticism. First, all literary forms have fixed patterns. In our culture, for example, a personal letter will usually contain (1) an indication of place and date, (2) the name of the recipient ("Dear Aunt Sue"), (3) an apology for not writing sooner, and (4) a statement of the writer's health and expression of hope that the recipient is in good health. As another example, we generally expect newspaper obituary notices to contain the following information: (1) name of the deceased, (2) brief description of life and career, (3) mention of surviving relatives, (4) age, (5) date of death, and (6) proposed funeral arrangements. These examples are typical of the way cultures have fixed patterns for their literary forms of communication.

Second, literary forms change throughout history. For example, a personal letter written in Egypt dating from 168 B.C. has features different from those of our own time and culture:

> *Greeting:* Isias to her brother Hephaestion, greeting.
> *Thanksgiving:* If you are well and other things are going right, it would accord with the prayer that I make continually to the gods. I myself and the child and all the household are in good health and think of you always.
> *Body:* When I received your letter from Horus, in which you announce that you are in detention in the Sarapeum at Memphis . . . when all the others who had been secluded there have come, I am ill-pleased . . . please return to the city, if nothing more pressing holds you back. . . .
> *Closing:* Goodbye. Year 2, Epeiph 30.
> (Addressed) To Hephaestion.

Although the basic pattern of a greeting, body, and closing is similar to our modern letter form, its basic arrangement and formal contents are different. The above features are typical of most personal letters written in the ancient Hellenistic world.[22]

Historians of literature, by studying the external and formal features (as well as language and style), can arrive at a relatively accurate date and location for the above literary forms, even when such information is not given overtly. Sensitivity to the changes of a literary form in the history of a culture is an important concern in form criticism.

A third characteristic of literary forms is that each form has a unique linguistic intent associated with it. For example, personal letters are intended to renew acquaintances, obituary notices serve as memorial notices for the deceased and family, dramatic plays entertain, and love poems usually endear one individual to another.

Although there may be exceptions to the above generalizations, every literary form has a specific intent. This linguistic intent or purpose is also fully understood by the specific audience addressed. The intent of a literary form is usually so familiar to the audience or readers that it signals certain expectations in them. We are so familiar with our literary forms that we have some idea of their contents even before reading them! For example, we approach a love poem differently than we would an obituary notice, a dramatic play with different expectations than a special documentary report. Each literary form has a specific intent that is fully understood by the audience addressed and triggers certain expectations in them.

A fourth characteristic of literary forms is that they are connected with certain social and institutional settings. The setting of a personal letter, for example, in most cases is a private relationship between two friends. The setting presupposed in an obituary notice is that of grief shared by friends and relatives of the deceased. The setting of a dramatic play, in our culture, would be on a stage in a public theater. The setting generally presupposed in a love poem is a private relationship between two

22. For the letter from Isias, see M. Gorman, *Apostle of the Crucified Lord: A Theological Introduction to Paul and His Letters* (Grand Rapids: Eerdmans, 2004), 81. For an additional example of the form of an obituary, see G. Lohfink, *The Bible, Now I Get It! A Form-Criticism Handbook* (New York: Doubleday, 1979), 19. For additional information on ancient letter forms, see J. L. White, *The Form and Function of the Body of the Greek Letter: A Study of the Letter-Body in the Non-literary Papyri and in Paul the Apostle* (Missoula, Mont.: Society of Biblical Literature, 1972) and *Light from Ancient Letters* (Philadelphia: Fortress, 1986); E. S. Meltzer, ed., *Letters from Ancient Egypt* (trans. E. F. Wente; Atlanta: Scholars Press, 1990); and J. A. D. Weima, *Neglected Endings: The Significance of the Pauline Letter Closings* (Sheffield: JSOT Press, 1994).

people in love. Literary forms are either the products of certain settings or are comprehensible only in certain contexts.

A fifth and final characteristic is that the setting for certain literary forms changes over a period of years, which we can illustrate from the broad category (or genre) of drama. The modern setting of a dramatic play is generally on the stage of a public theater, a secular or popular setting. Originally, however, drama did not have such a setting. Both tragedy and comedy originated in the religious festivals of Greek cities of the classical and Hellenistic periods. Despite their diverse themes and plots, dramatic plays were performed in honor of the Greek god Dionysius, and they generally followed a private religious ceremony of the cult in a nearby temple of the god. Consider the origins of this literary category the next time you watch your favorite television drama! The settings of literary forms change in the history of a culture. This is an important observation in the study of the traditional units of folk literature that presuppose an oral setting (e.g., poems, songs, riddles). When these oral forms are put into writing, the literary context often differs from its original oral setting.[23]

NT Case Studies Our discussion about the nature and significance of literary forms is a relevant preface to the form-critical study of the NT. This method was first applied to old European folk literature before its use in biblical writings.[24]

---

23. For a similar example taken from a love poem, see Lohfink, *Now I Get It!* 45-51. See also C. S. Lewis, *The Allegory of Love: A Study in Medieval Tradition* (London: Oxford University Press, 1936, 1938).

24. Two examples of early works that influenced the form criticism of the Bible are L. von Ranke, *Geschichte der romanischen und germanischen Völker* (1824), and E. Nordern, *Agnostos Theos* (1913). The following studies pioneered the approach in biblical studies: H. Gunkel, *Genesis* (1901) and *Ausgewählte Psalmen* (1917); M. Dibelius, *Die Formgeschichte des Evangeliums* (1919); and Bultmann, *Synoptic Tradition* (1921). For later research on form criticism, see B. Gerhardsson, *Memory and Manuscript* (trans. E. Sharpe; Lund: Gleerup, 1961); R. H. Lightfoot, *History and Interpretation in the Gospels* (London: Hodder & Stoughton, 1935); H. Riesenfeld, *The Gospel Tradition and Its Beginnings* (London: A. R. Mowbray, 1957); and V. Taylor, *The Formation of the Gospel Tradition* (London: Macmillan, 1933), which offers helpful insight into both the benefits and the limitations of form criticism, particularly as employed by R. Bultmann. For surveys, see Harrington, *IntNT*, 70-84; McKnight, *What Is Form Criticism?* S. H. Travis, "Form Criticism," in Marshall, *NTI*, 153-64; M. J. Buss, *Biblical Form Criticism in Its Context* (Sheffield: Sheffield Academic Press, 1999); and Marvin A. Sweeney, ed., *The Changing Face of Form Criticism for the Twenty-first Century* (Grand Rapids: Eerdmans, 2003).

The popular and social character of both types of literature almost required such a method. Because of the nature of literary forms (as we have seen), form criticism seeks to comprehend the following: (1) the character of each literary form and the fixed patterns in which it is framed, (2) the linguistic intent that the readers were accustomed to expect, and (3) the social and institutional setting that produced the literary form. These three concerns of form criticism will be applied to two traditional forms found in Mark's gospel: the miracle story of the healing of the leper (1:40-45) and the parable of the mustard seed (4:30-32). Each is a prevalent form in the Synoptic Gospels; each reflects an oral setting and has been the focus of much form-critical research.

Like all literary forms, the account of the healing of the leper in Mark 1:40-45 follows a fixed pattern, characteristic of most miracle stories of that period:

Diagnosis: a leper in need of cleansing (v. 40)
Therapy: the healing touch of Jesus (v. 41)
Proof of restoration: the leper left — cleansed! (v. 42).

Reading the entire account, one will note that the story centers on this basic three-point pattern. All details are reduced to essential descriptions. Nothing is known of the leper's name or of the specific time or place, nor is anything else mentioned of him after his restoration to health. Why? Assuming that healings took place in the ministry of Jesus, the incident was probably reduced after years of oral circulation to a simple fixed pattern so that the story could be remembered easily and transmitted to others. This was an acceptable way of telling miracle stories in the ancient Mediterranean world (and elsewhere). For example, many similar stories with the same fixed forms were circulated about the healer-philosophers Pythagoras and Apollonius.[25] Ancient Christian tradition also recognized that Mark's gos-

---

25. Iamblichus, *Life of Pythagoras* 36, 60-61, 134-36; Philostratus, *The Life of Apollonius* 2.4; 3.38; 4.20, 45; see also the healing accounts at the temple of Asclepius in the Epidaurus inscriptions (4th cent. B.C.). All of the above healing accounts are found in D. R. Cartlidge and D. L. Dungan, eds., *Documents for the Study of the Gospels* (Philadelphia: Fortress, 1980), 151-55, 220, 225-26, 229-31. For studies on NT miracles, see R. H. Fuller, *Interpreting the Miracles* (London: SCM Press, 1963); H. C. Kee, *Miracle in the Early Christian World* (New Haven: Yale University Press, 1983); E. Keller and M.-L. Keller, *Miracles in Dispute: A Continuing Debate* (trans. M. Kohl; London: SCM Press, 1969); G. Thiessen, *The Miracles of the Early Chris-*

pel was the literary transmission of well-worn oral traditions that had long been shaped by the shifting needs of preaching and teaching. As the fourth-century Christian historian Eusebius explains: "Whatever [Mark] recorded, he wrote down accurately, but *not in the order in which it was spoken or performed by our Lord*. For Mark did not hear the Lord, nor did he follow him, but he was a later follower of Peter, *who fashioned the teachings according to the needs of the moment*" (*Ecclesiastical History* 3.39.15).

The essential points to which this miracle story is reduced make plain the linguistic intent of this form. The healing of the leper story seeks to glorify Jesus as the instrument of God's power. It might also have sought to encourage its hearers by impressing them with Jesus' special ability to relieve a human affliction.

The sociological setting that produced the present framework of the miracle story is more difficult to ascertain. There are at least three stages in the history of the transmission of this gospel tradition (i.e., Jesus-church-gospel), and we will concentrate on the stages preceding the Gospel of Mark.[26] According to most form critics, many of the miracle stories of Jesus were widely circulated among urban Gentile communities that were attracted to Jesus as a divine miracle-worker superior to other healer-philosophers. The concluding proof of restoration in the story, however, indicates that it probably originated in a Jewish-Christian community of Palestine: "Go, show yourself to the priest, and offer for your cleansing what Moses commanded" (Mark 1:44). Although the literary framework of the story is characteristic of many miracle stories in the ancient Mediterranean world, the vocabulary and religious contents reflect the beliefs and perceptions of Jewish Christians of Palestine. This proposed setting also

---

tian Tradition (trans. F. McDonagh; Philadelphia: Fortress, 1983); D. Wenham and C. Blomberg, eds., *The Miracles of Jesus* (Sheffield: JSOT, 1986); M. D. Hooker, *The Signs of a Prophet: The Prophetic Actions of Jesus* (London: SCM Press, 1997); G. H. Twelftree, *Jesus the Miracle Worker: A Historical and Theological Study* (Downers Grove, Ill.: InterVarsity Press, 1999); E. Eve, *The Jewish Context of Jesus' Miracles* (Sheffield: Sheffield Academic Press, 2002); and J. Pilch, *Healing in the New Testament: Insights from Medical and Mediterranean Anthropology* (Minneapolis: Fortress, 2000).

26. If we were to trace the history of the tradition from its inception to its final shape in the Gospels, it would be more appropriate to posit four or more stages, for example: (1) the ministry of Jesus, (2) the earliest followers after Jesus, (3) early Christianity adjusting to its environment, and (4) the writing of the Gospels. See chart 2.1 earlier in this chapter on the development of the Gospels.

lends some credibility to the view that the story points back to an incident that took place in the ministry of Jesus.[27]

The saying in Mark 4:30-32 is called a parable. Beginning in the nineteenth century, NT scholars attempted to distinguish the "simplicity" of Jesus' parables from the "complexity" of traditional allegory. According to this view, allegory encodes an elaborate set of symbolic comparisons into the numerous details of a story, whereas a parable focuses attention on only one central message illustrated by a familiar life-situation.[28] More recent studies, however, regard this view as too reductionistic. The insistence on one point per parable appears to be a modernistic reaction to a less disciplined, ahistorical reading popularized by medieval allegory, where even the tiniest details carried great spiritual significance. Many contemporary scholars now urge a more flexible understanding of parable as an evocative metaphor, sufficiently imprecise that it will draw the hearer's/reader's mind and imagination to actively wrestle with its elusive message.[29] Still others argue for striking a balance between the allegorical and the parabolic by allowing Jesus' parables to make at least as many points as there are main characters in the story.[30]

27. See the following studies, which argue that the gospel tradition was derived from Jesus himself: Riesenfeld, *Gospel Tradition;* Gerhardsson, *Memory and Manuscript;* Hooker, *Signs of a Prophet;* and Twelftree, *Jesus the Miracle Worker.*

28. See the important work of A. Jülicher, *Die Gleichnisreden Jesu* (2 vols.; Freiburg and Leipzig: J. C. B. Mohr [P. Siebeck], 1899). For studies on parables, see C. H. Dodd, *The Parables of the Kingdom* (London: Nisbet, 1935; New York: Charles Scribner's Sons, 1936); J. Jeremias, *The Parables of Jesus* (trans. S. H. Hooke; 2d rev. ed.; New York: Charles Scribner's Sons, 1972; trans. of *Die Gleichnisse Jesu* [Zürich: Zwingli, 1947]); A. M. Hunter, *Interpreting the Parables* (Philadelphia: Westminster, 1960); J. D. Crossan, *In Parables: The Challenge of the Historical Jesus* (New York: Harper & Row, 1973); N. Perrin, *Jesus and the Language of the Kingdom: Symbol and Metaphor in NT Interpretation* (Philadelphia: Fortress, 1976); M. Tolbert, *Perspectives on the Parables: An Approach to Multiple Interpretations* (Philadelphia: Fortress, 1979); D. B. Gowler, *What Are They Saying about the Parables?* (New York: Paulist Press, 2000); R. N. Longenecker, ed., *The Challenge of Jesus' Parables* (Grand Rapids: Eerdmans, 2000); C. W. Hedrick, *Many Things in Parables: Jesus and His Modern Critics* (Louisville, Ky.: Westminster John Knox, 2004); L. Schottroff, *Envisioning the Reign of God through Parables* (trans. L. M. Maloney; Philadelphia: Fortress, 2006); and K. R. Snodgrass, *Stories with Intent: A Comprehensive Guide to the Parables of Jesus* (Grand Rapids: Eerdmans, 2008).

29. R. W. Funk, *Language, Hermeneutic, and Word of God* (New York: Harper & Row, 1966); S. M. TeSelle, *Speaking in Parables: A Study in Metaphor and Theology* (Philadelphia: Fortress, 1975); Perrin, *Jesus and the Language of the Kingdom;* J. R. Donahue, *The Gospel in Parable* (Philadelphia: Fortress, 1988).

30. See R. W. Funk, *Parables and Presence* (Philadelphia: Fortress, 1982); F. H. Borsch,

Despite the above controversy, Mark's parable of the mustard seed is simple enough to contain the following fixed pattern: (1) a starting point, usually with the opening phrase "the kingdom of God is like . . ."; (2) the illustration from life (e.g., a mustard seed); and (3) a central point (e.g., miraculous growth). The one-central-point aspect of this fixed pattern becomes problematic in the longer parables of Jesus that have more than one main character or theme (e.g., Luke 10:25-37; 16:19-31).

Many form critics believe that Jesus taught about the kingdom of God using concise and simple parables like that of the mustard seed (Mark 4:30-32). If this parable stems from the ministry of Jesus (as most scholars believe), it was probably intended as a defense of Jesus' ministry against Jewish critics. Many Jews of Jesus' day did not see the end-time glories of God's kingdom that they anticipated in Jesus' ministry. Telling a parable like the mustard seed would be an appropriate response of Jesus to that situation.

The following interpretation is a possible rendering of the original intent of Jesus' parable of the mustard seed. Although it is small and insignificant when it is planted, the mustard seed miraculously grows into a large bushy shrub providing shelter for the birds. So it is with the kingdom of God in Jesus' ministry. Even though it appears small and insignificant, when God's reign is truly recognized in the ministry of Jesus, it will become something great, providing shelter for people. This emphasis on the small beginnings of God's kingdom, with the promise that it would develop into something great, would be an appropriate response of Jesus to the charges of his critics.

Form Criticism: Conclusions Although much form-critical research has been done in the Synoptic Gospels, attention has also been directed to other areas, such as early Christian hymns (e.g., Phil 2:6-11; Col 1:15-20; 1 Pet 3:18-22; 1 Tim 3:16) and household rules (e.g., Col 3:18–4:1; Eph 5:21–6:9; Titus 2:1-10). Most of the hymns emphasize the divine mission of Christ and presuppose original oral settings in the life and worship of early communities.

Many Things in Parables: Extravagant Stories on New Community (Philadelphia: Fortress, 1988); and esp. C. L. Blomberg, *Interpreting the Parables* (Downers Grove, Ill.: InterVarsity Press, 1990). For example, the parables of the hidden treasure and the pearl of great price (Matt 13:44-46) each make one point, since there is only one "character" in the story. Parables such as the Pharisee and the tax collector (Luke 18:9-14) make two points, and the parable of the prodigal son (Luke 15:11-32) makes three points, one for each character (father, prodigal, and elder son).

The household rules are drawn from the traditional ethics of the Hellenistic world. Other traditional forms analyzed in the NT Epistles are creeds, confessions, baptismal formulas, catechetical teachings, diatribes (or philosophical dialogues), and pareneses (i.e., moral exhortations).[31]

The special concerns of form criticism are significant for the study of early Christianity. First, it seeks to get behind the sources discovered by source criticism to learn something about the earliest communities and Jesus. Second, it takes seriously the fixed literary forms of the NT and seeks to understand their practical function within the communities that produced them. Third, it takes seriously the preliterary period of oral transmission as a time of growth and adaptation for the literary forms within the communities who used them. Finally, form criticism regards many of these literary forms with their long preliterary history as "windows" from which to view and study the existence of early Christian communities.

Redaction Criticism

"Redaction" is the process of putting information into a suitable literary form, that is, the act of revising or editing. Using an example from our modern day, redaction is the work of a newspaper reporter who selectively organizes information from an interview and brings it together into a final written report. It is also the task of anyone today who revises a written proposal from a committee meeting by correcting it or adding important information that was overlooked. Redaction is concerned with the selection, omission, addition, correction, or abridgement of information to produce a final written document.

---

31. For surveys of the various early Christian forms, see W. G. Doty, *Letters in Primitive Christianity* (Philadelphia: Fortress, 1973), 55-63; G. W. H. Lampe, "The Evidence in the NT for Early Creeds, Catechisms, and Liturgy," *ExpTim* 71 (1959-60): 359-63; and C. J. Roetzel, *The Letters of Paul: Conversations in Context* (4th ed.; Louisville, Ky.: Westminster John Knox, 1998), 51-78. For specific form-critical studies, see D. L. Balch, *Let Wives Be Submissive: The Domestic Code in 1 Peter* (Chico, Calif.: Scholars Press, 1981); R. P. Martin, *Carmen Christi: Philippians 2:5-11 in Recent Interpretation and in the Setting of Early Christian Worship* (rev. ed.; Grand Rapids: Eerdmans, 1983); V. H. Neufeld, *The Earliest Christian Confessions* (Leiden: Brill, 1963); J. T. Sanders, *NT Christological Hymns* (Cambridge: Cambridge University Press, 1971); and S. K. Stowers, *The Diatribe and Paul's Letter to the Romans* (Chico, Calif.: Scholars Press, 1981); also see n. 21.

Basic Concerns In the NT, redaction criticism is concerned with the activity of the final writer of a book. It examines (1) how the writer employed (revised, edited) sources, (2) his or her particular emphases and distinctive viewpoint, and (3) the author's own life-setting and the needs of the specific audience being addressed.[32]

Redaction criticism both draws upon the literary and historical concerns of source and form criticism and also goes beyond them by focusing on a different aspect of the text. It presupposes source criticism by investigating the author's use of sources but goes beyond this method by concentrating on the work of the final author. It serves as a complement to form criticism because it concerns the final stage of the history of tradition. It distinguishes itself from form criticism, however, on at least three points: (1) redaction criticism focuses on the final text, not the preliterary history of tradition; (2) it works toward a synthesis of the smaller literary units that form criticism seeks to analyze; and (3) it deals only with the final author's life-setting and not the various oral and written settings of the traditions.

A Case Study from Luke Let us again look at our comparison of the Synoptic Gospels, concentrating on Luke 3:1-6 and its use of Mark. (See table 2.4 on p. 65.) We see from the comparison chart 2.2 that our analysis will presuppose from form criticism that Mark is a source for Luke. Even though redaction criticism can be undertaken with documents whose sources are not clearly delineated (e.g., Mark's gospel and the Acts of the Apostles), the evidence of defined sources makes the analysis less complicated. Mark is a complete work in itself, but in the history of the Synoptic tradition it, along with Q, functions as a precursor to the completed stages of the Synoptic tradition in which the Gospels of Matthew and Luke are classified.

As we concentrate on Luke's use of Mark, we can point out five redactional techniques employed by Luke: addition, omission, expansion,

---

32. For redaction-critical studies, see H. Conzelmann, *The Theology of St. Luke* (trans. G. Buswell; New York: Harper & Row, 1961; Philadelphia: Fortress, 1982); G. Bornkamm et al., *Tradition and Interpretation in Matthew* (trans. P. Scott; Philadelphia: Westminster, 1963); Harrington, *IntNT*, 96-107 (survey); W. Marxsen, *Mark the Evangelist* (trans. J. Boyce; Nashville: Abingdon, 1969); N. Perrin, *What Is Redaction Criticism?* (Philadelphia. Fortress, 1969); J. Rohde, *Rediscovering the Teaching of the Evangelists* (trans. D. M. Barton; London: SCM Press, 1968); R. H. Stein, "What Is Redaktionsgeschichte?" *JBL* 88 (1969): 45-56; and R. H. Stein, *Gospels and Tradition: Studies on Redaction Criticism of the Synoptic Gospels* (Grand Rapids: Baker, 1991).

TABLE 2.4. MARK AND LUKE: JOHN THE BAPTIST (3)

Mark 1:1-4	Luke 3:1-6
1The beginning of the good news of Jesus Christ, the Son of God.	
	1In the fifteenth year of the reign of Emperor Tiberius, when Pontius Pilate was governor of Judea, and Herod was ruler of Galilee, and his brother Philip ruler of the region of Ituraea and Trachonitis, and Lysanias ruler of Abilene, 2during the high priesthood of Annas and Caiaphas, the word of God came to John son of Zechariah in the wilderness. 3He went into all the region around the Jordan, proclaiming a baptism of repentance for the forgiveness of sins,
2As it is written in the prophet Isaiah, "See, I am sending my messenger ahead of you, who will prepare your way; 3the voice of one crying out in the wilderness: 'Prepare the way of the Lord, make his paths straight,'"	4as it is written in the book of the words of the prophet Isaiah, "The voice of one crying out in the wilderness: 'Prepare the way of the Lord, make his paths straight. 5Every valley shall be filled, and every mountain and hill shall be brought low, and the crooked shall be made straight, and the rough ways made smooth; 6and all flesh shall see the salvation of God.'"
4John the baptizer appeared in the wilderness, proclaiming a baptism of repentance for the forgiveness of sins.	

rearrangement, and inclusion. Some overlap may occur among these techniques.

Let us look at *addition*. It is clear from the chapter headings that Luke does not begin his gospel at the same place that Mark does. Luke adds to his source two chapters of material not found elsewhere: a prologue with birth and infancy narratives (Luke 1:1–2:52) and a historical preface (3:1-2a). Luke's prologue (1:1-4) introduces not only his gospel but also his second volume, Acts of the Apostles (see Acts 1:1). The birth narratives also include accounts of John the Baptist (Luke 1:5-25, 57-80), who is also the subject of our comparison table 2:4. This background of John is not found in Mark. Luke's additions (1:1–3:2a) provide much that is lacking in his Markan source and give Luke's gospel ancient biographical or historical characteristics. The historical notations, found in 2:1-3 and 3:1-2, may signify Luke's special concern to place the stories of John and Jesus in the context of Roman secular history, since similar notations are found elsewhere (e.g., Acts 11:28; 18:2, 12).

The second technique concerns a Lukan *omission*. Looking at our comparison table, we note that Luke omits the Malachi passage found in his source (Mark 1:2b / Mal 3:1a). Luke's omission was probably influenced by Q, since the Malachi passage appears elsewhere in a tradition common to both Luke and Matthew (Luke 7:27 and Matt 11:10 = Q).

Lukan *expansion* of his source is the third redactional technique. In Luke 3:5-6 the author expands his source by quoting more extensively the Isa 40 passage found in his Markan source. Luke continues to follow a Greek text similar to Mark. In his expanded citation of Isa 40:3-5, Luke omits a word ("all") and a phrase ("the glory of the Lord") and appears to underscore the statement "all flesh shall see the salvation of God." This statement in the Greek resembles both Luke 2:30 (God's salvation anticipated) and Acts 28:28 (God's salvation extended to all people). This theme of worldwide salvation (for Jews and Gentiles) is an important concern for the author of Luke-Acts (e.g., Luke 2:32; 24:47; Acts 13:47; 26:23). On the basis of historical clues and such Lukan emphases as worldwide salvation, tension with Judaism, and appeals for Roman tolerance, one can draw some tentative conclusions about the situation of Luke and his readers. They appear to be part of a growing Gentile-Christian community that is experiencing a loss of identity or purpose as a result of both Jewish and pagan antagonism (ca. A.D. 80-90).

The fourth device used by Luke in this passage is the *rearrangement* of his source. Luke makes it clear to his readers about whom this prophet speaks by relocating his source about John's preaching (Mark 1:4) before the Isaiah passage is cited (Luke 3:3). Luke also prefaces this Markan preaching summary with an introduction that appears to identify John as a prophet: "the word of God came to John" (3:2). John is identified as a prophet elsewhere (e.g., Luke 7:26-27; 20:4-6). By rearranging his source, Luke provides a "topical sentence" to introduce and preview the discussion on John that follows.

Luke uses a fifth redaction technique in this passage: *inclusion*. Luke not only begins his discussion of John with a description of John's preaching (3:3) but concludes with it as well (v. 18). Substantial blocks of material on John's preaching are also included from Q, Luke's second source (Luke 3:7-9 / Matt 3:7-10), and from L, Luke's own special material (Luke 3:10-14). All of this extra material probably serves as Luke's interpretation of the Markan source. According to Luke, John is the prophet who preaches "repentance for the forgiveness of sins" in anticipation of God's worldwide salvation. John is both subordinate to Jesus the Messiah (3:15-16) and is united with Jesus in his preaching and prophetic role (cf. 3:2b-20 with 4:16-30).

It has been evident from our study that much of the information on Luke's redactional activity was collected by approaching the text from two perspectives. First, by looking *in* the text for redactional changes, and then, by looking *through* the text into the entire literary work to verify whether the themes of the text are typical emphases and concerns of the author. From this last perspective we sought to reconstruct the author's life-setting.

Redaction Criticism: Conclusions As we have mentioned, redaction criticism can be applied to other books of the NT. It is relevant for books that have no clearly delineated sources, such as Mark's gospel and the Acts of the Apostles. Here, where close comparison of a specific written source is not possible, concentration must be placed on the unique vocabulary, style, structure, and key themes of each author. Redaction-critical study of the NT letters and homilies has also been done, especially where the use of traditional material can be detected (e.g., hymns, confessions, household rules).[33]

---

33. Redaction-critical research of the NT epistles is evident, for example, in the following commentaries of the Hermeneia series (Philadelphia: Fortress, 1971-): Conzelmann, *First*

The method of redaction criticism concentrates on the time of the final authors, their setting and audience, and their special concerns and intentions. It is not concerned with the preliterary oral traditions but with the literary text in its final form. This focus of redaction criticism has also prepared the way for more recent methods of literary criticism pioneered by scholars of European literature, including genre, style, and poetic analysis. All of these methods are concerned with the language, diction, structure, and imagery of the literary work in its final form. These new methods are often helpful for understanding the intrinsic qualities of the NT writings, regardless of the historical-critical problems.[34]

Corinthians; Betz, Galatians; Lohse, Colossians and Philemon; Dibelius and Conzelmann, Pastoral Epistles; and Dibelius and Greeven, James.

34. Examples of the new literary-critical approaches to NT study include W. A. Beardslee, The Literary Criticism of the NT (Philadelphia. Fortress, 1970); Crossan, In Parables; R. W. Funk, Jesus as Precursor (Missoula, Mont.: Scholars Press; Philadelphia: Fortress, 1975); D. O. Via, Kerygma and Comedy in the NT (Philadelphia: Fortress, 1975); D. Patte, What Is Structural Exegesis? (Philadelphia: Fortress, 1976); N. R. Petersen, Literary Criticism for NT Critics (Philadelphia: Fortress, 1978); R. Alter, The Art of Biblical Narrative (New York: Basic Books, 1981); E. V. McKnight, The Bible and the Reader: An Introduction to Literary Criticism (Philadelphia: Fortress, 1985); S. D. Moore, Literary Criticism and the Gospels: The Theoretical Challenge (New Haven: Yale University Press, 1989); S. Prickett, ed., Reading the Text: Biblical Criticism and Literary Theory (Cambridge, Mass.: Blackwell, 1991); A. Loades and M. McLain, eds., Hermeneutics, the Bible, and Literary Criticism (New York: St. Martin's Press, 1992); M. A. Powell, ed., The Bible and Modern Literary Criticism: A Critical Assessment and Annotated Bibliography (New York: Greenwood Press, 1992); C. Focant, ed., The Synoptic Gospels: Source Criticism and the New Literary Criticism (Leuven: Leuven University Press, 1993); E. V. McKnight and E. S. Malbon, The New Literary Criticism and the NT (Valley Forge, Pa.: Trinity Press International, 1994); S. E. Porter, The Paul of Acts: Essays in Literary Criticism, Rhetoric, and Theology (Tübingen: Mohr Siebeck, 1999); R. W. Tate, Interpreting the Bible: A Handbook of Terms and Methods (Peabody, Mass.: Hendrickson, 2006); and vols. 2-6, 10, 14, 20, 23, 26, 29, 30-32, 62-65, 69-70, 89 of Semeia: An Experimental Journal for Biblical Criticism (Atlanta: Scholars Press, 1972-2002).

CHAPTER 3

The Gospel of Mark

Our study of source criticism in chapter 2 showed that Mark was probably the first written gospel and served as a source for both Matthew and Luke. Along with an analysis of literary forms and themes, this chapter includes a survey on how Mark might have compiled his narrative from earlier traditions. These insights on the "making of Mark" are derived from the results of both form and redaction criticism.

Mention has already been made of the popular misconceptions about the Gospels as detailed itineraries of the life of Jesus. Although they do provide historical data, careful study suggests that the *specific* chronological ordering of each gospel is chiefly due to the creative work of the authors. Perhaps we should imagine the Synoptic writers inheriting an overarching framework of Jesus' life and ministry, which *each author* then fleshed out with topical collections, thematic units, and pericopae (individual sections) as he saw fit.[1]

Our study of Mark will employ an analytic definition that can be summarized as follows: Mark's gospel is (1) a collection of independent sayings and stories (2) grouped together by literary and thematic devices and (3) placed in a geographic framework for the specific religious purposes of the author. Mark is hardly neutral in his concerns. His gospel weaves together both history and interpretation, tradition and redaction, as does

---

1. In this case, Mark's basic outline may indeed "represent a genuine succession of events, within which movement and development can be traced" (C. H. Dodd, "The Framework of the Gospel Narrative," in *NT Studies* [Manchester: Manchester University Press, 1953], 11).

any good piece of historical writing.[2] He intends to relay the story of Jesus, not out of mere historical curiosity, but in order to persuade his readers to eventually share his faith in Jesus. It is no accident that the gospel writers have traditionally been called the Evangelists. Our study of Matthew and Luke-Acts, in the next three chapters, will follow a similar analysis based on history, interpretation, tradition, and redaction.

The Major Markan Literary Forms

The gospel of Mark is, first of all, a collection of independent sayings and stories. Papias made this observation (as Eusebius noted) toward the close of the first century, which has since been confirmed by the research of form criticism.[3] This method indicates that most of the utterances of Jesus and the narratives about him originated orally in the settings of both Jesus and the early church, decades before Mark compiled them into his own narrative. Sayings of Jesus are various kinds of direct discourse. Some are attached to stories about him, whereas others stand alone in the narrative. These sayings and stories have their own prehistory and make complete sense outside the narrative framework of Mark. After listing some of these literary forms, examples will be given to show their independence from the narrative of Mark.

Apothegms

Short, instructive sayings attached to certain situations or scenes are called apothegms. The stories or scenes, also called pronouncement stories, are illustrative of the utterances of Jesus highlighted in the narrative. Examples of such stories are controversy dialogues of Jesus with the Jewish leaders (e.g., Mark 2:1-12, 23-28; 3:1-6), scholastic dialogues of Jesus with various inquirers (10:17-22; 12:28-34), and biographical statements about Jesus (6:1-6; 10:13-16).

---

2. How many historians of World War II fail to begin their work already convinced that Adolf Hitler and his Nazi regime were a consummate evil? Does this "prejudice" disqualify them from writing an accurate, even an illuminating, biography of Hitler?

3. See ch. 2, n. 24, for an extensive bibliography on form criticism.

Dominical Sayings

Whereas pronouncement stories or apothegms are connected to background scenes, so-called dominical sayings of Jesus (from Lat. *dominus,* "lord") stand alone in the narrative. Examples of dominical sayings in Mark are prophetic and apocalyptic sayings (1:15; 9:1; 13:5-27), legal sayings and church rules (2:10; 3:28-29; 10:3-9; 11:25), "I" sayings (1:38; 8:31, 38; 9:37; 13:23, 31, 37), proverbs or wisdom sayings (2:17; 3:27; 10:25), and parables or similitudes (4:3-20, 26-32; 12:1-11).

Proverbs

Wisdom sayings and proverbs are the best examples of sayings whose meaning does not depend on immediate context. The sayings about salt in Mark 9:49-50, for example, which are loosely attached by the catchwords "salted with fire" and "salt," could be placed anywhere in Mark's outline of Jesus' ministry. The same observation applies to Jesus' sayings about entry into God's kingdom (10:15, 23). Each saying probably had a separate origin in the oral teachings of Jesus or early Christianity.

Stories

The stories about Jesus are various forms of indirect discourse or narrative. Most of these stories probably existed independently of each other before Mark compiled them. Two basic types of narrative material are miracle stories (4:35–5:20; 5:25-43; 7:24-37) and historical stories or legends (Jesus' baptism and temptation, 1:9-13; his transfiguration, 9:2-4; his triumphal entry, 11:1-11; and his passion, death, and resurrection, 14:1–16:8). Some stories, such as the pre-Markan traditions of Jesus' passion and death, properly belong at the end of Mark's book.[4] Other stories have been placed at different points in the outline of Jesus' ministry.

4. Is the Gospel of Mark a passion narrative with an extended introduction? See M. Kahler, *The So-Called Historical Jesus and the Historic Biblical Christ* (trans. C. Braaten, from 1896 ed.; Philadelphia: Fortress, 1964), 80 n. 11. Did Mark inherit a primitive passion narrative, which is the basis of all four gospels? For strong arguments in favor of this view, see V. Taylor, *The Formation of the Gospel Tradition* (2d ed.; London: Macmillan, 1935), 44-

A comparison of similar stories in the Gospels of Mark and John substantiates this observation. For example, Mark places the story of Jesus' cleansing of the Jerusalem temple near the end of his ministry (Mark 11:15-17), whereas John places it at the beginning (John 2:13-17). The similar actions and words in both stories present real difficulties for those who view Mark and John as reporting on two different events in Jesus' life. It is more probable that the story of Jesus' cleansing of the temple is from an independent tradition that Mark and John both utilized for their respective literary purposes.

The Markan Literary Devices

Second, the independent sayings and stories in Mark are grouped together according to certain literary and thematic devices.[5] We list here six examples of these Markan techniques.

62; and J. B. Green, *The Death of Jesus: Tradition and Interpretation in the Passion Narrative* (Tübingen: Mohr Siebeck, 1988). Even though these complex questions cannot be fully answered here, we note four places where there seems to be Markan redaction of an earlier passion narrative: (1) the anointing at Bethany (14:3-9), which contains the Markan motif of discipleship (vv. 8-9; see also 8:34-38; 14:17-21, 27-51, 54, 66-72) and is framed by 14:1-2 and vv. 10-11 (a typical Markan device called intercalation); (2) the early tradition of the Passover meal (Mark 14:12-25; see also 1 Cor 11:23-26), which contains the Markan motif "deliver up" or "betray" (*paradidōmi*, Mark 14:18, 21; see also 1:14; 3:19; 9:31; 10:33; 13:9, 11-12; 14:10-11, 41-42, 44; 15:1, 10, 15) and his typical use of the kingdom-of-God theme (14:25; see also 1:14-15; 15:43); (3) the Sanhedrin trial (14:53-65), which is also part of a Markan intercalation: 14:54 (55-65) 66-72, and contains the Markan themes of Jesus' relationship to Jerusalem and the temple (14:58; see also 11:1-20; 15:29-30, 38), discipleship (14:54), and Jesus' messianic identity (14:62; see also 8:27-30); and (4) the account of Jesus' crucifixion, which includes favorite Markan Psalms (22; 69) and his characteristic use of the kingdom-of-God theme (Mark 15:43). Both oral and written traditions of Jesus' passion and death were undoubtedly shaped by the primitive kerygma and catechesis (e.g., Gal 1:3-4 and 1 Cor 15:3-4; cf. Acts 2:23; 3:13-15), early hymns (e.g., Phil 2:6-11), sacramental practices (e.g., Rom 6:4-5 and 1 Cor 11:23-26), and recollections of eyewitnesses (Luke 1:1-2; Acts 1:21-22; Heb 2:3). Despite the immense challenge of distinguishing "literary chickens" from "historical eggs," it is certain that whatever early traditions Mark inherited, he thoroughly reworked them for his gospel.

5. For Mark's techniques of grouping, intercalation, and general composition, see R. Bultmann, *The History of the Synoptic Tradition* (trans. J. Marsh; New York: Harper & Row, 1963; trans. of *Die Geschichte der synoptischen Tradition* [4th ed.; Göttingen: Vandenhoeck & Ruprecht, 1958]), 322-51; V. Taylor, *The Gospel according to Mark* (London: Macmillan, 1959), 48-54, 628-32; W. Marxsen, *Mark the Evangelist* (trans. J. Boyce et al.;

First, Mark arranges his material according to themes, literary forms, and catchwords that have elements in common. Regarding Mark's *arrangement of material around common themes,* one notes (1) sayings about riches (10:23-27) and rewards (10:28-31) that are combined with the story about the rich young man (10:17-22) and (2) sayings about outward observance of the law (7:9-13) and inward defilement (7:14-16) that are added to the controversy story about purity (7:1-8).

Concerning common literary forms, most of the controversy stories (2:1–3:6), parables (4:2-34), and miracle stories (4:35–5:20) are grouped together in blocks of material. This formal arrangement either was done by Mark or existed in an earlier cycle of tradition that he inherited.[6]

Material is also grouped together by catchwords. Thus parables in Mark 4 are linked by the word "seed." The name "Elijah" ties together the transfiguration and the subsequent discussion on his end-time role (9:2-8 and 11-13). Finally, the word translated "sin" or "cause to stumble" (Gk. *skandalizō*) forms the link for the sayings about the "little ones" and the offending members of the body (9:42-47).

Second, Mark groups together his material by *summary statements* or various linking devices. The summaries in Mark are brief editorial comments that introduce, conclude, divide, or connect various stories, and they often contribute to the general movement of the narrative. Examples of these summary reports are Mark 1:14-15, 21-22, 39; 2:13; 3:7-12; 5:21; 6:6, 12-13, 30-33, 53-56; 10:1. Some also coincide with geographic references (1:14-15; 3:7-12; 6:6). Others include action words that give the narrative a movement of progression (1:29; 2:13; 5:1; 6:1, 34).

A third device that Mark employs to connect his materials is *parataxis,* in conjunction with place or time connectives. Parataxis (from Greek

---

Nashville: Abingdon, 1969); J. R. Donahue, *Are You the Christ?* (Missoula, Mont.: Scholars Press, 1973), 36-45; P. J. Achtemeier, *Mark* (Philadelphia: Fortress, 1975), 22-30; D. J. Selby, *Introduction to the NT: "The Word Became Flesh"* (New York: Macmillan, 1971), 83-88; R. A. Guelich, *Mark 1–8:26* (WBC 34A; Dallas: Word Books, 1989), xxxv-xxxvii; J. R. Edwards, "Markan Sandwiches: The Significance of Interpolations in Markan Narratives," *NovT* 31 (1989): 193-216; and R. H. Stein, "The Cleansing of the Temple in Mark (11:15-19): Reformation or Judgment?" in *Gospels and Tradition: Studies on Redaction Criticism of the Synoptic Gospels* (Grand Rapids: Baker, 1991).

6. It is plausible that these groupings of parables (Mark 4:2-32), miracle stories (4:35–5:20), and controversy stories (2:1–3:6) were already cycles of tradition before the writing of Mark's gospel. See N. Perrin and D. C. Duling, *The NT, an Introduction: Proclamation and Parenesis, Myth and History* (2d ed.; New York: Harcourt Brace Jovanovich, 1982), 233-34.

words meaning "to place beside") consists of the simple coordination of sentences and paragraphs with the connective *kai* ("and"; e.g., 1:16, 40; 2:23; 3:20; 7:1, 32). Place or time connectives generally consist of verbal constructions indicating certain changes in action, such as "as soon as they left . . . they entered . . ." (1:29) and "when he returned . . . after some days . . ." (2:1). These linking devices indicate transitions from one episode to the next. Many also occur in summary statements, which serve this same function in the narrative.

Fourth, Mark groups his material by using *framing and bracketing techniques* (i.e., inclusion or intercalation).[7] In Mark 2:1–3:6 the controversy dialogues have been framed by two miracle stories in which Jesus heals a paralytic (2:1-12; 3:1-6). These two framing stories appear to be deliberate comments on the actions that take place between them: Jesus' opponents in the controversy dialogues are like the paralyzed men. Another set of healings, the cures of two blind men (8:22-26; 10:46-52), frames the central section of Mark, where Jesus seeks to instruct his disciples on the necessity of his suffering and the true nature of discipleship. Since the disciples do not understand these teachings, they too are blind. Finally, Jesus' cleansing of the temple (11:15-19) is bracketed by the story of the cursed and withered fig tree (11:12-14, 20-25). Within this framework, Jesus is not merely purging the temple; even more, his indicting words (v. 17) prefigure its destruction. Other occurrences of intercalation are 3:20-21 (22-30) 31-35; 5:21-24 (25-34) 35-43; 6:7-13 (14-29) 30-32; 14:1-2 (3-9) 10-11; 14:12-16 (17-21) 22-25; and 14:54 (55-65) 66-72.

Mark's framing devices have additional stylistic functions. For example, the healing of the woman with the issue of blood (5:25-34) is framed by the healing story of Jairus's daughter (5:21-24, 35-43). Perhaps the inserted account of the woman's healing provides time in the narrative for Jairus's daughter to die. It may also serve to bracket a story that speaks of faith (v. 34) with one that does not mention it.

Fifth, Mark arranges his material in *pairs or doublets*. We find double parables that make the same point, such as the new patches and new wine (2:21-22) and the divided kingdom and divided house (3:24-25). Two further examples are Jesus' words on greatness (9:35-36; 10:42-44) and (with significant differences) the two stories of a storm at sea (4:36-41; 6:45-52).

---

7. See Edwards, "Markan Sandwiches"; and Stein, "The Cleansing of the Temple in Mark."

A further noteworthy example is the double feeding of the multitude: the 5,000 (6:35-44) and the 4,000 (8:1-10). Both feedings are followed by a cycle of stories that are also found in John's account of the feeding of the 5,000 (John 6:1-14). Table 3.1 shows an outline of this common material. The materials in both gospels appear to follow a similar pattern. Are these both Markan and Johannine versions of some earlier cycle of tradition? If there was an earlier tradition, did it contain the double cycle that we find in Mark, or did he create it himself? These particular source-critical questions are difficult to answer.[8]

TABLE 3.1. MARK AND JOHN: FEEDING OF THE MULTITUDE

Event	Mark	John
1. Feeding	6:30-44 (5,000); 8:1-10 (4,000)	6:1-14 (5,000)
2. Lake crossing	6:45-56; 8:10	6:16-21
3. Controversy	7:1-13; 8:11-13	6:15
4. Bread discourse	7:14-23 (food); 8:14-21 (no bread)	6:22-51

The sixth and final literary device is the use of *repetition and recurring refrains*. An example of repetition is the three passion predictions (8:31; 9:31; 10:33-34), which define and unify Mark (8:31–16:8). Recurring refrains are found in the mention of Jesus' command for silence (1:25, 34, 44; 3:12; 5:43; 7:36; 8:30, which culminate in 9:9), the spread of Jesus' fame (1:28; 2:2, 13, 15; 3:7), and the amazement at the mighty works of Jesus (4:41; 5:20, 42; 6:2, 51; 7:37). All of the above examples have a specific function in Mark's gospel. Some of them will be further explained in our discussion of Mark's religious themes and concerns.

The Markan Geographic Scheme

The third aspect of our analytic definition of Mark's gospel concerns the geographic scheme in which it was ordered. Mark not only grouped together these independent sayings and stories by literary and thematic devices, he also placed them in a particular geographic framework. In Mark 11–13 the narrative takes place along the Jordan River and in the Judean

---

8. See Perrin and Duling, *NT Intro*, 233-35, 332-35.

wilderness. Mark 1:14–9:50 focuses on Galilee, with some brief departures outside that region (7:31; 8:27). Mark 10:1–11:10 deals with Jesus' journey to Jerusalem, and 11:11–16:8, his entry and stay in Jerusalem.[9]

Although geographic and chronological concerns are not dominant in Mark, locations like Capernaum of Galilee, the Sea of Galilee, and Jerusalem link together various stories and help to unify the narrative. And even though Mark had overriding thematic concerns, he leaves us a significant chronological sketch. His gospel begins with the preaching of John and the baptizing of Jesus along the Jordan River. He begins Jesus' ministry of teaching and healing in Galilee and restricts the conclusion of Jesus' work to Jerusalem. Mark's geographic and sketchy chronological scheme provides the basis for the narratives as developed in Matthew and Luke-Acts. In agreement with the Synoptic accounts, John's gospel ends the work of Jesus in Jerusalem, although the earlier part of his narrative is organized under a different geographic-chronological scheme.

The Major Themes

The fourth aspect of our analysis deals with the religious themes and concerns that dominate Mark's work. Many of the literary and thematic devices already discussed reflect these special concerns of the author. Also, the geographic framework is subordinate and may contribute to the author's purpose. For example, Mark's use of "Galilee" in 14:28 and 16:7 may reflect his concern for a mission outside of Judea before the exalted Christ returns.

The themes to be examined are the kingdom of God, the hidden and suffering Messiah, miracles, discipleship, and the end times.[10] The first

---

9. C. W. Hedrick, "What Is a Gospel? Geography, Time, and Narrative Structure," *PRSt* 10 (1983): 255-68; E. S. Malbon, "The Jesus of Mark and the Sea of Galilee," *JBL* 103 (1984): 363-77; B. M. F. van Iersel, "Locality, Structure, and Meaning in Mark," *LB* 53 (1983): 45-54.

10. For the theology of Mark, see Achtemeier, *Mark*, 41-110; T. J. Weeden, *Mark — Traditions in Conflict* (Philadelphia: Fortress, 1971); R. P. Martin, *Mark: Evangelist and Theologian* (Grand Rapids: Zondervan, 1972); Marxsen, *Mark the Evangelist*; J. Rohde, *Rediscovering the Teaching of the Evangelists* (trans. D. M. Barton; London: SCM Press, 1968), 113-52; E. Best, *Following Jesus: Discipleship in the Gospel of Mark* (Sheffield: JSOT Press, 1981); J. L. Mays, ed., *Interpreting the Gospels* (Philadelphia: Fortress, 1981), 115-82 (several studies on Mark); M. D. Hooker, *The Message of Mark* (London: Epworth, 1983); C. S. Mann, *Mark*

theme has two aspects: the present inauguration and the future establishment of God's universal rule through Jesus. Mark's view of messiahship has a similar two-sided development: the progressive unveiling of Jesus as the Son of God and the necessity of his suffering and death. Our discussion of miracles concerns Mark's reinterpretation of Jesus' miracles in the broader context of his messianic mission. The topic of discipleship underscores Mark's teaching on the sacrifice and suffering involved in following Jesus. Mark's interest in the end times centers on preparation for the near return of the risen Christ (the "imminent parousia").

A dominant motif recurring in these themes is that of suffering and death. It pervades Mark's Christology (lit. "study of Christ"), provides the context for interpreting Jesus' miracles, characterizes the cost of discipleship, and is said to increase among believers before the return of the risen Christ. This preoccupation with suffering and death colors the author's religious concerns for writing his work and may provide some information about the situation of his audience.

The Kingdom of God

"The time is fulfilled, and the kingdom of God has come near; repent, and believe in the good news" (Mark 1:15). With these few words, Mark distills the essence of Jesus' initial public proclamation. The remainder of his gospel is basically a narrative explanation of these opening words. Jesus also repeats this message with power and authority, eventually commissioning twelve apostles (or emissaries) to do the same (1:21-22, 27, 38-39; 2:2, 12-14; 3:14-15; 4:1-2, 11, 26-32).

(AB 27; Garden City, N.Y..: Doubleday, 1986), 104-58; M. R. Mansfield, *"Spirit and Gospel" in Mark* (Peabody, Mass.: Hendrickson, 1987); T. J. Geddert, *Watchwords: Mark 13 in Markan Eschatology* (Sheffield: JSOT Press, 1989); C. D. Marshall, *Faith as a Theme in Mark's Narrative* (Cambridge: Cambridge University Press, 1989); W. R. Telford, *Mark* (Sheffield: Sheffield Academic Press, 1995) and *The Theology of the Gospel of Mark* (Cambridge: University Press, 1999); Telford, ed., *The Interpretation of Mark* (2d ed.; Edinburgh: T&T Clark, 1995); R. E. Watts, *Isaiah's New Exodus and Mark* (Tübingen: Mohr Siebeck, 1997); D. H. Juel, *The Gospel of Mark* (Nashville: Abingdon, 1999); C. A. Evans, *Mark 8:27–16:20* (WBC 34B; Nashville: Thomas Nelson, 2001), lxvii-lxxx; M. N. Sabin, *Reopening the Word: Reading Mark as Theology in the Context of Early Judaism* (Oxford: Oxford University Press, 2002); and I. H. Marshall, *NT Theology* (Downers Grove, Ill.: InterVarsity Press, 2004), 51-94.

Grasping the significance of the kingdom of God in Mark's gospel involves a variety of issues. First, the word "kingdom" (Gk. *basileia*) can designate both a *reign* and a *realm*. In other words, it may refer either to royal authority or to the territory under royal control. This ambiguity explains how Jesus could sometimes promise that the kingdom was coming (i.e., God's kingship is being implemented: 1:15; 9:1; 11:10) but at other times warn that the kingdom must be entered (9:47; 10:15, 23-25). Second, the common denominator in this equation is the earthly appearance of God's heavenly rule. When the Markan Jesus announces that "the time is fulfilled," he is drawing from a deep well of Jewish expectation that longed for the historical reestablishment of God's dominion over, not just the people of Israel, but all the earth.[11] Third, Jesus easily slips back and forth between announcing the kingdom's immediate presence (10:14-15, 23-25; cf. 3:24; 4:11, 26-32) and promising its future appearance (1:15; 9:1; 11:10; 14:25; 15:43). Contrary to many of Mark's contemporaries, who looked for God's kingdom to miraculously invade human history wholesale, Jesus planted only the "seed" of the kingdom, knowing that its fruition would appear in the future.[12]

Fourth, in the meantime, Jesus' actions do demonstrate the validity of his proclamation (3:23-27). Each exorcism proves that God's power is now driving Satan's power out of this world. The healing miracles demonstrate the health and wholeness that comes with the kingdom, while Jesus' controversial habit of dining with "tax collectors and sinners" (2:15-17) illustrates the new community created by the kingdom. Finally, Mark makes it clear that, not only is Jesus the kingdom's messenger, he is also God's messianic agent of the kingdom. The good news, the "gospel," is that the king-

---

11. For literature on the kingdom of God, see G. Lundström, *The Kingdom of God in the Teaching of Jesus: A History of Interpretation from the Last Decades of the Nineteenth Century to the Present Day* (Edinburgh: Oliver & Boyd, 1963); R. Schnackenburg, *God's Rule and Kingdom* (trans. J. Murray; New York: Herder & Herder, 1963); N. Perrin, *Jesus and the Language of the Kingdom: Symbol and Metaphor in NT Interpretation* (Philadelphia: Fortress, 1976); B. Chilton, *God in Strength: Jesus' Announcement of the Kingdom* (Freistadt: F. Plöchl, 1979); G. R. Beasley-Murray, *Jesus and the Kingdom of God* (Grand Rapids: Eerdmans, 1986); B. Chilton and J. I. H. McDonald, *Jesus and the Ethics of the Kingdom* (Grand Rapids: Eerdmans, 1987); and B. Chilton, *Pure Kingdom: Jesus' Vision of God* (Grand Rapids: Eerdmans, 1996).

12. This concept is often referred to as inaugurated eschatology, or the "already/not yet" tension; see W. G. Kümmel, *Promise and Fulfilment: The Eschatological Message of Jesus* (trans. D. M. Barton; London: SCM Press, 1957); O. Cullmann, *Salvation in History* (London: SCM Press, 1967); and G. E. Ladd, *The Presence of the Future: The Eschatology of "Biblical Realism"* (Grand Rapids: Eerdmans, 1974).

dom arrives with Jesus himself. To follow Jesus as Messiah is to enter into the kingdom of God.

The Messiah's Identity: Is It a Secret?

The first christological concern of Mark that we consider is the progressive unveiling of Jesus' identity as the Son of God. The announcements in the prologue (1:1, 11) alert Mark's readers to Jesus' messianic identity, but only the demonic powers recognize it in the narrative that follows (1:24-25; 3:11). At midpoint in the book, Peter acknowledges Jesus as Messiah (8:27-29), but he fails to comprehend the necessity of his mission as a suffering and dying Messiah (vv. 31-33). Jesus' injunctions to silence (noted above as an example of repetition in Mark) sharpen this focus on the progressive unveiling of Jesus' identity. Because the contemporaries of Jesus fail to recognize him and harbor misconceptions about his identity, Jesus enjoins his witnesses to silence.

These commands for silence were given a special theological significance by the nineteenth-century German scholar William Wrede, when he identified them as part of a Markan creation that he labeled "the messianic secret."[13] In Wrede's reconstruction, the historical Jesus never claimed to be the Messiah and certainly never predicted his death or resurrection. Consequently, the Christian proclamation of Jesus' messiahship found no precedent in Jesus' own teaching. According to Wrede, Mark invented the various components of hiddenness, obscurity, secrecy, parabolic confusion, and misunderstanding in order to provide the fledgling church with a cover story explaining why their kerygma, or proclamation, about Jesus was so different from anything the general public had ever heard Jesus say about himself.

Although most scholars today would thank Wrede for his powers of observation (he was the first to piece together the various components of Mark's secrecy theme), his explanation remains debatable. A number of scholars argue that Mark may have preserved a genuine aspect of Jesus' teaching and that his concern for secrecy is more plausibly explained by a

---

13. William Wrede, *The Messianic Secret* (trans. J. C. Greig; Cambridge: James Clarke, 1971; trans. of *Das Messiasgeheimnis in den Evangelien: Zugleich ein Beitrag zum Verständnis des Markusevangeliums* [Göttingen: Vandenhoeck & Ruprecht, 1901]).

combination of historical and religious factors: (1) it was common for demons to be silenced in ancient stories of exorcism, which was a sign of the exorcist's superiority over the powers of evil; (2) within certain apocalyptic circles, the Messiah's identity remained a secret until his final unveiling from heaven; (3) since the Roman authorities were highly sensitive to alternative claims of kingship, and since Jesus' kingdom was "not of this earth," he may have been hesitant to attract unwanted Roman attention; and (4) there was no Jewish precedent for Jesus' idea of a suffering Messiah, a concept that the disciples could grasp only in retrospect.[14]

The Messiah's Suffering

Closely related to the progressive revealing of Jesus' identity is the emphasis on his mission to suffer and die. This second christological emphasis of Mark makes Peter's acknowledgment (8:29) only a partial recognition of Jesus as Messiah. By the passion predictions (8:31; 9:31; 10:33-34) and forebodings of death (10:45; 12:1-12; 14:21-27), Mark underscores the divine necessity of Jesus' suffering and death. Without a true perception of Jesus' mission, one cannot correctly understand his identity as Messiah.

The title preferred by Mark in his presentation of Jesus as suffering Messiah is "Son of Man." This title is unique in the gospel tradition for, with one exception (Acts 7:56), it is used only by Jesus as his preferred way of referring to himself. The title is generally recognized as having three distinct, yet related, references: (1) the authoritative, earthly Son of Man (Mark 2:10, 28); (2) the suffering Son of Man (8:31; 9:9, 12, 31; 10:45; 14:21, 41); and (3) the coming Son of Man (8:38; 13:26; 14:62).

Why would Jesus refer to himself in this way? There are basically three schools of thought, which need not be mutually exclusive. First, the title may be a generic reference to humanity or a human being (Ps 8:4; 80:17). Second, it may render an Aramaic circumlocution for the first-person personal pronoun "I" (see Mark 2:10 and the parallels Mark 8:27 / Matt 16:13). Third, it may be drawn from Dan 7:13-14 and a few related apocalyptic

14. See J. L. Blevins, *The Messianic Secret in Markan Research, 1901-1976* (Lanham, Md.: University Press of America, 1981); C. M. Tuckett, ed., *The Messianic Secret* (Philadelphia: Fortress, 1983); F. B. Watson, "The Social Function of Mark's Secrecy Motif," *JSNT* 24 (1985): 49-69; H. Räisänen, *The "Messianic Secret" in Mark* (trans. C. M. Tuckett; Edinburgh: T&T Clark, 1990); and Telford, *The Theology of the Gospel of Mark*, 41-54.

texts of a victorious conquering ruler appearing from heaven at the end of the age.[15] Because "Son of Man" was an unusual title with no previous connection to an earthly deliverer, it was probably less susceptible to misinterpretation than "Christ" (Messiah) or "Son of God," since it was uncommon and had few presuppositions attached. Thus it gave Jesus more flexibility in adopting it for his own purposes; he was free to redefine the associated imagery and fill the title with his own content, namely, that he was the suffering Messiah, the ruler who conquers through humiliation and death before he is finally exalted and returns from heaven.

The Miracle Theme

Even though Mark includes many stories and summaries of Jesus' miracles in the first half of his gospel, he did not seem to regard them as messianic credentials. They visibly demonstrate the coming of God's kingdom through Jesus, suggesting the fall of Satan and the dawning of a new age, but they do not convey the essence of his messiahship. This view of miracles as credentials of the Messiah was a misconception entertained by Jesus' contemporaries (8:11-12), and possibly Mark's readers (13:22), but it is Jesus' suffering and death that provide the proper context for understanding his messianic identity and mission (8:27-33).

The Discipleship Theme

Another Markan theme related to Christology is that of discipleship. Since according to Mark the disciples had misconceptions about Jesus' identity and mission, they also misunderstood their own identity and task. This misunderstanding led to disputes over who was the greatest disciple (9:33-37) and requests for honored positions (10:35-45). In contrast to these delusions, Jesus issues a call for suffering discipleship (8:34-37; 9:33-42; 10:35-45; 13:9-13). For Mark, authentic Christian existence finds fulfillment in suffering servanthood. Perhaps Mark's audience was threatened by mis-

---

15. For a useful summary, see G. B. Caird, *NT Theology* (Oxford: Clarendon Press, 1994), 369-80. See also our discussion on "The Final Destiny" under "Persistent Faith of Judaism" in chap. 1.

conceptions similar to those attributed to the disciples in Mark. If so, this gospel would serve as corrective teaching, as well as a forceful presentation of Mark's religious convictions.

The Eschatological Theme

The final Markan theme to be examined is eschatology. Here we are concerned with the apocalyptic discourse in Mark 13, which is a complete literary unit like the passion narrative (14:1–16:8). Since Mark 13 is concerned with events after Jesus' resurrection and before his return, it provides special insights into the situation of Mark and his readers, who also exist in this same time frame. The references to being led astray by false Christs (vv. 5-7, 22-23) and undergoing tribulation and persecution (vv. 8-13) seem to echo the situation of Mark's readers. The reference to the "desolating sacrilege" in verse 14 is derived from the apocalyptic book of Daniel (11:31; 12:11) and alludes either to the desecration of the Jerusalem temple by the Seleucid ruler Antiochus IV Epiphanes in 167 B.C. (1 Macc 1:54) or to the destruction of the temple by the Romans in A.D. 70 (Josephus, *War* 6.220-270). Much tribulation and persecution followed the Roman destruction, and many Christians fled Judea (Mark 13:14; Eusebius, *Hist. eccl.* 3.5).

Whether or not the historical Jesus could have anticipated Jerusalem's destruction by Rome and what Mark's convictions may have been are both subject to scholarly debate. Many insist that Mark's gospel, with its apparent description of Roman siege and attack, could only have been written shortly after the events (a *vaticinium ex eventu*, or statement after the fact). Others, however, defend a pre-70 date for Mark 13, insisting that any Jewish prophet who felt rejected by the city's leaders would naturally warn of impending judgment, as had the OT prophets. Josephus, for instance, tells of another Jesus, son of Ananias, who predicted Jerusalem's destruction in A.D. 62 (*War* 6.300-309).[16] One need not believe that Jesus could foresee future events, only that he understood himself to stand in the prophetic

---

16. See the neglected insights of C. H. Dodd, "The Fall of Jerusalem and the 'Abomination of Desolation,'" *JRS* 37 (1947): 47-54, reprinted in *More NT Studies* (Manchester: Manchester University Press, 1968), 69-83; also B. Reicke, "Synoptic Prophecies on the Destruction of Jerusalem," in *Studies in NT and Early Christian Literature* (ed. D. W. Aune; Leiden: Brill, 1972); and J. A. T. Robinson, "The Significance of 70," in *Redating the NT* (Philadelphia: Westminster Press, 1976), 13-30.

tradition of Isaiah, Jeremiah, and others who had similarly warned of Jerusalem's destruction by Babylon.

In any event, despite these traumatic events, with their accompanying apocalyptic speculations, Mark writes to assure his readers that the end is near and that the Son of Man will soon return in power and glory (13:26); therefore, "beware, keep alert/keep awake" (vv. 33-37). In the face of the near return of the Lord, Mark encourages his readers to wait and hope. He also instructs them that, as Jesus himself had gone through passion to glory, so too they must be prepared for discipleship that involves suffering and death.

The Markan Structure

As we noted from our study of the major themes in Mark, the arrangement of this gospel is the result of Mark's own religious interests interacting with the established traditions that he received. His emphasis on the motif of suffering and death (1) might reflect the distinctiveness of Jesus' own messianic self-consciousness and (2) was reapplied to the challenges facing Mark's own situation — namely, persecution by Romans and Jews, plus misunderstandings about the Messiah. Through his presentation of the disciples, who consistently wrestle with Jesus' difficult teaching about servant-leadership, Mark conveys both negative and positive examples for his readers, men and women who identify with the disciples in their own ongoing attempts to "follow after Jesus."[17]

The literary, thematic, and geographic features in Mark's gospel suggest at least two possible outlines of its structure.[18] The first is geographic and can be arranged as in outline 3.1 on page 84.

17. An earlier generation of scholars imagined each gospel writer composing for a specific, localized, community audience. It has increasingly been suggested, however, that this tendency led researchers to an unnecessary restriction of the author's concerns; see R. Bauckham, ed., *The Gospels for All Christians: Rethinking the Gospel Audiences* (Grand Rapids: Eerdmans, 1998).

18. The geographic outline is derived from Hedrick, "What Is a Gospel?" 255-68; and van Iersel, "Locality," 45-54. The literary and thematic outline is adapted from Perrin and Duling, *NT Intro*, 239-40, 243-54; G. G. Bilezikian, *The Liberated Gospel: A Comparison of the Gospel of Mark and Greek Tragedy* (Grand Rapids: Baker, 1977), 51-106; and M. P. Scott, "Chiastic Structure: A Key to the Interpretation of Mark's Gospel," *BTB* 15 (1985): 17-26. Scott's study generally substantiates the view that the entire Gospel of Mark can be outlined in a chiastic A-B-C pattern similar to Bilezikian's "complication-crisis-denouement" scheme.

OUTLINE 3.1. MARK (GEOGRAPHIC)

Prologue: Jesus and John along the Jordan River; Jesus in
    the Judean wilderness   1:1-13
1. Galilean ministry of Jesus, including some brief
    departures outside that region (7:31; 8:27)   1:14–9:50
2. Jesus' journey to Jerusalem   10:1–11:10
3. Final events in Jerusalem   11:11–16:8

Although outline 3.1 closely follows Mark's geographic notations, its strict geographic scheme lessens the full impact achieved by Mark's literary techniques and thematic emphases. For example, it disregards both Mark's focus on the suffering Messiah (8:31; 9:31; 10:33-34, 45) and the bracketing device of the two healing stories that frame the central section of Mark (8:22-26; 10:46-52). Outline 3.2 presents an alternative along literary and thematic lines.

OUTLINE 3.2. MARK (LITERARY)

Complication of plot

Prologue	Introducing Jesus the Messiah	1:1-13
	Transitional summary	1:14-15
Scene 1	The authority of Jesus the Messiah	1:16–3:6
	Transitional summary	3:7-12
Scene 2	The unrecognized Messiah among his people	3:13–6:6a
	Transitional summary	6:6b
Scene 3	The Messiah unrecognized by his disciples	6:7–8:21
	Transitional story: restoring sight	8:22-26

Crisis

Scene 4	The messianic identity and mission revealed	8:27–10:45
	Transitional story: restoring sight	10:46-52

Denouement

Scene 5	Conflicts expediting the Messiah's death	11:1–12:44
	Introduction to apocalyptic discourse	13:1-5a
Scene 6	Opponents denounced (apocalyptic discourse)	13:5b-37
	Introduction to passion narrative	14:1-12
Scene 7	The suffering and death of the Messiah	14:13–15:47
Epilogue	The vindication of the Messiah	16:1-8

This outline includes the "complication-crisis-denouement" plot structure scheme of Aristotle's *Poetics* 18:1-3, which was well known in the ancient world. The outline also recognizes the crucial significance of Peter's confession of Jesus as the Messiah in 8:27-30, which functions as a crucial turning point in the narrative. From this point onward, Jesus gives less attention to the crowds and focuses more on his disciples; he especially highlights the inevitability of his suffering in Jerusalem, while the conflict with Israel's leadership increases. Finally, redaction criticism supports the basic premise behind the above outline: thematic and not geographic concerns seem to influence the composition of Mark's gospel.[19]

The Authorship and Date of Mark

Many argue that the Gospels were originally composed and handed down anonymously, while the "superscriptions," or titles attributing authorship to Matthew, Mark, Luke, and John, were not attached until the second century. A good case can be made, however, for the originality of each superscription, which would mean that none of the Gospels ever circulated without the titles that we know them by today.[20] In any event, whether Mark's gospel ever circulated anonymously or not, the NT describes Mark as a traveling companion of Paul (Phlm 24; Col 4:10; 2 Tim 4:11; Acts 12:25; 15:37-39), who was also believed to have been with Peter in Rome (1 Pet 5:13).[21]

All we can definitively know about the author is what can be deduced from the gospel itself. The author's emphasis on Galilee may suggest some

19. The view that Mark's composition is determined by thematic rather than geographic concerns is supported by the following works: Achtemeier, *Mark* 22-39; Mann, *Mark*, 84-99; Marxsen, *Mark the Evangelist*; D. E. Nineham, "The Order of Events in St. Mark's Gospel: An Examination of Dr. Dodd's Hypothesis," in *Studies in the Gospels* (Oxford: Blackwell, 1955), 223-39; N. Perrin, *What Is Redaction Criticism?* (Philadelphia: Fortress, 1969); Weeden, *Mark — Traditions in Conflict*; and Wrede, *The Messianic Secret*.

20. See M. Hengel, *Studies in the Gospel of Mark* (London: SCM Press, 1985) and *The Four Gospels and the One Gospel of Jesus Christ: An Investigation of the Collection and Origin of the Canonical Gospels* (trans. J. Bowden; Harrisburg, Pa.: Trinity Press International, 2000), 34-60. See also R. Bauckham, *Jesus and the Eyewitnesses*, 300-305.

21. See J. A. T. Robinson, *Redating the NT* (Philadelphia: Westminster Press, 1976), 95, 107-17, for an extensive discussion of the ancient testimony from Papias, Irenaeus, Clement of Alexandria, the Anti-Marcionite Prologue, Eusebius, and Jerome as to Mark's association with the apostle Peter.

close ties with this region. He shares the early Christian hope in the soon return of the risen Christ and other related apocalyptic beliefs (Mark 13). His concern for Gentiles (5:1-20; 7:24-30; 15:39) and a continuing work in ethnically mixed Galilee (14:28; 16:7) reveal an interest in a mission to Gentiles. Mark's portrait of Jesus' authority to annul Jewish law (2:15–3:6; 7:1-13) and his efforts to explain Jewish customs for his audience may also presuppose a Gentile audience.

Suggested dates of composition range from as early as the mid-50s to the late 70s, with the majority of scholars opting for a date ranging somewhere between shortly before to shortly after A.D. 70.[22] As mentioned earlier, a key factor in answering this question is how one chooses to relate Mark 13 to the destruction of Jerusalem in A.D. 70.

The Markan Text

The original ending of Mark was probably 16:8. The longer endings are absent from the earliest Greek manuscripts (א, B). The literary connections between v. 8 and the later 16:9-20 are awkward, and much of the terminology in vv. 9-20 is foreign to the rest of the gospel. Although the original ending appears abrupt, it has an effective dramatic function. The brief and sudden ending evokes a dramatic suddenness that leaves readers pondering over the meaning of the story. The motifs of fear and misunderstanding, found in 16:8, are also characteristic of Mark (4:40-41; 5:33; 6:50; 9:6; 11:18; 14:50-52).[23] Also, remember that ultimately Mark writes in the hope

22. See Hengel, *Studies in the Gospel of Mark*, 21-28; D. Guthrie, *NT Introduction* (Downers Grove, Ill.: InterVarsity Press, 1990), 72-76; and J. G. Crossley, *The Date of Mark's Gospel: Insight from the Law in Earliest Christianity* (London: T&T Clark, 2004). In *Redating the NT*, J. A. T. Robinson, who insists that all of the Synoptic Gospels were composed between the early 40s to the mid-60s, is influenced by the work of T. Zahn, *Introduction to the NT* (trans. J. M. Trout et al.; 3 vols.; Grand Rapids: Kregel, 1953; trans. of *Einleitung in das Neue Testament* [Leipzig: Deichert, 1900]), 2:394-95, 427-56; 3:484.

23. The following studies argue for the Mark 16:8 ending on linguistic, textual, and theological grounds: B. M. Metzger, *A Textual Commentary on the Greek NT* (2d ed.; Stuttgart: Deutsche Bibelgesellschaft, 1994), 102-6 (a text-critical analysis); C. F. D. Moule, "Mark XVI.8 Once More," *NTS* 2 (1955): 58-60; R. P. Meye, "Mark 16:8 — the Fading of Mark's Gospel," *BR* 14 (1969): 33-43; E. LaVerdiere, "The End, a Beginning," *Emmanuel* 90 (1984): 484-91; and J. C. Thomas, "A Reconsideration of the Ending of Mark," *JETS* 26 (1983): 407-19. The additions of Mark 16:9-20 and the so-called Freer Logion demonstrate the com-

of persuading his readers to share his belief in Jesus as the Messiah. The questions left unanswered by the gospel's abrupt ending may serve a deliberate part in his strategy as an evangelist. Why was the tomb empty? What happened to Jesus' body? Where were the other disciples? Learning the answers to these questions required a face-to-face conversation with members of the local Christian community.

Summary

In conclusion, Mark's gospel is a collection of independent sayings and stories grouped together by literary and thematic devices, placed in a geographic scheme for the specific religious purposes of the author. Although there is a history of tradition in the gospel, the final product is the direct result of the author's creative activity. Mark was not a mere compiler of tradition but a literary artist and proclaimer of the good news of Jesus Christ. For this reason we learn something about the author and his audience, along with the basic story line, when we read the gospel. This book provides us with important information about the concerns and insights of the ancient Christian community, including their memories of Jesus of Nazareth, as well as those of the first gospel writer himself.[24]

---

plex history of transmission of the Gospel of Mark (e.g., see W. L. Lane, *The Gospel according to Mark* [Grand Rapids: Eerdmans, 1974], 601-11).

24. Standard commentaries on the Gospel of Mark include C. E. B. Cranfield, *The Gospel according to Saint Mark: An Introduction and Commentary* (Cambridge: Cambridge University Press, 1959); V. Taylor, *The Gospel according to St. Mark* (1959); Lane, *Mark;* Mann, *Mark;* D. E. Nineham, *The Gospel of St. Mark* (Baltimore: Penguin Books, 1964); E. Schweizer, *The Good News according to Mark* (trans. D. Madvig; Richmond: John Knox, 1970); Guelich, *Mark 1–8:26;* D. Juel, *Mark* (Minneapolis: Augsburg, 1990); M. Hooker, *The Gospel according to St. Mark* (London: A&C Black, 1991); R. H. Gundry, *Mark: A Commentary on His Apology for the Cross* (Grand Rapids: Eerdmans, 1993); B. M. F. van Iersel, *Mark: A Reader-Response Commentary* (Sheffield: Sheffield Academic Press, 1998); J. Marcus, *Mark 1–8: A New Translation, with Introduction and Commentary* (AB 27; New York: Doubleday, 2000); Evans, *Mark 8:27–16:20;* B. Witherington, *The Gospel of Mark: A Socio-rhetorical Commentary* (Grand Rapids: Eerdmans, 2001); and R. T. France, *The Gospel of Mark* (Grand Rapids: Eerdmans, 2002).

87

CHAPTER 4

The Gospel of Matthew

No other gospel is so shaped by the thought of the church and so constructed for use by the church as is the Gospel of Matthew. It was probably for this reason that Matthew was placed at the beginning of the NT collection and became the most useful, and the most widely used, of all texts for the Christian church through the centuries. In fact, Mark's gospel was rather neglected by the church once Matthew's work became readily available.[1] Matthew is a masterful adaptation and supplementation of Mark, drawing also on a collection of Jesus' sayings (Q) and additional traditions (M), arranged according to specific religious and thematic purposes.

As in our study of Mark's gospel, here we look at Matthew's use of his traditional materials, his techniques of grouping, and his religious and thematic concerns in writing his gospel. In this analytic study of tradition and redaction, we will note that (1) Matthew extends Mark's narrative backward (chs. 1–2) and forward (ch. 28); (2) he rearranges thematically, abridges stylistically, clarifies ambiguities, and both omits and substitutes his traditional material (Mark, Q, M); and (3) he does so with the overriding religious concern of presenting Jesus as the Messiah and Son of God, who fulfills the Jewish Scriptures and properly interprets the law for the church. We also give some attention to the situation of the author and his readers.

---

1. D. A. Hagner, *Matthew 1–13* (WBC 33A; Dallas: Word Books, 1993), xlvii; M. Hengel, *The Four Gospels and the One Gospel of Jesus Christ* (trans. J. Bowden; Harrisburg, Pa.: Trinity Press International, 2000), 67, 71-72n.296.

The Matthean Redaction

Matthean Additions to the Markan Source

In Matthew, Mark's framework is extended backward and forward.[2] Before the account of John the Baptist, Matthew includes biographical material about Jesus: his ancestry (beginning with Abraham and leading up to Joseph, 1:2-17), a birth story (in which Joseph's fatherhood is expressly disputed, 1:18-25), stories about the Magi from the East (2:1-12), the flight to Egypt (2:13-15), the massacre of infants in Bethlehem (2:16-18), and the return to Nazareth (2:19-23). All of this material is from Matthew's own traditions (M). From chapter 3 onward, Matthew basically follows Mark's outline, except for those instances where the order and grouping are changed. At the conclusion of the book, after altering and expanding on the empty-tomb account (28:1-15), Matthew moves forward the narrative of Mark with the appearance of the risen Lord, who gives a missionary charge (28:16-20).

The Matthean Thematic Rearrangements of Sources

The Thematic Rearrangement of Mark   In Matthew we can also trace a rearrangement of material according to theme. On the one hand, we see this process in the bringing together of miracle stories (chs. 8–9) that were scattered in Mark and, on the other, in the formation of six larger complexes of discourses: the Sermon on the Mount (chs. 5–7), the mission charge (ch. 10), the parables discourse (ch. 13), community rules (ch. 18), denouncement of the Pharisees (ch. 23), and discourses on the end times and final judgment (chs. 24–25). Five of the discourses close with the same formula (7:28; 11:1; 13:53; 19:1; 26:1); the other has a formal, although not usual, ending (23:37-39).

The Thematic Rearrangement of Q   Matthew's use of Q, the sayings source common to Matthew and Luke (see table 2.3 above), is also affected

---

2. This survey assumes the priority of Mark as a source for the Synoptic Gospels; note our discussion in ch. 2. See the analytic treatment of Matthew in W. Marxsen, *Introduction to the NT* (trans. G. Buswell; Philadelphia: Fortress, 1968), 146. For differing views on Matthew's sources, see, e.g., Reicke, *Roots of Synoptic Gospels;* Farmer, *The Synoptic Gospels;* and Thomas, ed., *Three Views on the Origins of the Synoptic Gospels.*

by his technique of thematic grouping. Most charts on the contents of Q follow Luke's order, which probably reflects the original order, since this is also the case with Luke's use of Mark. By comparing Matthew's use of Q with Luke's, we note that Matthew makes selective use of this document in a different order than Luke does. For example, see (1) the discourse against the Pharisees (Luke 11:37–12:1; Matt 23); (2) the parables on watchfulness (Luke 12:39-46; Matt 24:43-51); (3) the sayings about agreement with adversaries (Luke 12:57-59; Matt 5:25-26); and (4) the discourse on the coming of the Son of Man (Luke 17:23-27, 33-37; Matt 24:17-18, 26-28, 37, 41). As we note from these examples, most of the Q material in Matthew is grouped with the major discourses.

Other Matthean Techniques of Redaction

In addition to extending the narrative of Mark and rearranging his source material thematically, Matthew employs four other redactional techniques: compression, clarification, omission, and substitution.[3]

Compression First, Matthew compresses his sources. For instance, the healing accounts of Jairus's daughter and the woman with a hemorrhage, which cover twenty-three verses in Mark (5:21-43), take only nine verses in Matthew (9:18-26); similarly, Jesus' healing of a demon-possessed boy covers sixteen verses in Mark (9:14-29) but only eight in Matthew (17:14-21). Matthew makes such changes both for the sake of economy and also to highlight certain aspects of the narrative that he regards as most important. Other examples of this same technique are found in 8:28-34 (cf. Mark 5:1-20), 12:15-16 (cf. Mark 3:7-12), and 14:1-12 (cf. Mark 6:14-29).

Clarification Another redactional technique is Matthew's clarification of his sources. Often this is a matter of style, as he smoothes Mark's awkward expressions (e.g., Matt 8:3 / Mark 1:42; Matt 8:16 / Mark 1:32; Matt 13:10 / Mark 4:10). In other cases, Matthew's clarification of his sources reflects his special concerns. For example, in the story of the woman with a hemorrhage (Matt 9:20-22 / Mark 5:25-34), Matthew has Jesus confront the woman and sanction the healing, which is only implicit in Mark's account (Matt 9:21-22 / Mark 5:28-29).

---

3. See J. D. Kingsbury, *Matthew* (Philadelphia: Fortress, 1977), 17-19.

Omission and Substitution The final two redactional techniques involve Matthew omitting material from his sources or substituting one piece of tradition for another.[4] An example of omission is Matthew's employment of Mark 3:13-22 (in Matt 10:1-4), omitting vv. 19b-21 because these derogatory remarks do not conform with Matthew's exalted view of Christ.

An example of substitution is found in Matt 13. In this chapter the author appropriates all of the parables of Mark 4, with one exception: we find the parable of the tares (Matt 13:24-30) instead of the parable about the seed growing secretly (Mark 4:26-29). In making this substitution, Matthew provides a new dimension to the disciple's life in the kingdom of God: all apparent members of the kingdom are not actual members (Matt 13:36-43).

The Matthean Structure

The literary and thematic features in Matthew's gospel suggest at least three possible outlines of the book's structure. The first (see outline 4.1) is based on the five discourses, which end in the fixed formula "when Jesus had finished" (7:28; 11:1; 13:53; 19:1; 26:1).[5]

OUTLINE 4.1. MATTHEW (DISCOURSES)

Prologue	The birth and infancy of Jesus the Messiah	1–2
Narrative	Ministry of John, commissioning of Jesus, and selection of Jesus' disciples	3–4
Discourse 1	Sermon on the Mount	5–7
Narrative	Ten miracle stories in Jesus' ministry	8–9
Discourse 2	The commission and instruction of Jesus' disciples	10:1–11:1
Narrative	Jesus in controversy with Jewish leaders	11:2–12:50
Discourse 3	Seven parables about the kingdom	13:1-52
Narrative	Opposition, faith, and the Messiah's mission	13:53–17:27
Discourse 4	Humility, forgiveness, and community rules	18
Narrative	Discipleship, the Messiah's mission, and controversies with the Jews	19–22

4. Kingsbury, *Matthew*, 17-19.

5. This outline is adapted from Pheme Perkins, *Reading the NT* (New York: Paulist, 1978), 208-9.

Discourse 5	Woes against the Pharisees and apocalyptic	
	discourse	23–25
Conclusion	Passion, resurrection, and Great Commission	26–28

However, because (1) many of the narrative segments also contain discourse, (2) there is some question about whether chapter 23 belongs to the fifth discourse, and (3) this fivefold outline renders the birth and passion narratives a mere prologue and epilogue to the story, an alternative outline is suggested here (see outline 4.2). Organized topically, it views the formulaic statements in 4:17 and 16:21 as sectional dividers.[6]

OUTLINE 4.2. MATTHEW (TOPICS)

1. The person of Jesus the Messiah — 1:1–4:16
2. The public proclamation of Jesus the Messiah — 4:17–16:20
3. The suffering, death, and resurrection of Jesus the Messiah — 16:21–28:20

Although the above outline correctly highlights Matthew's Christology, it does not fully take into account the large blocks of teaching on discipleship and the church in section 3, or the significance of the ten miracle stories in section 2. More recently, commentators have revisited the structural importance of Matthew's successive blocks of narrative (N) and discourse (D) material, suggesting a simple alternation between Jesus' deeds and words.[7] (See outline 4.3.)

OUTLINE 4.3. MATTHEW (NARRATIVE AND DISCOURSE)

N	Introduction: the main character (Jesus) introduced	1–4
D	Jesus' demands upon Israel	5–7

---

6. This outline was first suggested by J. C. Hawkins, *Horae Synopticae* (Oxford: Clarendon Press, 1899), and was adopted and developed by J. D. Kingsbury in *Matthew: Structure, Christology, Kingdom* (Philadelphia: Fortress, 1975), 7-37; in *Matthew*, 24; and in *Matthew as Story* (2d ed.; Philadelphia: Fortress, 1988); and by D. R. Bauer, *The Structure of Matthew's Gospel* (Sheffield: Almond, 1988). F. Neirynck has demonstrated the structural limitations of this outline in his "*AΠO TOTE HPΞATO* and the Structure of Matthew," *ETL* 64 (1988): 21-59.

7. See D. C. Allison, "Matthew: Structure, Biographical Impulse, and the *Imitatio Christi*," in *The Four Gospels, 1992* (ed. F. Van Segbroeck et al.; 3 vols.; Leuven: Leuven University Press, 1992), 2:1208; and Hagner, *Matthew 1–13*, liii.

N	Jesus' deeds within and for Israel	8–9
D	Extension of ministry through words and deeds of others	10
N	Israel's negative response	11–12
D	Explanation of Israel's negative response	13
N	Establishment of the new people of God, the church	14–17
D	Instructions to the church	18
N	Commencement of the passion, the beginning of the end	19–23
D	The future: judgment and salvation	24–25
N	Conclusion: the passion and resurrection	26–28

Because of both its simplicity and its fullness, this final outline is favored here.

The Major Matthean Themes

Matthew's redactional techniques and structure are primarily determined by his thematic concerns, many of which are christocentric: Jesus' inauguration of the kingdom of heaven, Jesus the Messiah and Son of God, the fulfillment of the Jewish Scriptures in the life of Jesus, Jesus as the true interpreter of the law for the church, and the church's mission to the Gentiles. As in laudatory biography, Matthew's gospel seeks to honor and glorify the central figure of the narrative.

The Kingdom of Heaven

Matthew's understanding of the kingdom of God is essentially the same as Mark's, although he does highlight some distinctive features. First, Matthew's kingdom teaching (forty-nine references) is much more prevalent than Mark's (fifteen references). Second, Matthew prefers the phrase "kingdom of heaven" (thirty times), probably because of the traditional Jewish aversion to pronouncing the name of God. Third, Matthew focuses attention on genuine membership in the kingdom, warning that many take their membership for granted and are in danger of losing it unexpectedly (7:15-27; 8:12; 13:47-50; 18:1-7; 19:14; 21:43; 25:1-13, 34-46). This final theme clearly refers to Jesus' rejection by the leaders of Israel. Matthew warns that the supposedly secure occupants of God's kingdom will find themselves replaced by the repentant sinners, prostitutes, and believing Gentiles who now receive Jesus as their Messiah (21:32; 22:1-10; 24:14).

Christ as Messiah-King

Matthew presents Jesus primarily as the Messiah-king who humbly suffers on behalf of, and is present with, his people. Some of the messianic titles employed by Matthew are "Christ" (1:1, 16-18; 2:4; 11:2; 16:16-20; 23:10; 26:63, 68; 27:17, 22), "king" or "king of the Jews/Israel" (2:2; 21:5-9; 27:11, 29, 37, 42), "Son of David" (1:1, 20; 9:27; 12:23; 15:22; 20:30, 31; 21:9, 15; 22:41-46), and "Emmanuel" (1:22-23). The last title is derived from Isa 7:14, a text used in early Christianity as a prophecy of Christ's unique birth and interpreted messianically (Luke 1:31, allusion). Each of these (except Emmanuel) is used frequently in public settings because the messianic-secret motif is not as prominent in Matthew as in Mark.

The title "Son of David" is used to show Jesus' royal descent from the Davidic line. Matthew employs this title more frequently than Mark,[8] while retaining the tradition that Jesus is greater than David (22:41-46 / Mark 12:35-37) and expanding upon Jesus' role as the humble king (Matt 21:4-5, with the fulfillment citation absent from the parallel Mark 11:1-10). In keeping with this tendency, Matthew's passion narrative retains all of Mark's references to Jesus the "king of the Jews/Israel" (Matt 27:11, 29, 37, 42 / Mark 15:2, 18, 26, 32). This Son of David suffers as the humble king of Israel who remains greater than David. The Greek title for the Messiah, "Christ," is used in public (23:10) and private (16:16-20) settings with its full messianic implications. Finally, the Matthean title "Emmanuel" ("God with us") forms an inclusion with 28:20 "remember, I am with you always," denoting the continual presence of the Messiah among his people.

Christ as Son of God

Matthew also refers to Jesus as the "Son of God" who is obedient to his Father's will. Although the title "Son of Man" is used frequently in Matthew, he deviates little from its Markan usage as a public title, describing Jesus'

---

8. The title "Son of David" appears three times in Mark and ten times in Matthew.

earthly authority, his suffering under the Jewish leaders and Gentiles, and his end-time return in glory. Matthew's favorite titles are "Son" or "Son of God" (e.g., 2:15; 3:17; 4:3, 6; 14:33; 16:16; 17:5; 26:63; 27:40, 54; 28:19). The designation "Son" finds its OT roots in Yahweh's covenant with Israel, who became God's "firstborn son" (Exod 4:22-23); in this way, Matthew uses the title "Son" to indicate Jesus' role as the true Israel.

"Son of God" is a confessional title, except when used by Jesus' adversaries (26:63; 27:40, 43). In Jewish tradition it often referred to Israel's king (see 2 Sam 7:14-16; Ps 2:6-9), as did "Son of David." Both the disciples (Matt 14:33; 16:16) and the confessing Roman soldiers (27:54) utter this title by a revelation from God (16:17).[9] Eventually the entire church, Jew and Gentile alike, will acknowledge Jesus as the Son of God, although here the title's significance extends beyond the original notions of kingship/ messiahship to focus on Jesus' unique relationship with God the Father. The title "beloved Son" ("my Son, the Beloved") appears in contexts where Jesus is completely obedient to his Father's will (3:15-17; 17:5); the same may also be said of "Son of God" in certain passages (4:3-10; 27:54). Because of Jesus' special relationship to God, he can address God as "my Father" (10:32-33; 12:50; 16:17). Disciples may also relate to God as "father" (5:16, 45, 48) when they become "children of God" (5:9, 45).

Christ as the One Who Fulfills Scripture

The fourth christological theme concerns the fulfillment of Scripture in the life of Jesus. In a manner similar to the Jewish Essenes, who made collections of scriptural passages about the Messiah, Matthew quotes from "the law and the prophets" to validate the messianic identity of Jesus.

Matthew does not imply that all of the Jewish Scriptures should be read in this manner; for Matthew, Jesus did not use Scripture as a checklist to follow in his ministry. Instead, Matthew used a proof-from-prophecy motif to show that events in Jesus' life, even the strange or offensive events, are in accord with God's pattern of salvation as revealed in sacred Scripture. The best examples of this motif are preceded by a fulfillment-formula quotation like "all this took place to fulfill what had been spoken by the Lord through the prophet," introducing an OT passage that is linked to a

---

9. Kingsbury, *Matthew,* 56.

narrative of Jesus' life. Matthew has ten of these specific prophetic-fulfillment citations, as listed in table 4.1.

TABLE 4.1. MATTHEW: PROPHETIC-FULFILLMENT CITATIONS

Incident	Matthew	OT
Miraculous birth	1:22-23	Isa 7:14
Flight to Egypt	2:15	Hos 11:1
Massacre of the infants	2:17-18	Jer 31:15
Residence in Nazareth	2:23	Isa 11:1
Move to Capernaum	4:14-16	Isa 9:1-2
Healing ministry	8:17	Isa 53:4
Healing ministry	12:17-21	Isa 42:1-4
Teaching in parables	13:35	Ps 78:2
Entry into Jerusalem	21:4-5	Isa 62:11; Zech 9:9
The fate of Jesus' betrayer	27:9-10	Zech 11:12-13; Jer 19; 32

Two additional passages use a variation of this specific fulfillment language: John the Baptist as the forerunner (Matt 3:3 / Isa 40:3), and the hard-heartedness of Jesus' opponents (Matt 13:14-15 / Isa 6:9-10).

Jesus' passion is twice described as the general fulfillment of Scripture (26:54, 56), although no OT passages are cited.

Finally, on three occasions the purpose of a fulfillment quotation is introduced with the simple alternative "it is written": Christ's birth in Bethlehem (Matt 2:5-6 / Mic 5:2), John the Baptist as the forerunner (Matt 11:10 / Mal 3:1), and the disciples' betrayal of Jesus (Matt 26:31 / Zech 13:7).

Although many OT passages considered to be messianic enjoyed a wide circulation among early Christians, the above examples signify Matthew's special concerns, emphases, and characteristic method of biblical interpretation. Frequently, the "fulfillment" accomplished by Jesus appears forced, hardly striking a dispassionate reader as the obvious meaning of the OT text. It is therefore not surprising that several of the OT passages cited by Matthew had never been read messianically by pre-Christian Judaism. For instance, Hos 11:1 recalls Yahweh's deliverance of Israel from Egyptian slavery as a precursor to Judah's eventual deliverance from Babylonian exile; it has nothing to do with the coming of a Messiah. Interpreting Jesus' flight into Egypt as the fulfillment of this passage makes sense only if the reader is already convinced that Jesus is the true Israel who now replicates, in general terms, the ancient pattern of Israel's life with God. Matthew sees Jesus fulfilling this OT pattern because he is rereading the history of Israel through the eyes of Christian faith.[10] The similar Essene method of interpretation, called *pesher,* also connected OT prophecy to the immediate details of their community life, which uniquely fulfilled God's promises, but in a way only they could understand. Whether Matthew exhibits literary dependence on a common collection of Scripture or close parallels to an Essene method of interpretation is difficult to establish.[11]

Christ as Interpreter of the Law

The fifth christological theme is Jesus as the true interpreter of the law. Unlike Mark, with its critique of the Mosaic law (e.g., Mark 7:1-23), Matthew affirms its enduring validity, as interpreted, or reinterpreted, by Jesus. For this reason, Matthew omits Mark's initial emphasis on the newness of Jesus' teaching (Mark 1:27) and occasionally adds Jesus' instruction about keeping Torah to Mark's story (Matt 12:12; 24:20).

According to Matthew, Jesus came to fulfill the law and exhorts others to obey it (5:17-20; 7:12; 19:17; 22:40). Even the legal teaching of the scribes and Pharisees is to be heeded, although they fail to practice their own precepts (23:2-3). For the church of Matthew, however, Jesus is the supreme arbiter of the law. Jesus at times therefore reinterprets the law of Moses on a higher ethical level (5:21-24, 27-29) or even radicalizes its demands to the point of revoking its original meaning (5:33-39). In fact, some scholars have suggested that outline 4.1 above of five discourses (in combination with other aspects of the gospel) intends to portray Jesus as the new Moses

---

10. See R. H. Gundry, *The Use of the OT in St. Matthew's Gospel: With Special Reference to the Messianic Hope* (Leiden: Brill, 1967), 189-234. D. L. Bock provides a good discussion of how another NT writer does something similar; see his *Proclamation from Prophecy and Pattern: Lucan OT Christology* (Sheffield: JSOT, 1987). The seminal work exploring Jesus' role as the true Israel is W. Trilling, *Das Wahre Israel: Studien zur Theologie des Matthäus-Evangeliums* (Munich: Kösel, 1964).

11. The *Testimonia* collection of Scriptures (a compilation of commonly used OT proof-texts) was popularized by C. H. Dodd, *According to the Scriptures* (London: Nisbet, 1961), although it was first suggested by J. R. Harris, *Testimonies* (2 vols.; Cambridge: Cambridge University Press, 1916-20). The school-of-Matthew thesis, which drew close parallels between Matthew and the Essene community, is found in K. Stendahl, *The School of St. Matthew and Its Use of the OT* (Philadelphia: Fortress, 1968).

offering a new law corresponding to the five books of the OT Pentateuch.[12] These two different emphases of reinterpreting and revoking the law may reflect separate traditions utilized by Matthew. They may have been combined in this gospel to show that Jesus' teachings both uphold and supersede the law of Moses. Jesus' teaching is clearly superior to the law of Moses, for whereas the law stands firm "until heaven and earth pass away" (Matt 5:18), Jesus' own words stand eternally: "heaven and earth will pass away, but my words will never pass away" (24:35).

For Matthew, the essence of the law is love; the two commandments to love God and to love others give decisive expression to the law and the prophets (7:12; 22:40). The scribes and Pharisees are indicted for neglecting these "weightier matters of the law" (23:23). In Matthew, love toward God and others is the hallmark of God's righteousness (5:44-48; 22:37-40) and of actions in obedience to God's will (5:43-48; 7:21). Through Jesus' teaching on love the will of God is revealed, and the law properly interpreted.

A "superior righteousness" is also demanded from the inhabitants of God's kingdom (5:20, 48). It is attained, not by a stricter legalism, but by following the way of Jesus. Disciples are the "poor in spirit" who belong to the kingdom of heaven (5:3, 8, 10). They are righteous because they follow the way of Jesus, unlike the Pharisees and teachers of the law, who remain in unbelief. This new righteousness sets the stage for Matthew's heightened emphasis on obedience. Whereas the children of Israel submitted themselves to the "yoke of the commandments" (*m. Ber.* 2:2), the followers of Jesus surrender to the yoke of Christ (11:28-30), which requires complete submission. Matthew frequently underscores this ethics of discipleship, reminding the reader that true disciples live transformed lives (6:10; 7:13-27; 12:33, 37; 13:44-46; 16:27; 18:17; 21:31, 43; 22:12). Although membership in the kingdom of heaven is not acquired by good works, it is certainly demonstrated by a disciple's "righteousness" (5:6, 10, 20; 6:1, 33; 21:32).[13] A good tree produces good fruit; a bad tree produces bad fruit (7:15-20).

---

12. B. W. Bacon, *Studies in Matthew* (New York: Holt, 1930); G. D. Kilpatrick, *The Origins of the Gospel according to St. Matthew* (Oxford: Clarendon Press, 1946); W. D. Davies, *The Setting of the Sermon on the Mount* (Cambridge: Cambridge University Press, 1964), 14-108; and D. C. Allison Jr., *The New Moses: A Matthean Typology* (Minneapolis: Fortress, 1993).

13. G. Barth, "Matthew's Understanding of the Law," in *Tradition and Interpretation in Matthew* (ed. G. Bornkamm, G. Barth, and H. J. Held; trans. P. Scott; Philadelphia: Westminster Press, 1963), 58-164; B. Przybylski, *Righteousness in Matthew and His World of Thought* (Cambridge: Cambridge University Press, 1980); R. Mohrlang, *Matthew and Paul:*

Mission to the Gentiles

Finally, Matthew's gospel contains a tension between the particularism of God's covenant with Abraham and the universalism of the church's mission to the Gentiles. On the one hand, Jesus twice explains that his ministry was limited to the Jews and was not for Gentiles (10:5-6; 15:24-26). On the other hand, there are numerous references to God's exclusion of stubborn Israel (3:9; 8:11-12; 11:20-24; 12:41-42; 13:14-15; 21:41-43; 22:3, 8; 23:5-38; 27:25), while believing Gentiles enter the kingdom. For example, Rahab and Ruth, both Gentiles, appear in Jesus' genealogy (1:5); the pagan "Magi" (the standard term for a magician or sorcerer) arrive to worship the infant Jesus, while Jerusalem's leaders remain unaware of his birth (2:1-12); and the gospel concludes with a charge for worldwide missions: "Go . . . and make disciples of all nations!" (28:19; see also 4:15-16, 25; 8:5-13; 10:18-20; 12:18-21; 13:37-38; 15:21-28; 21:43; 22:1-10; 24:14; 27:54).

The apparent tension is resolved in Matthew's conviction that the OT hope of God's kingdom becoming a light for all nations is now realized in Jesus (12:15-21, in fulfillment of Isa 42:1-4).[14] The Messiah offered himself first to the children of Abraham, Isaac, and Jacob, in fulfillment of God's covenant promises. After Jesus' final rejection in Jerusalem, however, the gospel is extended universally to all "outsiders."[15] This gospel mission created an ongoing challenge for Matthew's community: offering a Jewish Messiah, largely ignored by Judaism, to the pagan Gentile world.

Is Matthew Anti-Semitic?

Matthew's strident condemnation of Jesus' enemies — the Pharisees, elders, teachers of the law, Sadducees, and chief priests — has led some read-

---

A Comparison of Ethical Perspectives (Cambridge: Cambridge University Press, 1984); and P. Luomanen, *Entering the Kingdom of Heaven: A Study on the Structure of Matthew's View of Salvation* (Tübingen: Mohr Siebeck, 1998).

14. R. Beaton, *Isaiah's Christ in Matthew's Gospel* (Cambridge: Cambridge University Press, 2002).

15. J. LaGrand, *The Earliest Christian Mission to "All Nations": In the Light of Matthew's Gospel* (Atlanta: Scholars Press, 1995); J. Riches, "Matthew's Missionary Strategy in Colonial Perspective," in *The Gospel of Matthew in Its Roman Imperial Context* (ed. J. Riches and D. C. Sim; London: T&T Clark, 2005), 128-42. See also B. J. Malina and R. L. Rohrbaugh, *Social Science Commentary on the Synoptic Gospels* (2d ed.; Minneapolis: Fortress, 2003), 70, 141-42.

ers to accuse him of anti-Semitism.[16] Although Matthew's criticism of Israel's leadership is consistently accusatory, we argue below that Matthew himself was almost certainly a Jewish Christian deeply concerned about the fate of Israel. His criticism is not of Judaism per se (remember the gospel's endorsement of the Pentateuch, the Mosaic law, and the prophets) but of the spiritual obstinacy that blinded the people of Israel to their promised deliverer. In this light, Matthew's critique of Jesus' contemporaries is similar to the criticism leveled against Israel by the OT prophets. Matthew is no more anti-Semitic than were Isaiah and Jeremiah. He is simply convinced that in rejecting Jesus, the Jewish people had repeated the apostasy of their forefathers. Therefore, just as Yahweh had once condemned Jerusalem through the Babylonians (Jer 19:14-15), so God has revisited judgment against Jerusalem through Rome (Matt 24:2).[17]

The Authorship and Setting of Matthew

The Author

Concerning Matthew's gospel, Papias wrote in A.D. 140: "Then Matthew put together the sayings in the Hebrew [Aramaic?] dialect and each one translated [interpreted?] them as he was able" (Eusebius, *Hist. eccl.* 3.39.16). This tradition and others based on it are referring to the tax collector and disciple of Jesus whom Matthew's gospel alone identifies as "Matthew" (9:9; 10:3).[18] There are a number of problems, however, with the Papias tradition. First, the gospel as we know it is not a collection of sayings. Second, it was not originally written in, or translated from, Hebrew or Aramaic; it was composed in Koine Greek.

Various explanations have been offered to account for the Papias tra-

---

16. See the discussion in R. T. France, *Matthew: Evangelist and Teacher* (Grand Rapids: Zondervan, 1989), 238-41; A. J. Saldarini, *Matthew's Christian-Jewish Community* (Chicago: University of Chicago Press, 1994), 66-67, 203-6; and U. Luz, *The Theology of the Gospel of Matthew* (trans. J. B. Robinson; Cambridge: Cambridge University Press, 1995), 11-13, 156-59.

17. D. C. Sim, "Rome in Matthew's Eschatology," in *The Gospel of Matthew in Its Roman Imperial Context*, ed. Riches and Sim, 91-106.

18. Irenaeus, *Against Heresies* 3.1.1 (also quoted by Eusebius in *Hist. eccl.* 5.8.2); Pantaenus (found in *Hist. eccl.* 5.10.2-3); Clement (*Hist. eccl.* 3.24.5-6); and Origen (*Hist. eccl.* 6.25.4). See Bauckham, *Jesus and the Eyewitnesses*, 108-13, 301-2.

dition. On the one hand, many suggest that since Matthew relies on Mark's gospel as a source, which would seem unlikely if the author was a disciple and eyewitness of Jesus' ministry, Papias is reflecting the second-century church's attempt to ascribe special authority to its favorite gospel. Others would point out, however, that if a traditional connection of Mark with Peter is plausible, and if Matthew found that he agreed with Mark's content, then adopting the earlier gospel as a framework for his own gospel would make some sense. Furthermore, Matthew's relative obscurity in the primitive church (unlike Peter, James, or John) made it unlikely that he would be named as the apostolic author of an anonymous gospel. Did Papias confuse the canonical Matthew with an earlier lost work similar to Q? Did Matthew compose an earlier, Aramaic collection of Jesus' sayings that went out of circulation after his Greek gospel became available? A variety of theories and queries can be raised, but few can be adequately demonstrated or answered.

What is reasonably certain is that the author of Matthew was a Greek-speaking Jewish Christian, whom ancient tradition suggests was writing from Antioch of Syria. His Jewish background may be deduced from his concern to preserve the authority of the Mosaic law (5:19; 23:3), his allusions to Jewish customs without explanation (15:2; 23:5, 7; 27:6), his leaving Aramaic terms untranslated (5:22), his accommodating arguments to a Pharisaic/rabbinic format (5:32; 19:3-9), his reverential substitution of "heaven" for the name of God (3:2; 4:17; 13:31, 33), and his consistent use of OT fulfillment themes. The Greek of Matthew is smoother than that of Mark and does not read like a Greek translation of an Aramaic original (contra Papias), which points to a Hellenistic Jewish author. His is also the only gospel to use the word "church" (16:18; 18:17) and to specify principles of ecclesiastical discipline and organization.

The Date

Matthew's gospel appears to have been written toward the end of the first century. It has made use of Mark,[19] and the statement about a king sending troops and burning a city (22:7) may allude to the fall of Jerusalem in A.D.

---

19. See the discussion of Mark's date of composition in ch. 3 in "The Authorship and Date of Mark."

70.[20] By the early second century, Ignatius of Antioch appears to cite Matthew in his letters (*Smyrn.* 1.1; 6.1; *Pol.* 1.2-3; 2.2; *Eph.* 5.2; 17.1), and a Syrian work known as the *Didache* (A.D. 100) refers to words of Matthew as "the gospel" (8.1).[21] The break between Judaism and Christianity, which became final by the late first century with the Jamnia (Jabneh) movement (ca. A.D. 90), also seems to be anticipated or even reflected in Jesus' condemnation of the Pharisees (ch. 23) and the repeated references to "their" teachers (7:29) and synagogues (9:35; 23:34).[22]

The Place of Composition

The setting of Matthew in Syrian Antioch has some internal and external support. In the gospel the author betrays his situation as near but not in Palestine. The First Gospel has definite links with Palestinian Christianity through Q and other early traditions. The author also appears near enough to Palestine to feel the aftereffects of the First Jewish Revolt (66-70) and some preliminary or immediate effects of Judaism's reorganization at Jamnia (Jabneh). Yet the author was remote enough from Palestine to speak of it as "that district/region" (9:26, 31; 14:35) and use "their" in describing Jewish synagogues and cities of Galilee (9:35; 11:1; 13:54). The author also betrays an urban consciousness (5:14; 10:14-15, 23; 21:34) and a cosmopolitan spirit (13:38; 24:14; 28:19-20). The Syrian origin of Matthew finds external support in the fact that it is quoted in the *Didache* and Ignatius of Antioch.

The situation Matthew addresses also appears to reflect its origin in Antioch of Syria. The emphases on obedience to the law interpreted by Jesus, continuity with the old Israel, as well as the discipline, organization, and universal mission of the church, reflect a Christian community of Jews and Gentiles seeking to overcome their differences. Antioch of Syria was

20. Some scholars suggest that several of Matthew's unique, non-Markan references to the temple (5:23-24; 17:24-27; 23:16-22) indicate that it was still standing when he wrote. This conclusion, however, is far from certain. The internal evidence for Matthew's being written after 70, however, is more compelling than similar evidence in Mark.

21. B. H. Streeter, *The Four Gospels: A Study of Origins* (London: Macmillan, 1924), 504-11, conveniently lays out the parallels between Matthew, Ignatius, and the *Didache*.

22. For more information, see D. Hill, *The Gospel of Matthew* (NCBC; Grand Rapids: Eerdmans, 1972), 48-55; C. S. Keener, *A Commentary on the Gospel of Matthew* (Grand Rapids: Eerdmans, 1999), 48-49; and R. T. France, *The Gospel of Matthew* (NICNT; Grand Rapids, Eerdmans, 2007), 15-18.

the location of the first Gentile mission (Acts 11:19-20; 13:1-3; 14:26-27), which also occasioned early Christian conflicts involving Gentile observance of the law (Acts 15:1-2; Gal 2:11-16).[23] Some of these conflicts may have continued among certain groups or may have been revived with the migration of many Christians from Palestine to Syria after the destruction of Jerusalem.[24]

Matthew may reflect the church's attempt to consolidate (1) its traditional, Jewish heritage with (2) the innovations of a highly successful Gentile mission, two wings of the early Christian community that often found themselves at odds regarding the observance of the law, the terms of Gentile acceptance, and numerous ethical concerns. Certainly the Jewish reorganization movement at Jamnia, with its pronouncement against Christians (*birkath ha-minim,* perhaps pre-Jamnian),[25] would intensify discussion of the law and Christian continuity with the old Israel. Matthew's focus on Christ as the supreme authority in church ethics and mission is a response to the problems of his day.

Summary

In our analysis of Matthew's gospel, we noted Matthew's numerous redactional techniques in the arrangement and interpretation of the traditions he used.[26] We also looked at key christocentric themes: Jesus is the

---

23. See the subsection "Mission to the Gentiles" above.

24. On Matthew's community, see R. E. Brown and J. P. Meier, *Antioch and Rome: NT Cradles of Catholic Christianity* (New York: Paulist Press, 1983), 45-72; S. H. Brooks, *Matthew's Community: The Evidence of His Special Sayings Material* (Sheffield: JSOT Press, 1987); J. A. Overman, *Matthew's Gospel and Formative Judaism: The Social World of the Matthean Community* (Minneapolis: Fortress, 1990); G. N. Stanton, *A Gospel for a New People: Studies in Matthew* (Edinburgh: T&T Clark, 1992); Saldarini, *Matthew's Christian-Jewish Community;* J. Riches, *Matthew* (Sheffield: Sheffield Academic Press, 1996), 52-78; and D. C. Sim, *The Gospel of Matthew and Christian Judaism: The History and Social Setting of the Matthean Community* (Edinburgh: T&T Clark, 1998).

25. On the Twelfth Benediction, see W. Horbury, "The Benediction of the Minim and Early Jewish-Christian Controversy," *JTS,* n.s., 33 (1982): 19-61; and D. Instone-Brewer, *Prayer and Agriculture* (vol. 1 of *Traditions of the Rabbis from the Era of the NT;* Grand Rapids: Eerdmans, 2004), 108-17.

26. Standard commentaries on the Gospel of Matthew include W. C. Allen, *A Critical and Exegetical Commentary on the Gospel of Matthew* (3d ed.; ICC; Edinburgh: T&T Clark,

Messiah and Son of God, who fulfilled Jewish prophecy and who properly interprets the law for the church. It was also noted that the author of Matthew, who probably lived in Syrian Antioch in the late first century A.D., seems to have had a great concern to consolidate and codify the traditions of his community. He presents the portrait of Christ as the supreme authority for Christian ethics and mission.

1912); F. W. Beare, *The Gospel according to Matthew* (San Francisco: Harper & Row, 1981; repr., Peabody, Mass.: Hendrickson, 1987); R. H. Gundry, *Matthew: A Commentary on His Literary and Theological Art* (Grand Rapids: Eerdmans, 1982); Hill, *Matthew;* J. P. Meier, *Matthew* (NT Message 3; Wilmington, Del.: Michael Glazier, 1980); R. H. Mounce, *Matthew* (GNC; San Francisco: Harper & Row, 1985); A. Plummer, *An Exegetical Commentary on the Gospel according to St Matthew* (2d ed.; London: Eliot Stock, 1910; repr., Grand Rapids: Eerdmans, 1953); E. Schweizer, *The Good News according to Matthew* (trans. D. E. Green; Atlanta: John Knox, 1975); D. Senior, *What Are They Saying about Matthew?* (Ramsey, N.J.: Paulist, 1983); W. D. Davies and D. C. Allison, *A Critical and Exegetical Commentary on the Gospel according to Saint Matthew* (3 vols.; Edinburgh: T&T Clark, 1988); U. Luz, *Matthew: A Continental Commentary* (trans. W. C. Linss; Minneapolis: Fortress, 1992); D. E. Garland, *Reading Matthew: A Literary and Theological Commentary on the First Gospel* (New York: Crossroad, 1993); D. A. Hagner, *Matthew 1–13* and *Matthew 14–28* (WBC 33; Dallas: Word Books, 1993-95); R. H. Gundry, *Matthew: A Commentary on His Handbook for a Mixed Church under Persecution* (Grand Rapids: Eerdmans, 1994); Keener, *Gospel of Matthew;* R. Schnackenburg, *The Gospel of Matthew* (trans. R. R. Barr; Grand Rapids: Eerdmans, 2002); F. D. Bruner, *Matthew: A Commentary* (2 vols.; Grand Rapids: Eerdmans, 2004); J. Nolland, *The Gospel of Matthew* (Grand Rapids: Eerdmans, 2005); and France, *The Gospel of Matthew* (2007).

CHAPTER 5

Literary Features of Luke-Acts

If Matthew is the most Jewish of the gospel writers, Luke is the most educated Gentile among them. The way he writes Greek, the literary conventions he employs, the details of the life of Jesus that interest him, and even the hints we get about his community suggest an educated author from an urban Hellenistic setting.[1]

The gospel of Luke and the book of Acts were originally written to be read together as a single work in two volumes (see Luke 1:1-4 and Acts 1:1-2). But when the NT texts were collected, the four gospels were grouped together, and the gospel of Luke was separated from the Acts of the Apostles. The title "gospel" probably came from the opening verse of Mark, and the title "Acts of the Apostles" originated simply from the contents of the second volume. We will therefore treat the two books as the two-volume work it was intended to be, Luke-Acts.[2] We first look at Luke's redaction of his sources separately in his gospel and Acts, then analyze his literary techniques in the two-volume work as a whole. We consider the thematic concerns of Luke-Acts in the following chapter.

1. For the style of Luke-Acts, see H. J. Cadbury, *The Style and Literary Method of Luke* (Cambridge, Mass.: Harvard University Press, 1919), 1-38; and *The Making of Luke-Acts* (New York: Macmillan, 1927), 213-53.

2. For classic arguments on the unity and common authorship of Luke and Acts, see J. C. Hawkins, *Horae Synopticae: Contributions to the Study of the Synoptic Problem* (2d ed.; Oxford: Clarendon Press, 1909), 174-88; and Cadbury, *The Making of Luke-Acts*, 8-11; also R. C. Tannenhill, *The Narrative Unity of Luke-Acts: A Literary Interpretation* (2 vols.; Philadelphia: Fortress, 1986-99); and J. Verheyden, ed., *The Unity of Luke-Acts* (Leuven: Leuven University Press, 1999). Further explanation for the unity of Luke-Acts will be given later in this chapter in our discussion of Lukan literary techniques.

The Lukan Redaction

The Sources of the Gospel

As Matthew does in his gospel, so Luke extends Mark's framework backward and forward.[3] Before the Markan account of John the Baptist, Luke includes biographical material about both Jesus and John: the birth of John and announcement of Jesus' birth (1:5-80), and then the birth and infancy of Jesus (ch. 2). Unlike Matthew, Luke inserts the genealogy of Jesus (3:23-38) between his baptism and his temptation. All of the above material is from Luke's own traditions (L). In chapters 3–21 Luke basically follows Mark's outline except for the omission and insertions that will be explained shortly.

In chapters 22–23 we note that Luke changes the emphasis in the Markan passion tradition more decisively than Matthew. First, Luke understands the passion as the unjust murder of Jesus by the Jewish leaders, because the Roman Pilate considered him innocent. Second, Luke does not seem to focus on the death of Jesus as an atonement for sin, as does Mark.[4] In chapter 24 Luke moves forward the Markan narrative with much of his own material: the appearance of Jesus on the road to Emmaus (vv. 13-35), the appearance to his disciples in Jerusalem (vv. 36-49), and Jesus' ascension (vv. 50-53).

In addition to extending Mark's narrative, Luke also inserts and omits sizable portions of material, as listed in table 5.1 on page 107.

Luke's lesser interpolation consists of a sizable portion of material from Q inserted after the call of the Twelve in the Markan narrative (Mark 3:13-19 / Luke 6:12-16). Luke's omission includes various miracles, beginning with Jesus' walking on water (Mark 6:45-52) and the healing of the

3. For further study on the sources of Luke's gospel, see J. A. Fitzmyer, "The Priority of Mark and the 'Q' Source in Luke," in *To Advance the Gospel: NT Studies* (2d ed.; Grand Rapids: Eerdmans, 1998), 3-40; and *The Gospel according to Luke* (2 vols.; AB 28-28A; Garden City, N.Y.: Doubleday, 1981-85), 1:63-106; J. C. Hawkins, *Horae Synopticae* (Oxford: Clarendon Press, 1899), 15-29, 54-113; Reicke, *Roots of the Synoptic Gospels*; M. Casey, *An Aramaic Approach to Q: Sources for the Gospels of Matthew and Luke* (New York: Cambridge University Press, 2002); and B. Shellard, *New Light on Luke: Its Purpose, Sources, and Literary Context* (London: Sheffield Academic Press, 2002).

4. Neither has the subject vanished in Luke, as many suggest; see J. Neyrey, *The Passion according to Luke: A Redaction Study of Luke's Soteriology* (New York: Paulist Press, 1985); and P. Doble, *The Paradox of Salvation: Luke's Theology of the Cross* (Cambridge: Cambridge University Press, 1996).

TABLE 5.1. MARK AND LUKE: STRUCTURAL DIFFERENCES

Mark	Luke	
1:2–3:19	3:2–6:16	
—	6:20–8:3	Luke's lesser interpolation
4:1–6:44	8:4–9:17	
6:45–8:26	—	Luke's omission
8:27–9:41	9:18-50	
—	9:51–18:14	Luke's greater interpolation
10:13–16:8	18:15–24:9	(with special Lukan emphases)

blind man of Bethsaida (Mark 8:22-26). A large collection of special Lukan parables and discourses in a journey-to-Jerusalem framework compose Luke's greater interpolation.[5]

The sayings source Q appears to have undergone fewer modifications in Luke than in Matthew. For example, we do not detect any thematic groupings of Q in Luke as we find in Matthew. For this reason, many scholars believe that the order of Q in Luke is closer to the original arrangement.

The Sources of Acts

The sources of Acts are much more difficult to detect and analyze. First, we do not possess any of its sources (such as we have Mark as the source of Matthew and Luke). Second, whatever sources were used are so dominated by the author's style that their detection can be only a matter of educated guesswork.[6] Three possible sources used in Acts are (1) a diary of Paul's travels, (2) early traditions about Paul, and (3) traditions about Peter and the Jerusalem church.

5. See B. S. Easton, "Linguistic Evidence for Lucan Source L," *JBL* 29 (1910): 139-80; Fitzmyer, *Luke*, 1:67, 82-85. In textual criticism, "interpolation" denotes material inserted into the text in the process of scribal transmission, thereby altering the original meaning.

6. For further discussion of this topic, see G. H. C. Macgregor, "Acts of the Apostles," *IB* 9:14-18; A. Harnack, *Acts of the Apostles* (trans. J. R. Wilkinson; London: Williams & Norgate, 1909); J. Dupont, *The Sources of Acts* (trans. K. Pond; New York: Herder & Herder, 1961); C. J. Hemer, *The Book of Acts in the Setting of Hellenistic History* (ed. C. Gempf; Tübingen: Mohr Siebeck, 1989), 308-64; and C. K. Barrett, *A Critical and Exegetical Commentary on the Acts of the Apostles* (2 vols.; ICC; Edinburgh: T&T Clark, 1994-98), 1:49-56; 2:xxiv-xxxii.

The Travel Diary The theory of a travel journal finds its support in the abrupt change to first person plural in the narrative of Paul's journeys (note "we" in Acts 16:10-17; 20:5-15; 21:1-18; 27:1–28:16, traditionally referred to as the we-sections). Earlier generations believed that the we-passages were evidence that the author of Acts was Paul's traveling companion, an eyewitness of the events he recorded, and that these sections were remnants of a personal diary. In the nineteenth and twentieth century, however, many scholars argued that (1) the exalted portrait of Paul found in Acts, (2) the author's apparent unfamiliarity with Paul's letters, and (3) the similarity of style with the rest of the book weigh heavily against this traditional conclusion.[7] More recently, it has been argued that the use of "we" is a literary device to tell how "we" as a Christian movement spread to the Gentile world.

The traditional historical argument may have more substance to it, however, than modern critics allow. By carefully tracing the story line of Acts, giving special attention to the we-sections, the reader will observe that the ancient diarist was not in Paul's company during the majority of his letter writing or the major events that prompted his correspondence with the newly founded, struggling communities.[8] Whatever the conclusion, it is evident from the detailed localities and provincial designations in the Aegean Sea narratives (chs. 16–21) that the author had access to specific information or was a native of that region.[9]

---

7. See, for example, E. Haenchen, *The Acts of the Apostles* (trans. R. M. Wilson; Oxford: Blackwell, 1971), 112-16; and P. Vielhauer, "On the 'Paulinism' of Acts," in *Studies in Luke-Acts* (ed. L. E. Keck and J. L. Martyn; Nashville: Abingdon, 1966; repr., Philadelphia: Fortress, 1980; henceforth, *SLA*). On "we" as literary device, see R. C. Tannehill, *The Acts of the Apostles: The Narrative Unity of Luke-Acts; A Literary Appreciation 2* (Minneapolis: Fortress, 1990), 2:246-47.

8. See Hemer, *The Book of Acts*, 244-76; and S. E. Porter, *The Paul of Acts: Essays in Literary Criticism, Rhetoric, and Theology* (Tübingen: Mohr Siebeck, 1999), esp. ch. 9, "The Paul of Acts and the Paul of the Letters: Some Common Conceptions and Misconceptions."

9. See the classic works of W. M. Ramsay, *St. Paul the Traveller and the Roman Citizen* (London: Hodder & Stoughton, 1895), *The Cities of St. Paul: Their Influence of His Life and Thought, The Cities of Eastern Asia Minor* (London: Hodder & Stoughton, 1907), and *The Bearing of Recent Discovery on the Trustworthiness of the NT* (London: Hodder & Stoughton, 1915); and, more recently, W. W. Gasque, *A History of the Criticism of the Acts of the Apostles* (Grand Rapids: Eerdmans, 1975); J. Fitzmyer, *Luke the Theologian* (New York: Paulist Press, 1989), 3-11; Hemer, *The Book of Acts*; I. A. Levinskaya, *The Book of Acts in Its Diaspora Setting* (Grand Rapids: Eerdmans, 1996); and Barrett, *The Acts of the Apostles*, 2:xxxiii-lxxxi.

The Early Pauline Traditions The author of Acts might have used traditions about Paul's conversion and early days in Antioch. Some have even postulated a Pauline source for his conversion (9:1-30) and an Antiochian source that supposedly dealt with the appointment of the Seven and the story of Stephen (6:1–8:4), the founding of the church of Antioch (11:19-30), and the early ministry of Barnabas and Saul (12:25–15:35). The nature and extent of these sources, however, are questionable.

The Petrine Traditions The book of Acts may have relied on traditions associated with Peter and the Jerusalem church. Scholars have also sought to delineate these traditions into a Jerusalem source with superior (3:1–5:16) and inferior (1–2; 5:17-42) versions, and a Jerusalem-Caesarea source containing the stories of Philip (8:5-40), Peter in Joppa and Caesarea (9:31–11:18), and the persecution under Herod (12:1-24). Although ingenious and insightful, these source constructions are speculative. Current scholarship highlights the creativity of the author who told his own story, using sources that are almost impossible to delineate.

The Lukan Style

Our discussion of Lukan style includes Luke's modes of discourse, patterns of balance, literary techniques, and figures of speech.

The Modes of Written Discourse

The key literary forms of speeches and travel narratives are surveyed under the broader category of Lukan modes of discourse. This procedure is followed to properly interpret them in their own narrative context.

Direct Discourse Luke makes significant use of speeches, especially in the book of Acts. Comparing Acts with ancient historiography suggests that, while the speeches may well preserve the ideas and intentions of the original speakers, Luke does more than merely record the past. He also uses the speeches for his own purposes: first to underscore his personal perspective, and then to benefit his readers by interpreting and illuminating the significance of events.

Two types of speeches are found in Acts: (1) those that proclaim the passion, resurrection, and exaltation of Jesus (e.g., Acts 2:14-39; 3:11-26; 4:18-22; 13:16-41), and (2) those that defend Paul and the Christian mission to the Gentiles (22:3-21; 26:1-23; 28:16-28). The speeches in Acts contain all or most of the following features: an occasion for the speech, identification of the speaker, a designated audience, an introductory statement that is generally a direct address to the designated audience, a body, and a conclusion usually giving the response of the audience.[10]

In addition to speeches, there are other forms of direct address in Luke-Acts: prayers, visions, and dreams (Acts 1:24-25; 4:24-30; 9:4-6; 10:3-6; 18:9-10); songs or hymns (Luke 1:46-55, 67-79; 2:28-32); and letters (Acts 15:23-29; 23:26-30).

Indirect Discourse An important type of indirect discourse used in Luke-Acts is that of the travel narrative.[11] In Acts it includes Paul's journeys to Jerusalem and Rome (19:21–28:31); both accounts are thoroughly Lukan in language and style. Even the journey of Jesus to Jerusalem (Luke 9:51–19:44), derived from the Markan tradition, is greatly expanded. Much of it has been designated Luke's "greater interpolation." Diverse literary forms of direct discourse, dialogues, and miracle stories linked by summaries in both Luke 9:51–19:44 and Acts 19:21–28:31 are loosely organized around this journey motif.[12]

---

10. For further study of Lukan speeches, see H. J. Cadbury, "The Speeches in Acts," in *The Beginnings of Christianity* (ed. J. F. Foakes Jackson and K. Lake; 5 vols.; London: Macmillan, 1920-33), 5:402-27; M. Dibelius, *Studies in the Acts of the Apostles* (trans. M. Ling; London: SCM Press, 1956), 138-91; P. Schubert, "The Final Cycles of Speeches in Acts," *JBL* 87 (1968): 1-16; E. Schweizer, "Concerning the Speeches in Acts," in *SLA*, 208-16; and M. L. Soards, *The Speeches in Acts: Their Content, Context, and Concerns* (Louisville, Ky.: Westminster John Knox, 1994).

11. On the use of travel narratives in ancient literature, as well as in Luke-Acts, see D. Marguerat, *The First Christian Historian: Writing the "Acts of the Apostles"* (Cambridge: Cambridge University Press, 2002), 231-56.

12. Luke 9:51–19:44 is loosely linked by such geographic notations as 9:51, 53; 13:22, 33; 17:11; 18:31; 19:11, 28, 41. Acts 19:21–28:31 is loosely connected by geographic markers (Jerusalem: 19:21; 20:16; 21:11-13, 15; Rome: 19:21; 23:11; 25:12, 25; 27:1, 24; 28:14-16).

The Principle of Balance

A second category of Lukan style is the principle of balance.[13] The two most prominent are regular and inverted parallelism.

Regular Parallelism Regular parallelism occurs when there is a recurrence of certain elements in a corresponding order. It is illustrated by the pattern A B : A′ B′. The parallelism is synonymous (making the same or a similar point) or antithetical (making a contrasting point), according to content. Often the parallelism in Luke-Acts involves a larger number of elements, some of which are not in an exact corresponding order. When the order of these recurring elements is in no particular arrangement, this pattern is called counterpoint and is illustrated by the sequence A B C D : C′ A′ D′ B′. Most of the examples provided are parallelisms, although some of the elements may not be in corresponding order. They are also usually synonymous and not antithetical. Where parallelism is disputed, it can still generally be shown that Luke is at least employing the use of doublets or pairs.

These recurring elements in a basic corresponding order can be seen in comparisons of the gospel and Acts, Peter and Paul, and Paul and Jesus. The elements of comparison are mostly thematic, but sometimes they concern similar language (e.g., trial scenes of Jesus and Paul) and style (e.g., prefaces of Luke and Acts). Some overlapping occurs in these comparisons. To what extent these parallelisms were unconscious or deliberate is not easy to ascertain. The amount of convincing evidence presented in them (esp. linguistic parallels) could point to deliberate design. (See table 5.2 on p. 112.)

The parallels between the gospel and Acts are general at some points (e.g., in the preface and preparation, as listed in table 5.2) and specific at others (e.g., the passion). The general correspondences may have been coincidental, but the specific parallels seem to reflect the deliberate work of the author (e.g., four trials, three declarations of innocence). It appears that Luke, by using these parallels, was attempting to ground the activity of the apostles in the deeds of Jesus.[14]

13. For further discussion on the principle of balance, see C. H. Talbert, *Literary Patterns, Theological Themes, and the Genre of Luke-Acts* (Missoula, Mont.: Society of Biblical Literature, 1974), 14n.70, 67-88; and K. Olrik, "Epic Laws of Folk Narrative," in *The Study of Folklore,* ed. A. Dundes (Englewood Cliffs, NJ: Prentice-Hall, 1965), 129-41.

14. For further discussion, see R. F. O'Toole, *The Unity of Luke's Theology: An Analysis of Luke-Acts* (Wilmington, Del.: Michael Glazier, 1984), 62-96, 261-65; Talbert, *Literary Patterns,*

TABLE 5.2. LUKE AND ACTS: PARALLELS

Preface		Luke 1:1-4 / Acts 1:1-5
Preparation	Jesus' baptism in water	Luke 3
	The church's baptism in the Spirit	Acts 2
Ministry	Inaugural sermon of Jesus at Nazareth	Luke 4:16-30
	Peter (the church) at Jerusalem	Acts 2:14-40
	Healing of a lame man	Luke 5:17-26 / Acts 3:1-10
	Early conflicts with Jewish leaders	Luke 5:29–6:11 / Acts 4:1–8:3
	Raising of the dead	Luke 7:1-10 / Acts 9:36-43
Journey	Jesus/Paul to Jerusalem	Luke 9:51–19:28 / Acts 19:21–21:16
	Fateful passion journey	Luke 12:50; 13:33; 18:31-33 / Acts 20:22-25, 37-38; 21:4, 10-11, 13
Passion	Seized by a mob	Luke 22:54 / Acts 21:30
	Slapped in the face	Luke 22:63-64 / Acts 23:2
	Four trials	Luke 22–23 / Acts 22–26
	Declared innocent three times	Luke 23:4, 14, 22 / Acts 23:9; 25:25; 26:31
Vindication	Person/message of Christ	Luke 24 / Acts 28

Some of the above parallels have been used of Jesus and Peter (or the early church), such as the healing of the lame man (Luke 5:17-26; Acts 3:1-10) and the raising of the dead (Luke 7:1-10; Acts 9:36-43). This implies a unity of procedure in the healing activities of Jesus, Peter, and Paul. In other parallels, it appears that Luke's portrait of the miraculous is similar in the ministries of both Peter and Paul. (See table 5.3 on p. 113.) For Luke, God worked wonders in the activities of both apostles, indicating that the ministry of Jesus continued within the early (Jewish) church, as well as in the subsequent Pauline (Gentile) mission.

15-23. The following study urges caution in defining the criteria for parallelisms (e.g., content, themes, language) and stresses the importance of knowing both the strengths and the weaknesses of those criteria: S. M. Praeder, "Jesus-Paul, Peter-Paul, and Jesus-Peter Parallelisms in Luke-Acts: A History of Reader Response," *SBL 1984 Seminar Papers* (Chico, Calif.: Scholars Press, 1984), 23-40.

TABLE 5.3. PETER AND PAUL IN ACTS: PARALLELS IN MINISTRY

Event	Peter	Paul
Healing	cripple at temple (3:1-10) Aeneas at Lydda (9:32-34)	cripple at Lystra (14:8-10) father of Publius (28:8)
Raising from the dead	Tabitha (9:36-41)	Eutychus (20:9-12)
Miraculous effects	Peter's shadow upon sick (5:15)	handkerchiefs and aprons touched by Paul (19:12)
Victory over opponents	Simon the magician (8:18-24)	Elymas (13:6-12) The possessed girl (16:16-18)
Divine punishment of offenders or opponents	Ananias and Sapphira killed (5:1-11)	Elymas blinded (13:6-12)

Most of the parallels between Jesus and Paul have already been presented in the comparison of Luke and Acts (e.g., journey to Jerusalem, passion, and final vindication).[15] Some of the closest parallels occur in the accounts of the passion and trial. From these parallels, it appears that Luke is presenting some of the tragic events of Paul's life (e.g., arrest and trial) in close conformity to those of Christ's life, thereby signifying both Paul's imitation of Christ and the fact that these tragic events were ordained by God. This method of presentation functions as an effective apology for Paul and his ministry.

Inverted Parallelism (Chiasm) A second major type of balance is that of chiasm, or inverted parallelism.[16] This pattern is evident when elements appear in inverted order, A B : B′ A′. Chiasm is seen in such passages as

15. See also A. J. Mattill, "The Jesus-Paul Parallels and the Purpose of Luke-Acts: H. H. Evans Reconsidered," *NovT* 17 (1975): 15-46; and R. B. Rackham, *The Acts of the Apostles* (1901 ed.; repr., Grand Rapids: Baker, 1978), xlvii-l.

16. K. E. Bailey, *Poet and Peasant: A Literary-Cultural Approach to the Parables in Luke* (Grand Rapids: Eerdmans, 1976), 44-85; D. R. Miesner, "Missionary Journeys Narrative: Patterns and Implications," in *Perspectives on Luke-Acts* (ed. C. H. Talbert; Macon, Ga.: Mercer University Press, 1978), 199-214 (some of these alleged chiastic patterns are unconvincing under close scrutiny); C. H. Talbert, *Reading Luke: A Literary and Theological Commentary on the Third Gospel* (New York: Crossroad, 1982), 54-55, 111-13; and P. Borgman, *The Way according to Luke: Hearing the Whole Story of Luke-Acts* (Grand Rapids: Eerdmans, 2006), 7-15, 31, 77-96, 203-14.

Luke 4:16-20, 9:51–19:44, and Acts 12:25–21:16. This particular pattern, as we will note, highlights the central point, A B C B′ A′, which functions similarly to the crisis or turning point in the structure of a Greek tragedy (complication-crisis-denouement).

The opening speech of Jesus at Nazareth, Luke 4:16-20, can be structured as in chiasm 5.1. The correspondence between panels A, A′, B, B′, and C, C′ is that of initiation-completion: Jesus stood up to read (A), Jesus sat down (A′); Jesus was given a book (B), Jesus gave it back to the attendant (B′); he opened the book (C) and closed it (C′). The types of correspondences in a chiastic pattern vary. There can be, for example, contrasting or synonymous parallels, correspondences of exact words, and similar thoughts. Between each set of corresponding panels (e.g., A, A′), some type of balance should exist: synonymous, antithetical, progressive, consequential, or climactic. Although it is better if fewer divergences are found in a chiasm, some passages or verses can be omitted in the arrangement. Furthermore, some elements in the construction may not be in exact order. In Luke 4 the turning point of the chiasm (D) is the reading from Isa 61 and 58, which is the focus of the passage according to this type of balance.

CHIASM 5.1. JESUS' FIRST SPEECH (LUKE 4:16-20)

A Jesus stood up to read (16c)
   B a book was given to him (17a)
      C opening the book (17b)
         D Isa 61:1-2, with 58:6 (18-19)
      C′ closing the book (20a)
   B′ he gave it back to the attendant (20b)
A′ he sat down (20c)

Chiasm can also be detected in larger passages like the travel narrative in Luke 9:51–19:44 of Jesus' journey to Jerusalem. The section begins and ends with a rejection scene (9:51-56; 19:41-44), and a chiastic pattern emerges in the overall arrangement.[17] (See chiasm 5.2.) Jesus' statements on Jerusalem's rejection of its prophets (13:31-35) surface as the center of the chiasm. Verification of this inverted parallelism can be undertaken by comparing the corresponding points (e.g., A and A′, B and B′, C and C′). As in most examples of ancient chiasm, the correspondence is not perfect. Some

17. Bailey, *Poet and Peasant*, 80-82; Talbert, *Reading Luke*, 111-13.

passages are omitted or overlooked in the outline. But the number of close correspondences in most of the outline is significant, especially since Luke 9:51–19:44 is part of Luke's so-called greater interpolation.[18]

CHIASM 5.2. JESUS' JOURNEY TO JERUSALEM (LUKE 9:51–19:44)

A to Jerusalem: rejection in Samaria (9:51-56)
  B following Jesus (9:57–10:20)
    C how to inherit eternal life (10:25-41)
      D prayer (11:1-13)
        E signs of the kingdom (11:14-32)
          F conflict with Pharisees (11:37–12:34)
            G present faithfulness and the coming kingdom (12:35-48)
              H healing followed by Jewish accusation (13:10-17)
                I entry to the kingdom: exclusion and inclusion (13:22-30)
                  J prophets perish in Jerusalem (13:31-35)
                I′ the messianic banquet: exclusion and inclusion (14:7-24)
              H′ healing followed by Jewish accusation (14:1-6)
            G′ present faithfulness and the coming kingdom (16:1-13)
          F′ conflict with Pharisees (16:14-31)
        E′ signs of the kingdom (17:11-37)
      D′ prayer (18:1-14)
    C′ how to inherit eternal life (18:18-30)
  B′ following Jesus (18:35–19:9)
A′ to Jerusalem: rejection by Jerusalem (19:11, 41-44)

Literary Techniques

From patterns of balance we move to the literary techniques of restatement, model portraits, thematic echo, anticipation, summary statements, fulfillment motif, and versatility.

Restatement Luke often retells a story in a later speech to underscore and interpret a key episode. For example, Paul's conversion is twice retold, once

---

18. See Miesner, "Missionary Journeys Narrative," 203-14, for a similar, lengthy chiasm in Acts 12:25–21:16, although his example is less persuasive.

in his defense before the mob in Jerusalem (Acts 22:1-21) and again before Agrippa (26:2-23). Peter also restates the story of the conversion of Cornelius before the apostles in Jerusalem (11:15-17) and makes some allusion to it at the Jerusalem Council (15:7-9). Other examples include the decision of James at the Jerusalem Council (15:19-22, 23-29; 21:25) and the summaries of Festus concerning his first contacts with Paul's case (25:1-12 with vv. 13-21, 24-27).[19]

Model Portraits Through extended treatment and dramatic emphasis, Luke highlights several characters who serve as models for his controlling interests. For example, there are three models of Christian conversion: the Ethiopian eunuch (8:26-39), the Roman centurion Cornelius (10:1-48; 11:1-18, extended treatment), and Paul (9:1-31; 22:1-21; 26:4-23, three accounts). Through extended treatment and dramatic emphasis, the ideal martyr is provided in the story of Stephen (6:1–8:1).[20] In the same manner, the Jewish leader Gamaliel (5:33-39) and the Roman officials Gallio (18:12-17) and Festus (25:1-12) appear to be models of fair treatment shown toward Christianity.[21]

Thematic Echo One device that Luke uses to develop a favorite motif is thematic echo; note, for example, its use in the development of the passion motif. At a number of key points in Acts, a saying or description occurs that contains a striking echo of the passion theme in the gospel. These are found in the stories of Stephen (countenance, Acts 6:15 / Luke 9:29; vision, Acts 7:55-56 / Luke 22:69; dying words, Acts 7:59-60 / Luke 23:34, 46) and Paul (passion predictions, Acts 20:22-25; 21:4, 10-12 / Luke 9:22, 44; 18:31-33; seized

---

19. See Cadbury, "The Speeches in Acts," 422-23; and Barrett, *The Acts of the Apostles,* 1:437-45, 491-98. Marguerat refers to this device as a narrative chain or redundancy (*The First Christian Historian,* 52-56).

20. See Marguerat, *The First Christian Historian,* 56-59. Regular parallels can also be detected between Stephen and Jesus; see O'Toole, *Unity,* 63-67; R. Maddox, *The Purpose of Luke-Acts* (Göttingen: Vandenhoeck & Ruprecht, 1982), 104; and Barrett, *The Acts of the Apostles,* 1:388.

21. For more discussion on this and other literary techniques of Luke-Acts, see H. J. Cadbury, "Four Features of Lucan Style," in *SLA,* 87-102; and *The Making of Luke-Acts,* 140-54, 213-38; F. W. Danker, *Luke* (Philadelphia: Fortress, 1976), 89-103; Fitzmyer, *Luke,* 1:81-82, 91-97, 107-27; D. J. Selby, *Introduction to the NT: "The Word Became Flesh"* (New York: Macmillan, 1971), 149-62, 282-91; L. T. Johnson, "Literary Aspects of Luke-Acts," *ABD* 4:408-412; and I. H. Marshall, *The Acts of the Apostles* (Sheffield: Sheffield Academic Press, 1992), 13-30.

by mob, Acts 21:30 / Luke 22:54; four trials, Acts 22–26 / Luke 22–23; declared innocent three times, Acts 23:9; 25:25; 26:31 / Luke 23:4, 14, 22). In these accounts of Stephen and Paul, Luke may be dramatizing the call to follow Jesus as a way that involves suffering and death (e.g., Luke 9:23-26).[22]

Anticipation The technique of anticipation introduces a theme that the author develops later in his narrative.[23] At the end of the gospel, three such anticipations — (1) worldwide proclamation (Luke 24:46-48), (2) the promise of the Spirit (v. 49), and (3) the Ascension (v. 51) — lead the reader to the opening chapters of Acts and some major emphases of that book. The reference in Acts 2:44-46 to the community of goods in the church at Jerusalem, for example, anticipates the story of Barnabas's generosity (4:32-37) and the duplicity of Ananias and Sapphira (5:1-11). The mention of Barnabas also anticipates his work with the Antioch church and Paul (9:27; 11:25-30; 12:25–15:39). The work of Peter with the Roman Cornelius (10:1–11:18) anticipates Paul's mission to the Gentiles (13–14; 16–28).

Summary Statements Luke relies on summary statements to (1) transition from one stage of his narrative to the next and (2) highlight crucial developments in his story line. In the gospel, Luke's special material underscores Jesus' physical and spiritual maturation three times (1:80; 2:40, 52; cf. 1 Sam 2:26), highlighting his unique, divine calling. Luke then retains three of Mark's summaries noting the progress and development of Jesus' adult ministry (Luke 4:37 / Mark 1:28; Luke 4:44 / Mark 1:39; Luke 5:15 / Mark 1:45), while adding two of his own (Luke 7:17; 8:1). Finally, he pointedly summarizes the growing hostility that eventually led to Jesus' demise (Luke 11:53-54).

Luke continues his summarizing technique in the book of Acts. Three

---

22. R. F. O'Toole, "Parallels between Jesus and His Disciples in Luke-Acts: A Further Study," *BZ* 27 (1983): 195-212; D. P. Moessner, "'The Christ Must Suffer': New Light on the Jesus–Peter, Stephen, Paul Parallels in Luke-Acts," *NovT* 28 (1986): 220-56; J. B. Green, "Internal Repetition in Luke-Acts: Contemporary Narratology and Lucan Historiography," in *History, Literature, and Society in the Book of Acts* (ed. B. Witherington; Cambridge: Cambridge University Press, 1996), 283-99; C. H. Talbert, *Reading Acts: A Theological and Literary Commentary on the Acts of the Apostles* (New York: Crossroad, 1997), 11-17.

23. Also called prolepsis; see Marguerat, *The First Christian Historian*, 49-52; Danker, *Luke*, 101-2; and Selby, *Introduction*, 287. The parallel patterns in Talbert, *Literary Patterns*, 35-36, 58-63, presuppose the device of anticipation.

passages describe the piety and communal life of the early Jerusalem church (Acts 2:42-47; 4:32-35; 5:12-16). Six further summaries track the unstoppable nature of the apostolic proclamation as the church expands throughout Jerusalem (6:7), spreads into Judea, Samaria, and Galilee (9:31), overcomes persecution (12:24), prospers among the Gentiles (16:5), overcomes paganism (19:20), and is finally proclaimed throughout Rome, the empire's capital (28:31).

Fulfillment Motif Linked closely to the technique of anticipation is the fulfillment motif. As in Matthew's gospel, this theme figures prominently in Luke-Acts.[24] In Luke's gospel, various events in the life of Jesus are regarded as fulfillments of Jewish prophecy (e.g., Luke 3:4-6 / Isa 40:3-5; Luke 4:17-19 / Isa 61:1-2; Luke 22:37 / Isa 53:12), and in Acts, the outpouring of the Spirit (Acts 2:17-21 / Joel 2:28-32), the resurrection of Christ (Acts 2:25-28 / Ps 16:8-11), mission to the Gentiles (Acts 15:15-18 / Amos 9:11-12), and the hardening of the Jews (Acts 28:25-27 / Isa 6:9-10) are also examples of prophetic fulfillment. In contrast to Matthew's use of this motif, Luke does not rely on fixed formulas to introduce the quotations, and he also expands the idea of fulfillment to include events in the early church (e.g., Acts 15:15-18 / Amos 9:11-12).

Luke's theme of fulfillment of Scripture is also related to his concept of divine necessity, usually indicated by the Greek verb *dei* ("it is necessary").[25] It is used in connection with the suffering and rising of Jesus (e.g., Luke 17:25; 24:7, 26, 44; Acts 3:21; 17:3), the apostasy of Judas and election of Matthias (Acts 1:16-21), the sufferings of Paul (Acts 9:16), and the trials of all Christians (Acts 14:22). For Luke this concept expresses the workings of God's will to bring to fulfillment all that Moses and the prophets have said.

---

24. D. L. Bock, *Proclamation from Prophecy and Pattern: Lucan OT Christology* (Sheffield: Sheffield Academic Press, 1987); M. L. Strauss, *The Davidic Messiah in Luke-Acts: The Promise and Its Fulfillment in Lukan Christology* (Sheffield: Sheffield Academic Press, 1995).

25. Most of the following works discuss fulfillment of Scripture with the notion of divine necessity: Cadbury, *The Making of Luke-Acts,* 303-6; H. Conzelmann, *The Theology of St. Luke* (trans. G. Buswell; New York: Harper & Row, 1961; Philadelphia: Fortress, 1982), 149-69; and N. A. Dahl, "The Story of Abraham in Luke-Acts," *SLA,* 139-58. For fulfillment of prophecy in the broader Greco-Roman context, see Talbert, *Reading Luke,* 234-40; and J. T. Squires, *The Plan of God in Luke-Acts* (Cambridge: Cambridge University Press, 1993), esp. ch. 7, "Fate: The Necessity of the Plan of God"; O'Toole prefers "continuation of Israel in the church" instead of "promise-fulfillment" (*Unity,* 17-32).

Divine necessity and fulfillment of Scripture are two central motifs in Luke's scheme of salvation history.

Versatility The final literary technique to be discussed is versatility.[26] Luke-Acts contains some of the most elegant Greek prose in the NT. At the same time, portions of the gospel also preserve such Semitic Greek that many scholars wonder if Luke translated from Hebrew or Aramaic originals.[27] The harsh shift from the formal, literary Greek of Luke's prologue (Luke 1:1-4) to the thick, Semitic flavor of the birth narratives (1:5–2:52) is the clearest example of Luke's stylistic versatility. Whether the less elegant Greek indicates Luke's dependence on Aramaic sources or his effort to emulate "biblical language" by using grammatical constructions typical of the Greek Septuagint (e.g., "and it came to pass") is difficult to determine.

Like other literary men of antiquity, Luke knew that the speeches for his characters had to be varied and appropriate to the different speakers and occasions, although, once again, it is difficult to judge the extent to which changes in style and vocabulary originated with Luke or with his divergent source materials. For example, the speeches of Peter and Paul before the Jews are pervaded with biblical texts, whereas Paul's speeches before non-Jewish audiences contain fewer scriptural quotes and more classical Greek rhetoric and idioms. In Acts 17 Paul speaks with Greek philosophers in Athens in appropriate classical expressions, and in Acts 24, using the appropriate courtroom rhetoric, the prosecutor Tertullus makes his case before Felix. Has Luke composed these speeches to fit their literary contexts? Or is he accurately reflecting the abilities of effective, ancient communicators? Or do the Acts speeches reflect some combination of both?[28]

---

26. Cadbury, *The Making of Luke-Acts*, 221-30.

27. See the list of names in J. Fitzmyer, *Luke*, 1:312; for a discussion of Lukan style in the gospel, see Fitzmyer, *Luke*, 1:107-27; for the style of Acts, see Haenchen, *Acts*, 72-81.

28. M. Dibelius, "The Speeches in Acts and Ancient Historiography," in *Studies in the Acts of the Apostles* (ed. H. Greeven; London: SCM Press, 1956), 138-85 (reissued as *The Book of Acts: Form, Style, and Theology* [ed. K. C. Hanson; Minneapolis: Fortress, 2004], 49-86); E. Schweizer, "Zu den Reden der Apostelgeschichte," *TZ* 13 (1957): 1-11 (reprinted as "Concerning the Speeches in Acts," in *SLA*, 208-16); Soards, *The Speeches in Acts*; E. Plümacher, "The Mission Speeches in Acts and Dionysius of Halicarnassus," in *Jesus and the Heritage of Israel: Luke's Narrative Claim upon Israel's Legacy* (ed. D. P. Moessner; Harrisburg, Pa.: Trinity Press International, 1999), 251-66.

The technique of versatility is also evident when Luke uses names appropriate to the setting. For example, when Paul begins his mission into the Gentile world, Luke changes his name from the Hebrew "Saul" to the Roman name "Paul" (Acts 13:9). Also at this stage in the story the author changes his customary name for Gentile adherents to Judaism, "God-fearers," to the less Semitic "God-worshippers."

Figures of Speech

Under this category we briefly discuss understatement, double entendre, irony, and satire.

Understatement A significant stylistic feature to be examined is understatement. Litotes is a form of understatement in which an idea is affirmed by stating the negative of its opposite. Litotes is frequently found in the works of classical and Hellenistic Greek authors like Euripides, Strabo, Polybius, Philo, and Josephus. Examples of litotes in Acts are (1) Paul's boast that he is "a citizen of *no unimportant city*" (21:39), (2) the mention that God did "not the ordinary" powerful deeds through the hands of Paul (19:11), and (3) Luke's favorite expression, "not a little," to convey large quantities (e.g., 12:18; 14:28; 17:4, 12; 19:23). By means of litotes, Luke seeks to affirm the importance or greatness of something by denying its opposite. This stylistic device helps us evaluate Luke's diction as educated and urbane.

Double Entendre Luke is fond of the double entendre, or a word with a double meaning.[29] We give four examples here. First, the word *pais*, "boy," denoting the twelve-year-old Jesus who stayed behind in Jerusalem (Luke 2:43), also connotes the appointed "servant" who fulfills God's mission (Luke 1:54; Acts 3:13, 26; 4:27, 30). Second, the "poor" of Luke 6:20 denotes the recipients of the promises described in Luke 4:18-19 / Isa 61:1-2 and also connotes those in a disadvantaged position who suffer oppression (e.g., Luke 18:22). Third, according to Luke 22:56, Peter faces the "light" of the fire, but Luke's audience knows that Peter is really in the presence of Jesus,

---

29. E. W. Bullinger, *Figures of Speech Used in the Bible* (1898; repr., Grand Rapids: Baker, 1968), 804-6; Danker, *Luke*, 102-3.

who was identified by Simeon as "a light for revelation to the Gentiles" (2:32) and who now turns to "look" at his cowardly disciple (22:61). Fourth, Paul appears to commend his Athenian listeners when he says, "I see how *extremely religious* you are in every way" (Acts 17:22), but Luke's readers know that these Greeks are superstitious and lacking in a knowledge of the true God and thus that there is an ironic sense to this word. See, for example, Acts 25:19 where the same word for "religion" is used in a derogatory sense.

Irony and Satire In the tradition of the Roman poet Horace, Luke also employs irony and satire.[30] Even though Jesus disclaims the role of judge in a court of petty claims (Luke 12:14), he is "the one ordained by God as judge of the living and the dead" (Acts 10:42). Intense pathos underlies the grim resolution in Luke 13:33, "Yet today, tomorrow, and the next day I must be on my way, because it is impossible for a prophet to be killed outside of Jerusalem." Luke approaches Horatian satire in his description of crowd psychology: "most of them did not know why they had come together" (Acts 19:32).

The Lukan Structure

Having discussed the Lukan literary and stylistic features, we turn our attention to the structure of Luke-Acts.

Geographic Movement

As mentioned earlier, travel or geographic movement is an important structural element in the narrative of Luke-Acts.[31] The two narratives of

---

30. Bullinger, *Figures of Speech*, 807-15; Danker, *Luke*, 103; Tate, *Interpreting the Bible*, 184, 328-29.

31. For Lukan geographic perspective, see Conzelmann, *The Theology of St. Luke*, 18-94; W. C. Robinson, "The Theological Context for Interpreting Luke's Travel Narrative (9:51ff.)," *JBL* 79 (1960): 20-31; F. V. Filson, "Journey Motif in Luke-Acts," in *Apostolic History and the Gospel* (ed. W. W. Gasque and R. P. Martin; Grand Rapids: Eerdmans, 1970), 68-77; I. H. Marshall, *Luke: Historian and Theologian* (Grand Rapids: Zondervan, 1970), 70-72; J. J. Navone, "The Journey Theme in Luke-Acts," *TBT* 58 (1972): 616-19; J. M. Scott, "Luke's Geo-

Jesus' journey to Jerusalem (Luke 9:51–19:44) and Paul's journeys to Jerusalem and Rome (Acts 19:21–28:31) each form complete structural units. In Luke's gospel, excluding 1:1–4:13 momentarily, material before the journey to Jerusalem narrative can be labeled "Jesus' ministry in Galilee" (4:14-16, 31; 5:1; 7:1, 11; 8:26; 9:10; with episodes in Judea, 4:44; 7:17; Gerasa, 8:26; and Bethsaida, 9:10), and material after his journey narrative can be designated "Jesus in Jerusalem" (19:45; 20:1; 21:37; 22:39; 23:7; 24:13, 18, 33; with an appearance in Bethany, 24:50). Now to return to Luke 1:1–4:13, we note that, although the geographic settings in this section vary, the scene inevitably returns to Jerusalem (1:8-9, 39; 2:22, 41; 4:9), which forms an inclusion with the last section (Luke 19:45–24:53).

In Acts the geographic movement follows, with some qualification, the outline conveyed by Acts 1:8, where Jesus commands his disciples to be his witnesses "in Jerusalem, in all Judea and Samaria, and to the ends of the earth." In Acts 1:12–8:3 the setting is Jerusalem, which then changes successively to Samaria (8:4-25), the coastal plain region (8:26-40; 9:32–11:1), Antioch (11:19-29; 13:1-3; 14:26-28; 15:30-35), Paul's first missionary journey from Antioch (13:4–14:25), Jerusalem (15:4-29), two journeys in the Aegean Sea region (15:36–19:20), and journeys to Jerusalem and Rome (19:21–28:31). As a result, Acts 1:6–8:3 can be seen as ministry in Jerusalem and Judea, 8:4–11:18 in Samaria (and coastal region), and 11:19–28:31 in the "end of the earth," or the Gentile world.

It has been shown in Luke's gospel how Jerusalem is a key setting to which much of the narrative returns. Thus we have the birth of John and visits of Jesus with his family to Jerusalem (1:5-25, 39-80; 2:22-38, 41-50; 4:9-13), Jesus' journey to Jerusalem (9:51–19:44), and Jesus in Jerusalem (19:45–24:49).

In Acts, Jerusalem becomes the focal point to which the mission returns and from which it rebounds farther and farther outward (1:12–8:3; 9:1-2, 26-29; 11:2-18; 11:30–12:25; 15:1-29; 21:17–23:21). Although Antioch appears to be the base of operation for many of Paul's missionary journeys (13:1-3; 14:26-28; 15:30-35; 18:22), it is not mentioned after Paul's third jour-

---

graphical Horizon," in *The Book of Acts in Its Graeco-Roman Setting* (ed. D. W. J. Gill and C. Gempf; Grand Rapids: Eerdmans, 1994), 483-544; M. C. Parsons, *The Place of Jerusalem on the Lukan Landscape: An Exercise in Symbolic Cartography* (Macon, Ga.: Mercer University Press, 1998); and D. P. Bechard, "The Theological Significance of Judea in Luke-Acts," in *The Unity of Luke-Acts* (ed. J. Verheyden; Leuven: Leuven University Press, 1999), 675-91.

CHART 5.1. GEOGRAPHIC EXPANSION IN ACTS

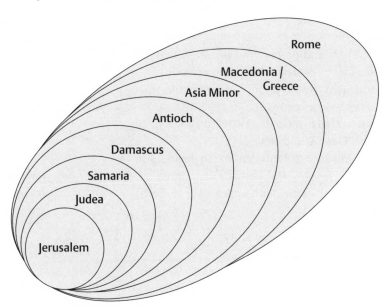

ney and gives way to the journeys to Jerusalem and Rome. Antioch appears to serve as a beachhead of operation for Paul's Gentile mission; however, the entire movement of the narrative is based on contact with Jerusalem, as if the holy city served as the common axis for a series of outward-expanding ellipses. (See chart 5.1 above.) Contacts with Jerusalem give the narrative impetus to go further out into the Gentile world.

Recommended Outlines of Luke and Acts

Noting the above discussion on the geography of Luke-Acts, outline 5.1 is recommended:[32]

32. The following works tend to support the outlines listed here: J. Dupont, *The Salvation of the Gentiles: Studies in the Acts of the Apostles* (trans. J. Keating, from 1967 French ed.; New York: Paulist Press, 1979), 11-33; Fitzmyer, *Luke,* 1:134-42; W. G. Kümmel, *Introduction to the NT* (trans. H. C. Kee; rev. ed.; Nashville: Abingdon, 1975), 125-28 (Luke), 154-56 (Acts); J. C. O'Neill, *The Theology of Acts in Its Historical Setting* (2d ed.; London: SPCK, 1970), 66-67; and Talbert, *Reading Luke,* vii-viii.

OUTLINE 5.1. LUKE-ACTS

The Gospel of Luke

Prologue	1:1-4
1. Prehistory and preparation for the activity of Jesus (focus on Jerusalem, with episodes in Bethlehem, Nazareth, Jordan riverbank, and Judean wilderness)	1:5–4:13
2. Jesus' activity in Galilee (with episodes in Judea, Gerasa, and Bethsaida)	4:14–9:50
3. Jesus en route to Jerusalem (with episodes in Samaria, Jericho, and Bethany)	9:51–19:44
4. Jesus in Jerusalem (with appearance in Bethany)	19:45–24:53

The Acts of the Apostles

Prologue and ascension story	1:1-11
1. Christianity in Jerusalem	1:12–8:3
2. Christianity in Samaria and the coastal plain region (with episodes in Damascus and Jerusalem, and concluding with the conversion of Cornelius)	8:4–11:18
3. Christianity in Antioch and Asia Minor (concludes with the Jerusalem Council)	11:19–15:35
4. Christianity in the Aegean Sea region (includes travel through Asia Minor and stops at Caesarea and Antioch)	15:36–19:20
5. Christianity en route to Rome via Jerusalem (the journey begins in the Aegean Sea region and returns to Palestine's coastal region and Jerusalem; from Jerusalem and Caesarea it goes out to the Mediterranean islands of Cyprus, Crete, Malta, and Sicily and then reaches Rome)	19:21–28:31

Alternative Outlines of Acts

Alternative outlines to the fivefold division that we have provided for Acts are the sixfold and twofold divisions indicated below. The sixfold division (outline 5.2) is based on the six progress-report summaries mentioned above (Acts 6:7; 9:31; 12:24; 16:5; 19:20; 28:31) that conclude each major section.[33]

OUTLINE 5.2. ACTS (SIXFOLD DIVISION: PERIODS)

1. Centering on the Jerusalem church and the preaching
   of Peter   1:1–6:7
2. Marking the extension of the church in Palestine, the
   preaching of Stephen, and conflict with the Jewish
   authorities   6:8–9:31
3. The extension of the church to Antioch, the conversion
   of a Roman officer, and further conflict with the Jewish
   authorities   9:32–12:24
4. The extension of the church to Asia Minor   12:25–16:5
5. The extension of the church to Europe, centering on
   Paul's work in Corinth and Ephesus   16:6–19:20
6. The extension of the church to Rome, centering on
   Paul's captivities   19:21–28:31

Although the above outline has been followed by many students of Luke-Acts, it ignores other significant summaries in the work (e.g., 2:41; 4:4, 32-35; 5:14; 11:21, 24). The summaries used in the outline 5.2 also do not display a regularity of form, as is found in Matthew's stereotyped phrases that conclude his blocks of teaching narrative (Matt 7:28; 11:1; 13:53; 19:1; 26:1).

A twofold division,[34] which has at least three versions (see outline 5.3), interprets Acts 1:8 as a programmatic statement of the Christian witness to Palestine and beyond.

---

33. C. H. Turner, "Chronology of the NT," *DB(H)* 1:421-22; further developed by D. Gooding, *True to the Faith* (London: Hodder & Stoughton, 1990).

34. See G. Krodel, *Acts* (Philadelphia: Fortress, 1981), 8-10; for additional suggestions, illustrating how difficult it is to find consensus on this matter, see I. H. Marshall, *The Book of Acts: An Introduction and Commentary* (Grand Rapids: Eerdmans, 1980), 51-54; L. T. Johnson, *The Acts of the Apostles* (Collegeville, Minn.: Liturgical Press, 1992); Marshall, *The Acts of the Apostles*, 29; and B. R. Gaventa, *Acts* (Nashville: Abingdon, 2003), 54-56.

Outline 5.3. Acts (Twofold Divisions: Place of Witness)

Version 1

1. Jerusalem and Palestine	1–11
2. Antioch to Rome	12–28

Version 2 (agrees with the fivefold division in outline 5.1)

1. Christian witness in Palestine and Asia Minor up to the Jerusalem Council	1:1–15:35
2. Christian witness in the Aegean Sea region and onward to Rome via Jerusalem	15:36–28:31

Version 3 (highlights the Cornelius narrative, with the Jerusalem Council as transitional)

Introduction	1
1. Witness in Jerusalem, Judea, and Samaria	2:1–9:43
2. Witness to the end of the earth: to Gentiles (10:1–19:20), to Christians (19:21–21:14), and to Jerusalem, Caesarea, and Rome (21:15–28:28)	10:1–28:28
Epilogue	28:30-31

Summary

In this first section of study on Luke-Acts, we examined Luke's redaction of his sources, his literary and stylistic features, and the structural arrangement of his two-volume work. In our discussion of Luke's sources, we treated the gospel and Acts separately. In the gospel, Luke makes use of Mark, Q, and his own special material (L). Luke extends Mark's narrative with biographical (Luke 1–2) and apologetic material (Luke 23–24). Luke also omits (Mark 6:45–8:26) and inserts (Luke 6:20–8:3; 9:51–18:14) sizable portions of material. His use of Q appears to have undergone fewer modifications than we find in Matthew. Three possible sources used for Acts are (1) a diary of Paul's travels, (2) traditions about Paul's conversion and early ministry, and (3) material on Peter and the Jerusalem church. The traditional material in Acts is so dominated by the author's vocabulary and style, however, that it is difficult to determine their nature and extent.

The literary and stylistic features that we examined included written discourse, the principle of balance, repetition and extended treatment, an-

ticipation, summary statements, a fulfillment motif, litotes, double entendre, irony, and satire. In addition to speeches (both kerygmatic and apologetic), other forms of direct address used by the author are prayers,
visions, dreams, hymns, and letters. Both Jesus' journey to Jerusalem (Luke
9:51–19:44) and Paul's journeys to Jerusalem and Rome (Acts 19:21–28:31)
are important types of indirect discourse employed in Luke-Acts.

After discussing the importance of geographic movement in Luke-
Acts and possible alternative outlines, we recommended structural arrangements that highlight the following: (1) Jesus' activity in Galilee and
his journey to Jerusalem in the gospel and, in Acts, (2) the progression
from Jerusalem and Judea to Samaria, the coastal regions, and the Gentile
regions.

CHAPTER 6

Key Themes of Luke-Acts

Imagine being part of a growing worldwide religious movement. You are becoming visible in the large urban centers of the world and are attracting devotees of all races from both upper and lower classes. You represent the third generation of adherents and are facing both external conflict and internal tension. The older established religions of the day mock your past as illegitimate. You are encountering some conflict with the state. These external conflicts have influenced and compounded your internal tension. As third-generation adherents with many new converts from different races and classes, you are experiencing an identity crisis. Who are we? How did our movement begin? Have we progressed or deviated from our founding fathers? Where do we go from here? These may have been some of the issues that Luke was addressing when he wrote his two-volume work. We may detect similar issues as we study the thematic concerns of Luke-Acts.

In this chapter we first discuss Luke's concept of history, then look at several themes that occupy Luke's attention. This chapter presupposes the discussion in chapter 5 on Luke's use of his sources, his literary and stylistic techniques, and the structural arrangement of Luke-Acts.

The Lukan Scheme of Salvation History

We have seen that Luke-Acts shares noteworthy characteristics with ancient history writing, containing more of what we know as historiography than any other NT book. Luke's concept of salvation history is closely related to the themes of fulfillment of Scripture and divine necessity, which were discussed in chapter 5 (see pp. 118-19). These themes connect Luke's salvation history with the utterances of prophets and the activity of God among his people, both of which are characteristics of Israelite, Jewish history.

Luke's scheme of salvation history may include four stages:[1] (1) John, the one who prepares the way; (2) Jesus, the Lord who has come; (3) the Twelve, Paul, and others, who embody the way of Jesus; and (4) the Gentile church of the postapostolic period, symbolized by the Ephesian elders (Acts 20), who are to embody the way of Jesus as perpetuated by the apostles. (See chart 6.1.)

CHART 6.1. LUKE: FOUR STAGES OF SALVATION HISTORY

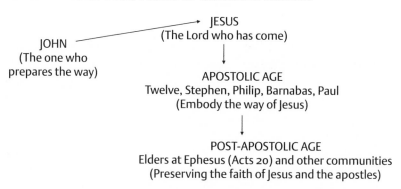

John the baptizer and the circles from which he comes symbolize the faithful of Israel. John's appearance fulfills prophecy (Luke 1–2), but his role is subordinate to that of Jesus. Jesus, whose appearance also fulfills prophecy, brings God's salvation, for which John prepares the way. Jesus also serves as the master to his pupils who succeed him (the Twelve, Paul, and others). Just as the Twelve and Paul are successors of Jesus, so the elders of the mixed, Jew-Gentile communities (symbolized by the Ephesian elders in Acts 20) are the successors of the apostles. For this church of the postapostolic period, the apostles provide the authentic examples of how to embody the way of Jesus.

1. Adapted from C. H. Talbert, *Literary Patterns, Theological Themes, and the Genre of Luke-Acts* (Missoula, Mont.: Society of Biblical Literature, 1974), 106. L. T. Johnson argues for a two-stage pattern: (1) Luke's Gospel describes Jesus' first offering to Israel, and (2) Acts tells of his second, post-resurrection, offering to the world; see *The Gospel of Luke* (Collegeville, Minn.: Liturgical Press, 1991), 15-21.

The Major Lukan Themes

We look here at seven major themes in Luke-Acts: (1) salvation to the Gentiles; (2) progression of the gospel; (3) the Holy Spirit; (4) prayer; (5) wealth, poverty, and the marginalized; (6) Christianity as the true Israel; and (7) fair treatment under Rome. These themes also provide some information on Luke's views of Christ, salvation, Christian piety, church community, and the Jewish law, and they offer some clues on the type of audience Luke is addressing.

Salvation to the Gentiles

How did Christianity ever become a Gentile religion separate from Judaism? It was originally a Jewish religion founded by a Jew who never left Israel, with Jewish followers who preached from a Jewish Bible. How did Christianity with its Jewish origins become a Gentile religion whose adherents, of different races and nationalities, can be found all over the Mediterranean world? In writing Luke-Acts as he did, the author appears to answer the above questions concerning the development of Christianity from a Jewish sect into a worldwide Gentile movement. He attempts to show how this development took place and why it was in accordance with the plan of God. In Luke-Acts we find a number of ideas expressing Luke's universalistic concerns, such as salvation for the Gentiles, light to the nations, and salvation for everyone.[2] These universalistic concepts indicate

---

2. For further studies, see J. Dupont, *The Salvation of the Gentiles: Studies in the Acts of the Apostles* (trans. J. Keating, from 1967 French ed.; New York: Paulist Press, 1979), 11-33; J. A. Fitzmyer, *The Gospel according to Luke* (2 vols.; AB 28-28A; Garden City, N.Y.: Doubleday, 1981-85), 1:187-92; J. Jervell, *Luke and the People of God* (Minneapolis: Augsburg, 1972), 41-74; S. G. Wilson, *The Gentiles and the Gentile Mission in Luke-Acts* (Cambridge: Cambridge University Press, 1973) (critique of Jervell); M. Kiddle, "The Admission of the Gentiles in St. Luke's Gospel and Acts," *JTS* 36 (1935): 160-73; I. H. Marshall, *Luke: Historian and Theologian* (Grand Rapids: Zondervan, 1970), 77-144; R. F. O'Toole, *The Unity of Luke's Theology: An Analysis of Luke-Acts* (Wilmington, Del.: Michael Glazier, 1984); D. Ravens, *Luke and the Restoration of Israel* (Sheffield: Sheffield Academic Press, 1995); D. Seccombe, "The New People of God," in *Witness to the Gospel: The Theology of Acts* (ed. I. H. Marshall and D. Peterson; Grand Rapids: Eerdmans, 1998), 349-72; R. Wall, "Israel and the Gentile Mission in Acts and Paul: A Canonical Approach," in *Witness to the Gospel,* 437-58; C. W. Stenschke, *Luke's Portrait of Gentiles prior to Their Coming to Faith* (Tübingen: Mohr

Luke's concern to present a Christianity that is not limited to a particular race or nation.

Christ's Arrival Universal salvation is clearly mentioned in Luke 2:32 / Isa 49:6 and Luke 3:6 / Isa 40:5 with the coming of Jesus as savior of the world. These texts are derived from passages in Second Isaiah that speak of Israel as a light to the nations. In Luke-Acts Jesus fulfills Israel's role as a bringer of salvation to the nations. These same Second Isaiah passages are later alluded to in the ministry of Paul (Acts 13:47 / Isa 49:6; Acts 28:28 / Isa 40:5), indicating that Christ's mission is carried out by his appointed followers.

Announced by Christ A mission to the Gentiles is also previewed in the opening sermon of Jesus before the commencement of his ministry (Luke 4:25-27). The passage refers to God's favor bestowed on outsiders. At the end of the gospel and the beginning of Acts, the resurrected Christ commands his disciples to preach salvation to the nations (Luke 24:47; Acts 1:8). In Luke-Acts "forgiveness of sins" and "salvation" appear to be synonymous concepts (e.g., Luke 1:77; Acts 5:31; 13:26, 38), and the phrase "to the ends of the earth" seems to indicate passage into the Gentile world (Acts 1:8; 13:47 / Isa 49:6). The *Psalms of Solomon,* a Pharisaic document written about 50 B.C., uses the same phrase — "the ends [Gk. *eschata*] of the earth" (8:15) — applying it to Rome. The Lukan Jesus also displays considerable concern for "the outsider," marginalized members of society, who are unexpectedly, even shockingly, included within God's kingdom, while "the righteous" find themselves excluded (Luke 2:8-12; 3:8-9; 7:1-10, 36-50; 8:2-3; 10:25-37; 13:22-30; 14:12-14, 15-24; 15; 17:11-19). Both the gospel and Acts make it clear that the boundaries of the kingdom will be much wider and more fluid than many Israelites had anticipated.

Pentecost The account of the Spirit's descent at Pentecost includes several universalistic allusions. The pilgrims in Jerusalem during the Feast of Pentecost who witness the event are from nations throughout the Mediterranean world (Acts 2:5-11). Representing a single ethnicity, they are Diaspora Jews, and their international composition offers a preview of things to come. In Peter's sermon on Pentecost, it is stated that "whoever calls on the

---

Siebeck, 1999); and C. B. Puskas, *The Conclusion of Luke-Acts: The Function and Significance of Acts 28:16-31* (Eugene, Ore.: Cascade Books, 2008).

name of the Lord shall be saved" (Acts 2:21 / Joel 2:32), and "the promise is to you and to your children and *to all that are far off, everyone* whom the Lord our God calls" (Acts 2:39). The international audience at Pentecost, the open invitations for "all" or "whoever" calls upon the Lord, and the possible reference to the Gentiles ("all that are far off") as recipients of God's promises are all universalistic allusions.

Paul's Conversion/Call   The first and subsequent narratives of Paul's conversion/call include references to a Gentile mission. Acts 9:15 states that Saul of Tarsus (Paul) is to carry the name of Jesus "before Gentiles and kings." This Gentile mission is also reiterated more explicitly in the other narratives of Paul's conversion/call (22:15; 26:17, 23).

Cornelius's Conversion   The long narrative of Peter and the Roman centurion Cornelius (Acts 10:1–11:18) prefigures the Gentile mission to be carried out by Paul. The conversion of Cornelius is regarded as an outpouring of the Holy Spirit on the Gentiles (10:44-45). Cornelius's reception of the Holy Spirit (cf. Acts 2) is associated with receiving the word of God (11:1) and being granted "repentance that leads to life" (11:18), all of which appear to be terminology of salvation in Luke-Acts. At the Jerusalem Council in Acts 15, Peter refers to the Cornelius episode in stating that "I should be the one through whom the Gentiles would hear the message of the good news and become believers" (15:7). At this conference, James endorses Peter's position by stating, "Simeon [Peter] has related how God first looked favorably on the Gentiles, to take from among them a people for his name" (v. 14).

Paul's Mission   In the mission of Paul, which precedes and follows the Jerusalem Council, the worldwide mission to the Gentiles becomes a major focus. After the Jews of Pisidian Antioch reject the gospel in Acts 13:45-47, Paul turns to the Gentiles in fulfillment of prophecy (Isa 49:6), which was introduced earlier with the arrival of the infant Jesus (Luke 2:32). Similar statements about the mission to the Gentiles are ascribed to Paul at Corinth (18:6) and Rome (28:28). Mention is also made of Paul's going to the Gentiles at Ephesus (19:9-10). As stated earlier, the second and third reports of Paul's conversion/call refer to his mission to the Gentiles (22:15; 26:17, 23).

Luke's Possible Intention   In presenting this theme of Gentile mission, Luke may have intended to show that the extension of God's salvation to the nations was the plan of God. It was the fulfillment of prophecy (Isa 40:5; 49:6), initiated by the appearance of Jesus (Luke 2:32; 3:6), previewed throughout Jesus' ministry (Luke 7:1-10; 14:15-24), commanded by the resurrected Christ (Luke 24:47; Acts 1:8), and to be carried out by his apostles (Acts 11:1; 15:7, 14) and appointed witnesses (9:15; 26:17, 23). The Gentile mission was therefore the plan of God, legitimized by Christ and his earliest followers. Christianity as a Gentile movement, which may have been the situation of Luke's day, was therefore a phenomenon intended by God. Although the salvation of individual Jews always remains a possibility for Luke (Acts 2:41, 44; 6:7; 15:5; 21:20; 24:14), the Jews as a nation have become hardened to the gospel (Acts 13:45; 14:1-2, 4-5; 17:4-5; 18:6; 19:9; 28:24-25); therefore the focus in the second half of Acts is on the movement of Christianity into the Gentile world (Acts 13:47; 18:6; 28:28).

Luke's portrait of the origin and development of Gentile Christianity may have been in reaction to accusations by Jews and Jewish Christians that Gentile Christians had no grounds for receiving the promises of God in the Law and the Prophets. Such accusations may help explain why the Spirit's initial outpouring among believing outsiders such as the Samaritans (8:14-17), Saul the persecutor (9:15-18), and the Gentiles (10:44-48) is delayed, separated from the moment of conversion, pending a personal visit and the laying on of hands by a leader from the Jewish church, preferably one of the apostles. Representatives of Jewish Christianity must be eyewitnesses to God's reception of their former enemies on equal terms.

Luke's presentation of the Gentile mission may have also been an attempt to inform his readers of the origins and heritage of their church. Perhaps the readers of Luke were undergoing an identity crisis and needed to know about their roots as a people.

The Progression of the Gospel

A devout Lutheran preacher and theologian of the eighteenth century, J. Albrecht Bengel, summarized the contents of the Acts of the Apostles as recounting "the victory of the gospel extending from one meeting, to temples, houses, streets, marketplaces, plains, inns, prisons, camps, palaces, chariots, ships, villages, cities and islands: to Jews, Gentiles, governors, generals, soldiers, eunuchs, captives, slaves, women, boys, sailors; to the

Areopagus in Athens, and eventually to Rome."[3] Is there support for Bengel's statement? In Luke-Acts considerable attention is given to the proclamation of the gospel.[4] Many of Luke's reports of preaching occur in brief narrative summaries that introduce (Luke 8:1; 20:1; Acts 8:4) or conclude (Luke 4:43-44; Acts 4:31; 15:35; 28:31) a story or speech.

This theme of gospel proclamation is developed in six ways. First, numerous witnessing terminologies are employed, especially "preach the gospel" (Gk. *euangelizomai*), "proclaim" (Gk. *kērussō*), "teach," and "testify."

Second, the objects of this diverse witnessing terminology are both Jesus Christ (e.g., Acts 5:42; 8:12; 18:5) and the kingdom of God (e.g., Luke 4:43; 8:1; 9:2, 11; Acts 19:8; 20:25). There is a progressive development from the good news of Luke's gospel to the good news of the book of Acts. Whereas the earthly Jesus announced the coming of God's kingdom, the church clarifies that the kingdom has now arrived with Jesus' resurrection (Acts 8:12; 28:23, 31).

Third, these accounts of preaching the gospel generally presuppose the contents of the evangelistic speeches in Acts (2:14-36; 3:11-26; 4:8-12; 10:34-43; 13:16-41). In these speeches we learn what Luke means by preaching Jesus, proving from Scripture that Jesus is the Christ, and proclaiming the kingdom of God.

Fourth, despite the diverse terminology and topics, a common message of the preaching summaries is conveyed: in the divinely willed events of Christ's life, death, and resurrection, God's reign has dawned for the salvation of both Jew and Gentile, and this message is to be proclaimed to all nations.

Fifth, most of the preaching accounts are narrated summaries that give a generalization or idealization of an adjacent scene or story (e.g., Luke 9:6; 13:22; Acts 5:42; 8:25; 19:8-10; 28:30-31). These summaries often in-

---

3. J. A. Bengel, *NT Word Studies* (trans. C. T. Lewis and M. R. Vincent from *Gnomon Novi Testamenti,* 1864 ed.; repr., 2 vols., Grand Rapids: Kregel Publications, 1971), 1:740.

4. See Fitzmyer, *Luke,* 1:145-64; E. Haenchen, *The Acts of the Apostles* (trans. R. M. Wilson; Oxford: Blackwell, 1971), 49; O'Toole, *Unity,* 75-79, 86-94; W. C. Van Unnik, "The 'Book of Acts' the Confirmation of the Gospel," *NovT* 4 (1960): 26-59; N. A. Dahl, *Jesus in the Memory of the Church* (Minneapolis: Augsburg, 1976), 87-98 (critique of Van Unnik); H. C. Kee, *Good News to the Ends of the Earth: The Theology of Acts* (Philadelphia: Trinity Press International, 1990); R. L. Gallagher and P. Hertig, eds., *Mission in Acts: Ancient Narratives in Contemporary Context* (Maryknoll, N.Y.: Orbis Books, 2004); and Puskas, *The Conclusion of Luke-Acts,* ch. 4.

troduce (e.g., Luke 8:1; 20:1; Acts 8:4) or conclude (Luke 4:43-44; 9:6; Acts 4:31; 15:35; 28:31) a narrative scene. Some also connect or divide the narrative (Acts 6:7; 9:31; 12:24; 16:5; 19:20; 28:30-31).[5]

Sixth, most of these preaching summaries give the narrative a continuity and forward movement. There is a progression of proclamation and a continuity of witness, begun by Jesus (Luke 4:43-44; 8:1; 20:1), continued by his disciples (Luke 9:6; 10:8-11), carried on by the early church (Acts 5:42; 8:12), and brought to a culmination by Paul (9:27-29; 15:35; 17:2-3; 18:5; 19:8; 28:23, 30-31). The message of God's reign in the deeds of Jesus is taught and proclaimed in Galilee and Judea (Luke 4:31, 44), Jerusalem (Luke 19:47–20:1; Acts 5:42; 9:26, 29), Samaria (Acts 8:4-5, 25), the coastal regions (8:40), Antioch (15:35), Asia Minor (13:49; 14:1; 19:8, 10), Greece (17:2-3; 18:5, 11), and Rome (28:23, 30-31). This survey thus offers clear support to Bengel's comments about the victorious progression of the gospel.

The Holy Spirit

The Acts of the Apostles has been renamed by some scholars as the Acts of the Holy Spirit because the activity of the Spirit permeates the book.[6] Mention of the Holy Spirit also occurs frequently in Luke's gospel: seventeen references in Luke, compared with twelve in Matthew and six in Mark. Unlike in Matthew and Mark, however, where the Spirit empowers Jesus for his ministry, only five of Luke's references concern the Spirit's work in Jesus (3:22; 4:1, 14, 18; 10:21). Previewing things to come in the book of Acts, the Spirit in Luke's gospel principally empowers others for their witness to Jesus' messiahship (1:15, 17, 35, 41, 67; 2:25-27; 11:13[?]; 12:12).

The activities of the Spirit are numerous in Luke-Acts. Jewish and Christian prophets prophesy by the Spirit (e.g., Luke 1:67; Acts 1:16; 11:28). The Spirit speaks to individuals (e.g., Acts 8:29; 10:19) and through the prophets (e.g., Acts 28:25). Specific activities of the Spirit are to teach (Luke 12:12), appoint (Acts 13:2; 20:28), forbid (16:6-7), and help in decision

---

5. See our sixfold division of Luke-Acts in "Alternative Outlines of Acts" in ch. 5. See also H. J. Cadbury, "The Summaries in Acts," *BC* 5:392-401.

6. J. D. G. Dunn, *Baptism in the Holy Spirit* (London: SCM Press, 1970); Dupont, *Salvation of the Gentiles*, 35-59; J. H. E. Hull, *The Holy Spirit in the Acts of the Apostles* (Cleveland: World, 1968); K. Lake, "The Holy Spirit," *BC* 5:96-111, and "The Gift of the Spirit on Pentecost," *BC* 5:111-21; O'Toole, *Unity*, 28-30.

making (15:28). The Spirit can also be blasphemed (Luke 12:10), lied against (Acts 5:3-9), and opposed (7:51), all of which are serious offenses, since the Spirit is a divine representative of the risen Christ (5:9; 16:7).

Function of the Spirit The basic functions of the Spirit in Luke-Acts are to bear witness to God's activity, empowering the church for its ministry.[7] The function of bearing witness to God's activity overlaps with other operations, since bearing witness often coincides with proclaiming the gospel (Acts 1:8), which is the major task of the church. The Spirit's activity of bearing witness to God's work is evident in passages where individuals prophesy by the Spirit: for example, Zechariah (Luke 1:67), Simeon (2:27-32), Agabus, and others (Acts 11:28; 21:4, 8-11). Empowerment for ministry is seen at the baptism of Jesus (Luke 3:22) and the parallel baptism of the church in Acts (2:1-4; see also 10:44-47; 19:4-6). The assistance of the Holy Spirit in the work of the church concerns diverse activities: proclaiming the gospel (Acts 4:31; cf. 2:1-4, 14-36), prophesying (19:6), appointing of missionaries (13:2, 4) and elders (20:28), assisting in the church's decision-making process (15:28), and guiding it in its missionary endeavors (16:6-7; 20:23). The unity between these activities and the original intentions of Jesus are underscored when the Holy Spirit is also identified as "the Spirit of Jesus" (Acts 16:6-7).

The Indwelling Spirit The Spirit is imparted to many individuals in the infancy narrative of Luke (1:41, 67; 2:25, 27), all of whom then speak some word of "prophecy" about God's impending work of salvation. Only Jesus possesses the Spirit during his ministry (Luke 3:22; 4:1, 14, 18; 10:21). In Acts Jesus fulfills his prior promise to share the Holy Spirit with the disciples (Luke 11:13; 12:12), beginning on the day of Pentecost (Acts 1:8; 2:32-33). Church communities and individual Christians share in the gift of the Spirit as they are "baptized with" (Acts 1:5; 11:16) or "receive" (10:47) the Spirit "poured out" upon them (2:17-18; 10:45). This flexible vocabulary designates the initial reception of the Spirit by all those who confess their faith in the resurrected Jesus. This Spirit baptism is a gift (Luke 11:13; Acts

---

7. R. Stronstad, *The Charismatic Theology of St. Luke* (Peabody, Mass.: Hendrickson, 1984); R. P. Menzies, *The Development of Early Christian Pneumatology, with Special References to Luke-Acts* (Sheffield: Sheffield Academic Press, 1991), and *Empowered for Witness: The Spirit in Luke-Acts* (Sheffield: Sheffield Academic Press, 1994); J. M. Penney, *The Missionary Emphasis of Lukan Pneumatology* (Sheffield: Sheffield Academic Press, 1997).

2:38; 8:19-20; 10:45; 11:16-17) foreseen by John the Baptist (Luke 3:16) and promised by the Father (Luke 24:49; Acts 2:33).

Being "filled" with the Spirit, in contrast, is a repeatable experience that signifies an empowerment for a specific moment of ministry and proclamation. "Even before his birth," John the Baptist will be "filled with the Holy Spirit" (Luke 1:15). Jesus launches his ministry only after he is "full of the Holy Spirit" (4:1). At Pentecost all of the apostles were "filled with the Holy Spirit and began to speak in other languages" (Acts 2:4). Peter is then filled twice more as the need arises (4:8, 31). Similarly, Paul is filled with the Spirit on three separate occasions (9:17; 13:9, 52).

Relation to Other Lukan Themes The activity of the Holy Spirit is associated with many key themes in Luke-Acts, including fulfillment of prophecy (Luke 1:67-71; 2:27-29; Acts 2:16-21; 28:25-27), the Gentile mission (Acts 1:8; 10:44-47; 11:15-18; 15:7-9; 28:25-28), and the proclamation of the gospel (Acts 4:31; cf. 2:1-4, 14-36). Through the Holy Spirit the risen Christ acts on behalf of the church (Luke 3:16; 24:49, with Acts 1:5, 8; 2:33).

Prayer

Luke's gospel also has more to say about prayer than either Mark or Matthew. Luke develops this theme through (1) his retention (9:16; 19:46; 20:47; 22:19) or expansion (22:40-42) of Mark's tradition, (2) editorial insertions into Markan material (3:21; 5:16; 6:12; 9:18, 28-29; 22:32, 44; 23:34, 46), and (3) the use of additional sources, whether Q or L (1:10; 10:21-24; 11:1-4, 5-8, 9-13; 18:1-8, 9-14; 24:30). Naturally, the story of apostolic mission and church expansion in Acts also contains numerous references to prayer (1:14; 2:42; 4:24-31; 6:4, 6; 7:59-60; 8:14-17, 22-24; 9:11; 10:2, 9, 30; 11:5; 12:5, 12; 13:3; 14:23; 16:13, 25; 20:36; 21:5; 22:17; 26:29).

Luke-Acts emphasizes several distinctive features in its theology of prayer.[8] First, Jesus is presented as the ideal man of prayer; the one who perfectly models and teaches what it means to be intimate with and to obey the

---

8. D. Crump, *Jesus the Intercessor: Prayer and Christology in Luke-Acts* (Tübingen: Mohr Siebeck, 1992; Grand Rapids: Baker, 1999) and *Knocking on Heaven's Door: A NT Theology of Petitionary Prayer* (Grand Rapids: Baker, 2006); J. Green, *The Theology of the Gospel of Luke* (Cambridge: Cambridge University Press, 1995), 58-60; R. J. Karris, *Prayer and the NT: Jesus and His Communities at Worship* (New York: Crossroad, 2000), 40-81.

Father (Luke 3:21-22; 4:42; 5:16; 11:1-4; 22:31-32, 39-46). Second, the direction and success of Jesus' ministry is due in large part to his own prayerfulness. He learns how to proceed in God's will as he prays, experiencing the divine fatherhood and exploring his own sonship (3:21-22; 5:16; 6:12-16; 10:21-22). Third, Jesus' intercessory prayers are essential to the disciples' understanding of Christ's true identity; Jesus' petitions overcome his followers' spiritual blindness (9:18-22, 28-36; 10:21-22). Fourth, Jesus prays for his people, not only during his earthly ministry, but also from his heavenly throne; his ongoing prayers secure the disciples against evil and foster spiritual longevity (Acts 7:56-60). Fifth, because the church and its leaders in Acts follow Jesus' model and apply his teaching, they too experience the Spirit's illumination, empowerment, guidance, and preservation. Persistent prayer sensitizes disciples to the ways of God, facilitating their participation in Christ's work in this world (Luke 18:1-8; Acts 1:14; 2:42; 4:23-31; 9:11-12; 10:1-10).

Wealth, Poverty, and the Marginalized

For whatever reason (perhaps Luke's community had a special sensitivity to society's downtrodden?), Luke-Acts preserves the bulk of NT teaching on the proper management of worldly resources and God's affinity for the poor.[9] Luke's gospel retains more stories about Jesus' contacts with women, prostitutes, Samaritans, tax collectors, and other marginalized members of Jewish society than any other gospel.[10] For instance, only Luke informs us that Jesus and his apostles were supported financially by a collection of wealthy women (Luke 8:1-3), a provocative arrangement in Jesus' day.

Not surprisingly, Luke's Jesus highlights an apocalyptic event sometimes called the eschatological reversal — that is, the moment of divine judgment reversing the eternal fortunes of the haves and the have-nots of

---

9. M. Hengel, *Property and Riches in the Early Church: Aspects of a Social History of Early Christianity* (Philadelphia: Fortress, 1974); L. T. Johnson, *Sharing Possessions: Mandate and Symbol of Faith* (Philadelphia: Fortress, 1981); D. P. Seccombe, *Possessions and the Poor in Luke-Acts* (Linz, Austria: A. Fuchs, 1982).

10. J. M. Ford, *My Enemy Is My Guest: Jesus and Violence in Luke* (Maryknoll, N.Y.: Orbis Books, 1984); J. Neyrey, ed., *The Social World of Luke-Acts: Models for Interpretation* (Peabody, Mass.: Hendrickson, 1991), 271-304; B. E. Reid, *Choosing the Better Part? Women in the Gospel of Luke* (Collegeville, Minn.: Liturgical Press, 1996); J. M. Arlandson, *Women, Class, and Society in Early Christianity: Models from Luke-Acts* (Peabody, Mass.: Hendrickson, 1997).

this world.[11] Luke's special material (either L or his unique version of Q) highlights God's eventual elevation of the poor and his dethronement of the rich (1:50-53). Luke's Beatitudes announce not only blessings upon the poor but eternal woes upon the rich (6:20-26). The parables of the rich fool (12:16-21) and the rich man and Lazarus (16:19-31) vividly depict this dramatic reversal when it happens.

Consequently, Jesus repeatedly warns his followers of materialism's inevitable power to corrupt (Luke 8:14; 12:13-15; 16:1-12; 18:25; 21:1). The only effective remedy is extreme generosity and profound humility (3:10-14; 11:41; 12:22-32; 14:7-14; 18:22). Jesus first announces his ministry in terms of the OT Year of Jubilee (4:14-21; see Lev 25:8-54; Isa 61:1-2), the year in which all debts were forgiven, slaves were freed, and property was returned to its original owner. He then requires every would-be disciple to leave everything behind, follow him, and give to the poor (Luke 5:11, 28; 9:61-62; 11:41; 12:33-34; 14:28-33), as is demonstrated by the unexpected generosity of a repentant tax collector named Zacchaeus (19:1-10).

The church in Acts then obediently implements Jesus' instructions. Twice the reader is told that the believers were united in heart and soul and had all things in common (Acts 2:44-45; 4:32). Patterning itself after the organizational model of the ancient synagogue, the Jerusalem church provides daily food rations for its widows (6:1-6). Luke is also at pains to highlight that Cornelius, the first Gentile believer, was highly regarded for his generosity to the poor (10:2, 4, 31).

Faithful Israel

Who are the people of God and the recipients of his divine promises as recorded in the Law and the Prophets?[12] Luke was very concerned with this

11. D. L. Mealand, *Poverty and Expectation in the Gospels* (London: SPCK, 1981).

12. J. Jervell, *Luke and the People of God: A New Look at Luke-Acts* (Minneapolis: Augsburg, 1972), 41-74, and *The Theology of the Acts of the Apostles* (Cambridge: Cambridge University Press, 1996), 18-94; J. B. Tyson, ed., *Luke-Acts and the Jewish People: Eight Critical Perspectives* (Minneapolis: Augsburg, 1988); Green, *The Theology of the Gospel of Luke*, 68-75; D. Ravens, *Luke and the Restoration of Israel* (Sheffield: Sheffield Academic Press, 1995); Seccombe, "The New People of God," 350-72; D. P. Moessner, "Driving to the Crux: Luke's Gospel-Acts and the Story of Israel," in *Jesus and the Heritage of Israel* (Harrisburg, Pa.: Trinity Press International, 1999), 307-57.

question, especially since the Jews of his day claimed exclusive rights to this title and its benefits. It was clear to Luke that in Israel's history the people of God were the faithful Israelites who obeyed the commandments of the Lord (Luke 1:6; 2:25, 36-37). The disobedient Israelites, according to Luke, were part of the Jewish nation but not members of God's people. It was therefore among the faithful of Israel that God's promises would be fulfilled. But who constitutes this people? The Jews of Luke's day claimed to be God's people and denied this status to the Christians, whom they probably regarded as the adherents of a Gentile religion founded by Jewish apostates. Luke, however, provides his own response to the question of who God's people are.

The author of Luke-Acts seeks to show that Jesus and his followers were faithful Israelites and therefore heirs to the promises of God. At the same time, he shows that the Jewish people of his day, while remaining a historical race, do not as a group constitute the faithful Israel. According to the Lukan Jesus and his apostles, since the Jews as a nation rejected the Christian gospel, they become descendants of the disobedient Israelites mentioned by the prophets (Luke 13:31-35; 19:41-44; 21:12-24; Acts 4:27-30; 7:51-53; 28:25-28) and thereby relinquish their claim to the divine promises. Hence in Luke's view the "people of God" is no longer a race or nation but comprises those Jews and Gentiles who believe the gospel. In Luke and Acts, many invitations to repent and believe are extended to the Jewish nation in order to gather the faithful Israelites before turning to the Gentiles (Luke 3:1-18; 4:14-30; 9:1-9; 10:1-17; Acts 13:13-52; 14:1-7; 15:14-18; 17:1-15; 18:1-8; 19:8-10) and pronouncing a judgment on the unbelieving Jews (Luke 7:1-10; 11:37-54; 13:1-9; Acts 13:46; 18:6; 28:25-28).

Let us now look at the Lukan theme of Christianity (see Acts 11:26) as the faithful Israel.[13] According to Luke, Christianity was founded by a faithful Jew (Jesus), carried on by loyal Jews who worshipped in the temple (the Twelve), and spread to the Gentiles (often faithful adherents to the Jewish synagogue) by a dedicated Pharisee, Saul of Tarsus. With this presentation, Luke makes his case for Christians as the people of God and recipients of God's promises. This Jewish portrait in Luke-Acts also conveys

---

13. Acts introduces the term "Christian," meaning "Christ-followers," as originating within the Syrian church at Antioch. By using this term, we do not intend to conjure the historic perception of Christianity and Judaism as mutually exclusive religions. We must remember that the emergent "Christianity" of the book of Acts was a mixed community, embracing both Jews and Gentiles, united by their common belief in Jesus as God's Messiah.

the piety of Jesus and his followers. For Luke and his readers, these examples of piety serve as paradigms to emulate but not precedents for returning to Jewish ritual. Luke makes it clear to his readers that membership in the people of God is determined not by identity with a particular race (i.e., Judaism) but by believing the gospel.

The Faithful Israelite The theme of Christianity as the faithful Israel begins with the portrait of its founder as a faithful Jew. Jesus' birth is shown to fulfill Jewish prophecy (Luke 1:31-33 / 2 Sam 7:12-16 and Isa 7:14; Luke 1:46-55 / 1 Sam 2:1-10). His faithful Jewish parents raise him according to the law of Moses (Luke 2:21-24, 27, 39, 41-43). During his ministry, Jesus preaches in the synagogues on the Sabbath (Luke 4:15-16, 31-33; 6:6; 13:10). Shortly before his death, he daily taught in the temple (Luke 19:47; 20:1; 21:37-38; 22:53). The entire life and work of Jesus are said to fulfill the Jewish Scriptures: both his ministry (Luke 4:18-19 / Isa 61:1-2) and his passion, death, and resurrection (Luke 24:27, 44-47). Luke is also unique in underscoring Jesus' similarities to both Moses and Elijah, emphasizing that his final rejection by Jerusalem's religious leaders fully conforms to ancient Israel's practice of persecuting its own prophets.[14]

The True Faith of Israel Second, Luke presents Christianity as the true faith of Israel. Both the origins and mission of Christianity — its initiation at Pentecost (Acts 2:1-4, 14-21 / Joel 2:28-32) and its mission to the Gentiles (Acts 13:47 / Isa 49:6) — are said to fulfill Jewish prophecy. The apostles are also portrayed as faithful Jews. They regularly attend the temple (3:1; 5:12, 25, 42) and are concerned about keeping the Jewish dietary laws (10:9-16; 15:19-21).

Paul the Loyal Pharisee Third, Luke presents Paul as a loyal Pharisee who regularly attends the synagogue and keeps the Jewish laws and feasts. In his

14. D. P. Moessner, "Luke 9:1-50: Luke's Preview of the Journey of the Prophet like Moses of Deuteronomy," *JBL* 102 (1983): 575-605; "Suffering, Intercession, and Eschatological Atonement: An Uncommon Common View in the Testament of Moses and in Luke-Acts," in *Pseudepigrapha and Early Biblical Interpretation* (Sheffield: JSOT, 1993), 202-27; and "Good News for the 'Wilderness Generation': The Death of the Prophet like Moses according to Luke," in *Good News in History* (Atlanta: Scholars Press, 1993), 1-34; see also R. J. Miller, "Elijah, John, and Jesus in the Gospel of Luke," *NTS* 34 (1988): 611-22; and J. S. Croatto, "Jesus, Prophet like Elijah, and Prophet-Teacher like Moses in Luke-Acts," *JBL* 124 (2005): 451-65.

missionary travels, Paul's regular procedure is to first attend the synagogues (Acts 13:14; 17:1-2; 18:4; 19:8). Paul also circumcises an associate (16:3), takes the Nazirite vow (18:18), and participates in a purification rite at the temple (21:26). In his defense speeches, Paul regards himself as a loyal Pharisee (23:6; 26:5) who obeys the Law and Prophets (24:14; 26:22-23) and stands for the hope of Israel (26:6; 28:20). A leading Pharisee named Gamaliel, a member of the Sanhedrin and (possibly) Paul's mentor, also lends his tacit blessing to the young church when he publicly defends the apostles' freedom to preach the gospel (5:34-40).

On the basis of the above portraits, Luke argues that Christianity fulfills the requirements as the people of God, the faithful Israel. It is therefore heir to the divine promises, which, according to Luke, are forgiveness of sins and the bestowal of the Spirit, both of which are accomplished through the suffering, death, and resurrection of Jesus Christ (Luke 24:49; Acts 1:4; 2:33-39; 13:32-39; 26:6-8; 28:28).

Roman Tolerance

Historical Background The Roman imperial government of Luke's day usually tolerated foreign beliefs and practices in the provinces as long as they were not politically disruptive.[15] In fact, Rome itself was regarded as a place where the superstitions and religions of the Mediterranean world found their center and became popular.[16] Nevertheless, the Roman government was suspicious of two phenomena often connected with religious gatherings: (1) secret meetings, because they could provide opportunities for plotting against the government;[17] and (2) any public gatherings, which could result in social disturbances.[18]

The Roman government also had certain reasons for being suspicious

---

15. F. F. Bruce, *The Acts of the Apostles* (Grand Rapids: Eerdmans, 1951), 30-32; H. J. Cadbury, *The Making of Luke-Acts* (New York: Macmillan, 1927), 308-16; B. S. Easton, *Early Christianity, the Purpose of Acts, and Other Papers* (ed. F. C. Grant; London: SPCK, 1955), 41-57; J. C. O'Neill, *The Theology of Acts in Its Historical Setting* (2d ed.; London: SPCK, 1970), 179-81; O'Toole, *Unity*, 160-66.

16. Tacitus, *Annals* 15.44.

17. *Pliny, Letter to Trajan* 97.

18. E.g., the alleged dispute between Christian missionaries and Jews of Rome in Suetonius, *Claudius* 25; and Acts 18:2.

of the Christian sect. Its founder had been sentenced to death by the Roman prefect Pontius Pilate. Emperor Nero had also inflicted penalties on the Christian sect in Rome for alleged crimes there (A.D. 64-68).[19] Two leaders of this sect, Peter and Paul, were probably executed at that time. And throughout its short history the Christian sect had been associated with the Jews (both in fellowship and in bitter conflict). After A.D. 70, the close of the First Jewish Revolt, Romans were suspicious of any Jewish gatherings, in Palestine or elsewhere. For many decades of the first century, Jews and Christians were indistinguishable to many Roman officials.

How should the Roman government regard Christianity — as a rebellious sect like the Jewish Zealots, or as a harmless religious group engrossed in theological debates with Jews and other inquirers? Luke appears to have addressed such questions in developing his theme of Christianity's fair treatment under Rome.

A Lukan Apology Even before examining the theme, we note features that reveal Luke's concern to win the sympathy of the secular Roman world. In his prefaces (Luke 1:1-4; Acts 1:1-2), the author appears to be addressing a Roman official, "most excellent Theophilus." This title and its function in the prefaces are similar to that in Josephus's *Ag. Ap.* 1.1 and 2.1, where he addresses his patron as "most excellent Epaphroditus." Theophilus may have been a patron to whom the work of Luke-Acts was dedicated, since a much larger audience is envisioned. The title "most excellent" probably indicates that Theophilus was a Roman official and may even have been a Christian (Luke 1:1-4). Luke's chronological notations also reveal his concern to narrate the stories of Jesus and Christianity in the context of secular Roman history (e.g., Luke 2:1-2; 3:1; Acts 11:28; 18:12-27; 24; 25:13-14).

The theme of fair treatment under Rome applies to the situation of both Jesus and Paul in Luke-Acts. In the trial narrative of Luke 23, the author has the Roman prefect of Judea, Pontius Pilate, exonerate Jesus. Although the Jewish leaders accused Jesus of religious apostasy and political sedition, the Roman prefect Pontius Pilate three times declared him inno-

---

19. Sulpicius Severus, *Chronicle* 2.29. Citing examples in Luke-Acts of Roman corruption (Acts 24:26), cruelty (Luke 13:1-3; 21:12-15, 23), or indifference (Acts 24:29), and of Jesus and his followers: the radical prophecies (Luke 1:52-53), teaching (22:25-26, 35-38), radical contacts (Luke 6:15; Acts 1:13), and actions (Acts 4:20-21; 5:29), R. Cassidy questions the idea of a Roman apology in Luke-Acts, in his *Jesus, Politics, and Society* (Maryknoll, N.Y.: Orbis Books, 1978), 20-76, 126-35.

cent of any crime (vv. 4, 14, 22). According to Luke, the influence of the Jewish leaders and the clamor of the city mob incited by them (vv. 1-5, 18-23) compelled Pilate, against his own better judgment, to pass the death sentence on Jesus (vv. 24-25). As Luke saw it, Rome wanted to release Jesus (vv. 15-16, 22) and thus, for Luke, the crucifixion of Jesus is regarded as a miscarriage of Roman justice (vv. 47-48; Acts 3:13-15).[20]

Roman officials are converted to Christianity, and Paul in his journeys receives favorable treatment from Romans. The Roman centurion Cornelius and his household receive the Spirit and are baptized in water under Peter's ministry (Acts 10:1–11:18). The proconsul of Cyprus, Sergius Paulus, favorably responds to the preaching of Paul and Barnabas (13:7-12). On the island of Malta (south of Sicily), Paul enjoyed the hospitality of the chief man of the island, whose father Paul had healed (28:7-10). Even in Luke's gospel, a God-fearing centurion impresses Jesus with his faith (Luke 7:1-10). According to Acts, Paul was a Roman citizen who exercised his right of appeal (Lat. *provocatio*) against punishment by scourging (Acts 16:37-39; 22:24-29) and a possible capital sentence (25:10-12, 21).[21] Paul was born a Roman citizen (22:28), and Luke underscores his privileged status by mentioning that the Roman tribune at Jerusalem had paid a large price for his citizenship.[22]

Favorable Roman treatment is shown to Paul on other occasions. In the scene before Gallio, the Roman proconsul of Achaia, political sedition charges brought against Paul by the Jews of Corinth are dismissed (Acts 18:12-16). The ruling of Gallio appears to establish a precedent that is followed by other Roman officials in the narrative of Acts. In Jerusalem and

---

20. The Lukan theme of Jesus' death as an unjust murder is further developed in C. H. Talbert, *Reading Luke: A Literary and Theological Commentary on the Third Gospel* (New York: Crossroad, 1982), 212-25. For a critique of this view, see R. J. Karris, "Luke 23:47 and the Lucan View of Jesus' Death," *JBL* 105 (1986): 65-74. Further discussion of this theme, with a distinctive interpretation, can be found in J. B. Tyson, *The Death of Jesus in Luke-Acts* (Columbia: University of South Carolina Press, 1986).

21. Under the Valerian (300 B.C.) and Porcian (199-198 B.C.) laws, a Roman citizen had the right of an appeal (Lat. *provocatio*) against both capital sentences and punishment by scourging. Luke's narration of Paul's appeals seems to betray some familiarity with such legislation; see *Leges Porciae and Valeriae* under "Lex, Leges," and "Provocatio," in *Oxford Classical Dictionary*, 601-5, 892-93; H. J. Cadbury, "Roman Law and the Trial of Paul," *BC* 5:312-19; and A. N. Sherwin-White, *Roman Society and Roman Law in the NT* (Oxford: Clarendon Press, 1963), 58-70, 115-19.

22. During the reign of Emperor Claudius, Roman citizenship was purchased by those provincials who could afford it; see Dio Cassius, *History* 60.17.5-6.

Caesarea, Paul is declared innocent of the Jewish allegations of sedition made against him (23:29; 24:22-23; 25:18-19; 26:31-32). The Jewish charges and the Roman declaration of innocence in the trial narrative of Paul (chs. 22–26) are similar to those in the trial narrative of Jesus (Luke 23).

On two occasions Paul is also rescued from death by Romans. First, Romans rescue Paul from a Jewish lynch mob at the outer court of the Jerusalem temple (Acts 21:30-32; cf. 23:10). Second, when Paul as a prisoner journeyed to Rome, his ship was beached at Malta. The soldiers aboard the ship wanted to kill the prisoners to prevent escape, but a Roman centurion, wishing to save Paul, kept them from carrying out this threat (27:42-43).

Even as a prisoner in Rome, Paul was granted special privileges by the Romans. He was permitted to live as a private resident under the custody of a guard (28:16), a privileged situation he also enjoyed in Caesarea (24:23). Finally, in the closing verses of Acts, Paul is pictured as enjoying a considerable degree of liberty. He remained two years in Rome at his own rented lodging, received visitors, and shared the gospel publicly without restriction (28:30-31).

With this theme of Roman tolerance, Luke makes an implicit appeal for Rome to continue its fair treatment toward the new, world-expanding religion. According to Luke, Rome should regard the Christian sect not as a rebel group (21:38-39) but as a harmless religious organization (18:14-15) propagating a teaching that is appealing even to Romans (e.g., Acts 10; 13:7-12). Some have suggested that Luke was arguing that the status of "legal religion" (Lat. *religio licita*) (supposedly) enjoyed by the Jews should be extended to include Christians. This conclusion is doubtful, however, since (1) first-century evidence for such a procedure is lacking, (2) Rome was generally tolerant to most provincial and ethnic religions, and (3) Rome became more suspicious of Judaism as a result of the revolts of A.D. 66 and 132. Luke did intend to show that most of the disturbances connected with early Christianity were caused by the opposition of contentious Jews throughout the Mediterranean world and that the private meetings of early

---

23. Acts 2:43-47; 4:32-37; Pliny, *Letter to Trajan* 97; also see R. MacMullen, *Enemies of the Roman Order: Treason, Unrest, and Alienation in the Roman Order* (Cambridge: Cambridge University Press, 1966). Because Luke's apology for Rome also contains so much religious material, Paul Walasky argues that a defense of Rome is made for the benefit of the church (e.g., Rome has been fair to us) and *not* for a sympathetic Roman official: *"And So We Came to Rome": The Political Perspective of St. Luke* (Cambridge: Cambridge University Press, 1983), 18-22, 59-62.

Christianity should not be viewed as a threat to the Roman government, since they were peaceful and socially constructive religious gatherings.[23]

If Theophilus (Luke 1:3; Acts 1:1) was a Roman official and patron to whom Luke dedicated his two-volume work, we could expect him to be impressed with the treatment that early Christianity received from Rome (in Acts) and to support a continued policy of tolerance toward the new sect. Nevertheless, we should not limit the purpose of Luke-Acts to that of pleasing one particular reader, i.e., Theophilus, whether he is a real person, publisher, or patron (L. Alexander, The Preface to Luke's Gospel [Cambridge: Cambridge University Press, 2000]).

The Authorship, Setting, and Date of Luke-Acts

Jerusalem's Destruction

The Roman destruction of Jerusalem in A.D. 70 is as relevant to dating the composition of Luke's gospel as it is to either Mark or Matthew.[24] In Luke's case, however, even more attention is typically given to his description of events in Luke 21. The majority of modern scholars argue that Luke's version of the story is more specific than Mark's, reflecting his knowledge of details after the fact. For instance, the mention of Jerusalem being encircled by armies (v. 20) and the building of palisades or ramparts around the city (19:43) are thought to be allusions closely coinciding with the accounts of Josephus (War 5.446-526). The statements about Jerusalem being leveled to the ground (Luke 19:44) and people slain by the sword and led away captive (21:24) again coincide with the reports of Josephus (War 6.220-357).

Other scholars, however, following the British scholar C. H. Dodd, share the view that the similarities are exaggerated. In fact, if "any historical event has coloured the picture, it is not Titus's capture of Jerusalem in A.D. 70, but Nebuchadressar's [sic] capture in 586 B.C. There is no single trait of the forecast which cannot be documented directly out of the Old Testament."[25] Furthermore, if Luke's depiction of Jesus as Israel's final prophet reflects an au-

24. See the earlier discussion of this event with respect to dating Mark's gospel in "The Eschatological Theme" in ch. 3.

25. C. H. Dodd, "The Fall of Jerusalem and the 'Abomination of Desolation,'" JRS 37 (1947): 52. It is interesting to note that Dodd dated Luke's gospel as post-70 on other grounds but insisted that the material concerning Jerusalem was decidedly a tradition from before 70.

thentic reminiscence of the historical Jesus, then condemning the city in which he is finally rejected and crucified, using language borrowed from his prophetic predecessors, is precisely what one would expect him to do.

Paul's Death

The conclusion of the book of Acts leaves Paul in the midst of a two-year Roman imprisonment, offering no indication of how his trial or the charges brought against him were finally resolved. This uncertainty has led to a variety of suggestions regarding the setting and date of Luke-Acts, none of them fully satisfactory.

One proposal is that Luke stopped writing because his story had caught up with current events. He did not know the outcome because Paul was still in prison. Some have even argued that Luke wrote Acts, at least in part, to influence the outcome of Paul's trial. This view also requires a very early dating for the book, since Paul's death is typically placed sometime during Nero's persecution (A.D. 64-68). Few scholars, however, are comfortable dating Luke-Acts this early. It is also difficult to explain how Acts 1–12 would have been relevant to Paul's defense.

A few suggest that Luke intended to write a third volume, picking up where Acts 28 leaves off. There is no evidence for this idea, however, and it ignores the obvious balance and symmetry evident between the two volumes as they are.

Third, some wonder if Acts 28:31 is intended to imply that Paul was released after two years and continued preaching elsewhere, as suggested by the pastoral letters 1 Timothy and Titus. In this case, Paul underwent two trials in Rome, was acquitted at the first (recorded in Acts 28), and was condemned at the second (see 2 Tim 4:6-8, 11, 16-18). Unfortunately, Paul's relationship to the Pastoral Letters is contested, leaving this suggestion ultimately to hang upon an argument from silence.

Finally, it is possible that Paul was executed in Rome, but for whatever reason, Luke preferred not to tell this part of the story. Perhaps Luke assumed that his readers were already familiar with the events, or perhaps relating the apostle's death simply did not suit his purposes. Some see hints of Paul's death in his farewell address to the Ephesian elders at Miletus, where he tells them that they will never see him again (Acts 20:25, 38). Similarly, why would Luke have Paul say anything like "there was *no reason for the death penalty* in my case?" (28:18) if he had not already died? Luke makes a similar statement about Jesus presupposing his death: "indeed, he has done nothing to deserve death" (Luke 23:15).

Third-Generation Perspective

Luke appears to be writing as a third-generation Christian. A line of succession from the apostles to their successors, ending with Luke and his community, seems presupposed in several passages. Luke 1:1-4 speaks of: (1) "eyewitnesses" (the apostles), (2) "servants of the word" (Paul and his peers and successors), and (3) "I" and "us" (Luke and his readers). It is uncertain here whether we have two or three generations of Christians as in Heb 2:3 and 2 Pet 3:2. Acts 2:39 speaks of the promises of God extended to (1) "you" (apostles and their contemporaries), (2) "your children," and (3) "all who are far away" (Luke and his readers?), which we can take as specifying three generations. The narrative of Paul addressing the Ephesian elders whom he appointed (Acts 20:17-38) seems to indicate a line of succession from (1) Paul to (2) the Ephesian elders, and ending with (3) Luke and his readers.

A Glorified View of the Past?

Determining the original setting of Luke-Acts also depends on reconstructing the nature of the relationship depicted between Paul's Gentile mission and the Jewish community centered in Jerusalem. In the past, scholars have argued that Luke presents an idealized portrait of Paul's relationship with Jerusalem, nostalgically depicting a harmonious, united church for a later generation. For example, Paul's mission to the Gentiles is sanctioned by Jerusalem's leaders (Acts 15), who soundly reject the opposition raised by former Pharisees (6:7[?]; 15:5, 24), thus presenting a united front in the missionary ventures ahead.

Conversely, other scholars point out that the evidence does not really support this conclusion. Acts portrays the church as a fallible human community, complete with sectarian tensions and unresolved conflict. Paul and Barnabas eventually part company because of their irreconcilable differences (15:36-40). Although the Jerusalem leaders endorse Paul's manner of preaching the gospel, the legalistic faction (and how many of the common people?) that disputes his methods continue their resistance (21:20-24), eventually aggravating the situation that leads to Paul's arrest in Jerusalem (21:27-36). Is Luke idealizing the past for a later generation, or is he describing the roots of a long-standing, unresolved tension within the church?

Date of Composition

We would therefore date Luke-Acts near the time of the destruction of Jerusalem (A.D. 70), yet before its earliest known use, which is by Justin Martyr (140) and Marcion (150). The dating range of A.D. 70-90 is recommended by most scholars. Luke-Acts appears to be characteristic of the time just before the early catholic writing of *1 Clement* (95) and works by Ignatius (115) and Justin Martyr (140). Luke-Acts was also written at a time when Paul's letters were not widely circulated, since the work reveals no direct dependence on or acquaintance with them.[26] The later one date's Luke's work, the more difficult it becomes to explain this lack of familiarity.

The Author

Although we have referred to the author as Luke, we have no definite means of knowing his or her real identity. The most reliable outside witness to Luke the beloved physician and companion of Paul as author is from Irenaeus, *Against Heresies* (A.D. 180).[27] Irenaeus refers to Luke as a "follower of Paul" who "wrote into a book the gospel Paul preached" (3.1.1). From the we-passages (Acts 16:10-17; 20:5-15; 21:1-18; 27:1–28:16) and

---

26. The view that Acts is independent of any detailed knowledge of the content of Paul's epistles is widely acknowledged today; see W. W. Gasque, *A History of the Criticism of the Acts of the Apostles* (Grand Rapids: Eerdmans, 1975), 18. R. I. Perro, however, has done extensive comparisons of Paul's letters and Acts in his *Dating Acts: Between the Evangelists and the Apologists* (Santa Rosa, Calif.: Polebridge Press, 2006), 51-148. He argues for a late date of A.D. 115.

27. Both the Muratorian Fragment and the so-called Anti-Marcionite Prologue to Luke support Irenaeus's claim of Lukan authorship, but the dates of these two works are probably later than the second century A.D. See Bauckham, *Jesus and the Eyewitnesses*, 426-27.

probably references in 2 Tim 4:10-11 and Col 4:14, Irenaeus showed that Luke was "always associated with him [Paul] and inseparable from him" (3.14.1). The argument by Irenaeus, however, contains nothing that could not have already been derived from Luke-Acts itself.

The Place of Composition

In our discussion of Lukan sources in chapter 5, we saw that the author had such detailed information about the localities and provincial designations in the Aegean Sea areas (Acts 16–21) that he either had access to specific information or was personally familiar with that region. Apart from the prelude to Paul's first journey, his work is largely limited to the Aegean Sea region. Acts 16:6-15 also appears to point to the real mission field for Luke: Europe.

Beyond this, estimating the location of Luke-Acts' composition is even more tenuous than estimating its date. Various arguments have been advanced in favor of a number of locations, all of which have their problems.

Some have suggested that Luke-Acts was written from Rome because the narrative ends there (Acts 28:30-31). But Luke betrays no special interest or concern for the church at Rome. In fact, the picture of Paul at Rome is very artificial and betrays a lack of knowledge of Rome and the local church (e.g., cf. Acts 28:14-15 with Rom 1:11-13; Acts 28:21 with Rom 3:1, 8-9; and Acts 28:22 with Rom 1:18; 16:19).

Caesarea is occasionally suggested, for at least the early drafting of Luke-Acts, if not the final composition. Assuming the traditional identification of "Luke" as Paul's traveling companion, Paul's two-year Caesarean imprisonment (Acts 23:23–26:32; see esp. 24:27) affords ample opportunity for a curious researcher to track down eyewitnesses and other participants in the life of Jesus and the history of the early church (Luke 1:2-3). At least the raw materials, if not the final version, of Luke-Acts may have been assembled in this time, provided one assumes the we-sections are the record of a Pauline companion.

Others have suggested Syrian Antioch, since some ancient traditions claimed that Luke was a native of that city.[28] Its church was the originator

---

28. I. H. Marshall, *The Book of Acts: An Introduction and Commentary* (Grand Rapids: Eerdmans, 1980), 45.

and the home base of the Pauline mission, so the believers there had a vested interest in preserving a record of both the origins of their community and the expansion of the Gentile mission.

Still other scholars suggest Troas as the point of origin, since the appearance of this port city in the first we-section (Acts 16:10-11) suggests that it may have been the native town for whoever composed the travel diary standing behind the we-sections of Acts.

Finally, others opt for the city of Ephesus as the place of composition. Given the prominence of this urban capital in Paul's third missionary journey, the unusually long period of time Paul devotes to establishing its Christian community, and the special meeting arranged between Paul and the Ephesian elders as he traveled to Jerusalem for the last time, Ephesus certainly looms large on the author's agenda.

At the end of the day, it is impossible to offer anything substantial or definite on the question of location.

The Historical Situation

The themes and concerns discussed in Luke-Acts give us some clues about the situation of Luke and his readers. They appear to be a growing community of Gentile believers and/or "God-fearers," that is, Gentile adherents to the synagogue, seeking to find stability and continuity in the midst of Jewish and pagan antagonism. That Luke's community was primarily Gentile may be reflected in his concern to legitimize the Gentile mission as the plan of God. At the same time, many aspects of Luke's story presume considerable familiarity with Judaism, indicating that his readers (such as Theophilus) were not entirely pagan but were poised between a prior attraction to Judaism and the newer appeal of the gospel.[29] In this environment, Luke-Acts serves to confirm that (1) an essential continuity exists between the life and ministry of Jesus of Nazareth and the life and ministry of the Christian churches now spread throughout the Roman Empire; (2) God intended these ethnically mixed communities, born of the Gentile mission, to be the offspring of faithful Israel, the next step in salvation history; and (3) the Christian movement, whether or not it is associated with Judaism, poses no threat to Rome.

---

29. J. Nolland, *Luke 1–9:20* (WBC 35A; Dallas: Word Books, 1989), xxxii-xxxiii.

Summary

Our treatment of the major themes presupposed some of the discussion of Lukan sources, style, and structure in chapter 5. Before discussing the themes, we briefly looked at the concept of salvation history in Luke-Acts. We showed how Luke's concept of salvation history is closely tied to the idea of fulfillment of Scripture, a feature that aligns Luke-Acts closely with Israelite/Jewish historiography. A fourfold scheme of salvation history in Luke-Acts was also proposed: (1) John, who prepares the way; (2) Jesus the Lord, who has come; (3) the Twelve, Paul, and others, who embody the way of Jesus; and (4) the Gentile-Jewish church, which is to embody the way of Jesus as exemplified by the apostles.

The seven major themes we examined were salvation to the Gentiles; the progress of the gospel; the Holy Spirit; prayer; wealth, poverty, and the marginalized; Christianity as the faithful Israel; and fair treatment under Rome. These themes also told something about Luke's view of Christ, the church, salvation, Christian piety, Jewish law, and the type of audience he was addressing.

To conclude our study, we made some observations on the date, authorship, and setting of Luke-Acts. This twin work appears to have been written after A.D. 70 and before 140, probably around 70-90. The author seems to have been a third-generation Christian from somewhere in one of the eastern provinces under Rome. He and the group he is addressing appear to be a growing Gentile community (some connected with the synagogue) in need of religious direction and encouragement because of Jewish and pagan antagonism.

CHAPTER 7

The Gospel of John

More than any other document of the NT, the Fourth Gospel invites readers of every century to approach it solely on its own terms. The very mention of this gospel causes many to recall timeless affirmations like "I am the way, and the truth, and the life." Some of John's words seem so free from their ancient setting (e.g., "You will know the truth, and the truth will make you free") that we chisel them into the walls of our university libraries from Chicago to Freiburg, implying that they are philosophical truisms, clearly understood in every age.[1]

Despite the universality and profundity of much of its teaching, the Gospel of John raises many difficult questions for critical readers. What is its relationship to the Synoptic Gospels? What sources were employed by the author? What is the literary character and structure of the gospel? To what kind of situation was it addressed? Who was the author, and what is the relationship between his original work and the postscript apparently added in chapter 21? When did he write, and where did he live? Although many of these questions cannot be answered with certainty, we address them here in our study of John's gospel.

1. The Johannine quotations are from John 14:6 and 8:32; the opening paragraph is adapted from J. L. Martyn, *History and Theology in the Fourth Gospel* (3d ed.; Louisville, Ky.: Westminster John Knox, 2003), 27.

John and the Synoptics

Differences

When we read the Gospel of John, we enter a different narrative world than that of the Synoptic Gospels. In contrast to the Synoptics, John introduces us to a distinctly different Jesus who is not only the promised, messianic king but also the preexistent Logos (Word), who is God's only Son and the Lamb of God sent into the world (John 1). In the Fourth Gospel, we do not find the straightforward Synoptic parables of Jesus but a few complex allegories. The concise Synoptic aphorisms have become extended discourses in the form of dramatic dialogues or monologues (chs. 4, 5, 6, 9, 10). The miracle stories are limited to seven "signs" that glorify Jesus, teach the meaning of belief, and serve as "enacted parables" symbolizing the spiritual significance of Jesus' person and behavior. John's emphasis on the Judean ministry of Jesus is evident by the five trips Jesus makes to Jerusalem (2:13; 5:1; 7:10; 10:22-23; 12:12), in contrast to one visit as an adult in Mark (ch. 11) and Luke (19:45; see also 4:9). In Mark 1:14 Jesus' ministry begins as John the Baptist is imprisoned, whereas in John 3:22-24 the two preachers work side by side.

According to the Synoptic Gospels, the temple was cleansed at the close of Jesus' ministry (Mark 11:15-19; Matt 21:12-13; Luke 19:45-46); in John's account it occurs at the beginning (2:13-22). The dialogue on the eating of flesh and drinking of blood (John 6) appears to replace the words of the Last Supper in the Synoptic tradition (e.g., Mark 14:17-25). John also includes a long farewell discourse of Jesus (chs. 13–17), replacing the Synoptic prayer in Gethsemane (e.g., Mark 14:32-42). The Synoptic Gospels agree that the crucifixion of Jesus took place on the Passover (Nisan 15), but John has it before the Passover to coincide with the sacrifice of lambs (John 1:29, 36; 19:30-37), which means that John's Last Supper is no longer a Passover meal. Finally, the length of Jesus' ministry in John is at least three years, whereas in the Synoptic tradition it appears to be only one.

It becomes evident from a comparison of John with the Synoptic Gospels that the structural arrangement and thematic emphases of the former is distinctive. John 1:19–12:50 seems to be built around the theme of signs (2:11; 4:54; 12:37); chapters 13–17 are thematic discourses and a prayer, and chapters 18–20 are a passion narrative. In distinction from the Synoptic tradition, we also find in John (1) a high Christology (e.g., the preexistent

Word, who has "come down" from heaven), (2) both a moral dualism (light/darkness, life/death) and a cosmic dualism (above/below, heaven/ earth), (3) an emphasis on faith (e.g., 1:7; 3:12-18), (4) the gift of the Paraclete (chs. 14–16), and (5) realized eschatology (e.g., 3:17-19; 11:25-26).[2]

The gospel of John also contains stories and discourses not found in the Synoptic Gospels: the wedding at Cana (2:1-11), the narratives concerning Nicodemus (3:1-21) and the Samaritan woman (4:7-42), the healing at the pool of Beth-zatha (5:1-9), the healing of the man born blind (9:1-12), the raising of Lazarus (11:1-44), Jesus' washing of the disciples' feet (13:1-17), the farewell discourse (13:18–16:33), and the so-called high priestly prayer (ch. 17). John, however, omits teaching and stories crucial to all three Synoptic story lines: Jesus' baptism (Mark 1:9-11), the temptation in the wilderness (Mark 1:12-13), the exorcisms (e.g., Mark 1:21-28), the transfiguration (Mark 9:2-8), warnings about the destruction of Jerusalem (Mark 13), Jesus' prayer in Gethsemane (Mark 14:32-42), and Peter's betrayal (Mark 14:66-72).

Similarities

Despite numerous differences, there are noteworthy similarities. Narratives that John has in common with the Synoptic Gospels are the call of the disciples (1:35-51); the healing of the official's son (4:46-53); the feeding of the multitude, followed by a sea-crossing miracle (6:1-21); Peter's confession (6:66-69); the entry into Jerusalem (12:12-15); the cleansing of the temple (2:13-22); the anointing at Bethany (12:1-8); the Last Supper, with a prophecy of betrayal (13:1-11); and the basic story of the passion. Events in John that follow Mark's sequence are the following:

1. The work of the Baptist
2. Jesus' departure to Galilee
3. The feeding of a multitude
4. Walking on water
5. Peter's confession
6. The departure to Jerusalem

---

2. "Realized eschatology" is the view that eternal decisions, such as the final judgment, are occurring here and now in the present.

7. The entry into Jerusalem and the anointing (order rearranged in John)
8. The Supper, with predictions of betrayal and denial
9. The arrest and the passion narrative

The feeding and sea miracles followed by a discourse on bread in John also have parallels with a double-cycle tradition in Mark, as seen in table 3.1 in chapter 3 above. Even though there are verbal differences in the accounts, the similar order and themes seem to indicate a common cycle of tradition.[3]

There are also similarities between the Markan and Johannine passion narratives, both in actions and in wording. Such parallels lend further support to the view that John was familiar with either Mark's gospel or traditions used by Mark.[4] (See table 7.1 on p. 157.)

John also shares some of the traditions found in the Gospel of Luke. For instance, compare the two stories of Jesus' anointing (John 12:3-8; Luke 7:36-50). In John 12 the two unusual actions of Mary are explainable if John knew Luke's simpler version. In John she *first* anoints the feet of Jesus then dries them with her hair(!), whereas in Luke the woman wipes Jesus' feet with her hair before anointing them. John's version seems more complicated and unusual. Luke's account is simpler and less problematic. Luke is also the earliest gospel to include the two ritualistic acts. In Mark 14:3-9, for example, the woman only anoints Jesus' head; there is no mention of her wiping his feet with her hair. It seems plausible, therefore, that the author of John derived both acts of foot washing and anointing from Luke and added his own curious changes, which we read in John 12:3-8. Furthermore, only in John and Luke do the two sisters Mary and Martha appear together (John 11:1-44; 12:1-8; Luke 10:38-42), and only in John and Luke does Pilate pronounce Jesus innocent three times (John 18:38; 19:4, 6; Luke 23:4, 14-15, 22).[5]

---

3. See N. Perrin and D. C. Duling, *The NT, an Introduction: Proclamation and Parenesis, Myth and History* (2d ed.; New York: Harcourt Brace Jovanovich, 1982), 234-35.

4. R. Bauckham, "John for Readers of Mark," in *The Gospels for All Christians: Rethinking the Gospel Audiences* (Grand Rapids: Eerdmans, 1998), 147-71, even argues that John knew that his audience had read Mark.

5. Additional similarities are discussed in J. Bailey, *The Traditions Common to the Gospels of Luke and John* (Leiden: Brill, 1963), and in D. M. Smith, *John among the Gospels: The Relationship in Twentieth-Century Research* (Minneapolis: Fortress, 1992), 85-110.

TABLE 7.1. MARK AND JOHN: PARALLELS

Action Parallels	Mark	John
1. The anointing for burial, with similar vocabulary	14:3-9	12:2-8
2. Prediction of betrayal and denial[6]	14:18-21, 27-31	13:21-30, 36-38
3. Trial before the high priest, in the context of Peter's denial	14:54 [55-65] 66-72	18:15-18 [19-24] 25-27
4. Pilate and the "king of the Jews"	15:2-15	18:33-39
5. Aspects of the crucifixion	15:20-37	19:16-30

Verbal Parallels		
1. "Stand up," "take your mat," and "go to your home"/"walk" (different paralytics addressed)	2:11	5:8
2. bread worth two hundred denarii	6:37	6:7
3. "an alabaster jar of very costly ointment of nard"/ "a pound of costly perfume made of pure nard"	14:3	12:3

Conclusions of the Comparison

Even though the evidence is not decisive, it appears that the author of John was familiar with certain traditions common to the Synoptic Gospels. He also may have been acquainted with the Gospel of Mark and possibly Luke, but if he was, he did not follow them closely.[7]

6. The bracketing of John's account of the trial by the narrative of Peter's denial, precisely as it appears in Mark, argues favorably for John's knowledge of Mark or a pre-Markan tradition.

7. See C. H. Dodd, *Historical Tradition in the Fourth Gospel* (Cambridge: Cambridge University Press, 1963); R. Kysar, *The Fourth Evangelist and His Gospel* (Minneapolis: Augsburg, 1975), 54-66, and "The Gospel of John in Current Research," *RelSRev* 9 (1983): 315-16; A. Denaux, *John and the Synoptics* (Leuven: Leuven University Press, 1992); B. Lindars, "John and the Synoptic Gospels: A Test Case," in *Essays on John* (ed. C. M. Tuckett; Leuven: Leuven University Press, 1992), 105-12; J. D. G. Dunn, "John and the Synoptics as a Theological Question," in *Exploring the Gospel of John* (ed. R. A. Culpepper and C. C. Black; Louisville, Ky.: Westminster John Knox, 1996), 301-13; and R. Brown, *An Introduction to the Gospel of John* (New York: Doubleday, 2003), 90-114.

The Sources of John's Gospel

Despite the consistent use of language and style in John, there are abrupt transitions and apparent dislocations, which imply a complex process of composition. Various theories have been formulated to explain these features.

Rudolf Bultmann's Theory

The most influential presentation of Johannine sources was made by Rudolf Bultmann (1884-1976).[8] He argued that the Fourth Evangelist drew upon three sources for his material, the first of which was a signs source. This source is reputed to be an early collection of Jesus' miracles from which John took the seven used in the first part of his gospel (chs. 1–12).[9] An indication of borrowing from a source may be seen in two observations: (1) the initial enumeration of signs mentions "the first" (2:11) and "the second" (4:54) sign, although 2:23 and 3:2 make it clear that additional signs were performed before the second, and (2) further references (6:2; 12:37; 20:30) make it clear that Jesus actually performed many more than seven. This piece of the theory has been widely accepted, although debate continues about isolating the contours of the signs source.[10]

The second source contained revelation discourse material. From this source the evangelist obtained the discourses ascribed to Jesus in the gos-

---

8. See R. Bultmann, *The Gospel of John: A Commentary* (trans. C. Beasley-Murray et al.; Philadelphia: Westminster, 1971), and *Exegetica* (ed. E. Dinkler; Tübingen: Mohr Siebeck, 1971), 124-97.

9. Although only the first two signs are enumerated, the seven signs appear in 2:1-11; 4:46-54; 5:1-15; 6:5-15, 16-21; 9:1-12; 11:1-44. An eighth sign, found in 21:1-14, was apparently added with the postscript in ch. 21.

10. R. Fortna, *The Gospel of Signs: A Reconstruction of the Narrative Source Underlying the Fourth Gospel* (Cambridge: Cambridge University Press, 1970); W. Nicol, *The Sēmeia in the Fourth Gospel: Tradition and Redaction* (Leiden: Brill, 1972); U. von Wahlde, *The Earliest Version of John's Gospel: Recovering the Gospel of Signs* (Wilmington, Del.: Michael Glazier, 1989); J. Ashton, *Studying John: Approaches to the Fourth Gospel* (Oxford: Clarendon Press, 1994), 90-113; G. Van Belle, *The Signs Source in the Fourth Gospel: Historical Survey and Critical Evaluation of the Semeia Hypothesis* (Leuven: Leuven University Press, 1994).

pel (e.g., in ch. 10, "I am the good shepherd"). The source began with a prologue and contained poetic discourses written in Aramaic.

Bultmann's third source contained the passion narrative. He argued that this source was non-Synoptic, although the Fourth Gospel has much in common with the Synoptic passion narratives.

The many reasons for criticizing Bultmann's source analysis of John include the following three observations. First, the book is so permeated with Johannine style and thought that it cannot be subjected to precise source delineations. Second, parallels to the Synoptic materials are found in both the alleged signs document and the discourse source. Finally, some signs and discourses are so closely bound together that the signs must be regarded as the source for the discourses; that is, the discourses often seem to be built around themes that the evangelist discovers in the signs (e.g., in chs. 9 and 11).[11]

An Alternate Theory

From our discussion of John and the Synoptics, the question of sources should also have some parallel to the development of the Synoptic tradition. We list here three possible traditions, oral and written, used in the composition of the Fourth Gospel.[12]

Synoptic-Type Sayings Sources Synoptic-type sayings are Jesus-sayings that probably originated independently and later became the nuclei of Johannine discourses and dialogues. Many of them are brief maxims, aphorisms (e.g., 3:6, 8), and sayings of Jesus prefaced by formulas like "very truly [*amēn amēn*], I tell you . . ." (3:3, 5, 11). There are also sayings that find some parallel in the Synoptic tradition, both Markan and Q: John 1:51 / Mark 14:62; John 10:15 / Matt 11:27 / Luke 10:22; John 12:25 / Matt 10:39; John 13:20 / Matt 10:40. In fact, the portion of Jesus' Synoptic (Q) prayer found in Matt 11:27 / Luke 10:22 has famously been described as "a lightning bolt fallen from the Johannine heaven."[13]

---

11. For a thorough critique of Bultmann's theory, see D. M. Smith, *The Composition and Order of the Fourth Gospel: Bultmann's Literary Theory* (New Haven: Yale University Press, 1965).

12. See chart 2.1 in ch. 2.

13. This much-repeated phrase was first coined by D. von Hase, *Geschichte Jesu: Nach*

Synoptic-Type Stories Source The Synoptic-type stories source includes the narratives that John has in common with the other gospels (e.g., cleansing of the temple, the anointing of Jesus) and Markan or pre-Markan material in John (e.g., feeding of multitude and sea-crossing miracles, Peter's denial in the context of Jesus' trial before the high priest). As we discussed earlier, the wording and sequence of these narratives in John presuppose some acquaintance with the Synoptic tradition.

Synoptic-Type Concepts Although John's gospel is distinctive in its emphasis on the immediacy of realized eschatology (e.g., in 3:18, 36, eternal life and the final judgment occur here and now), the author also preserves the "already/not yet" tension more typical of the Synoptic Gospels (e.g., in 12:25, 48, eternal life and final judgment are delayed until the future).[14] In addition, while John develops an elaborate, unique series of "I Am" statements,[15] identified by the awkward Greek phrase *ego eimi,* the identical construction, complete with christological overtones, appears less frequently but just as significantly in the Synoptic Gospels (Mark 13:6 / Luke 21:8; Mark 14:62). In fact, the absolute "I Am" statement in John 6:20 is identical to Jesus' words in Mark 6:50 / Matt 14:27.

Conclusions Our theory of the Synoptic-type traditions in John qualifies the arguments for two of Bultmann's more acceptable source theories. First, much of the pre-Johannine passion material appears to be derived from Mark and Luke or traditions used by them (e.g., the anointing in Luke and John, Peter's denial in Mark and John).[16] It therefore cannot be regarded as a source unique to John. Second, the nature and contents of the signs source are still debated, and parallels with the Synoptic miracle

---

akademische Vorlesungen (Leipzig: Breitkopf & Hartel, 1876), 422; see also M. Sabbe, "Can Mt 11,25-27 and Lc 10,22 Be Called a Johannine Logion?" in *Logia: Les paroles de Jésus = The Sayings of Jesus* (ed. J. Delobel; Leuven: Leuven University Press, 1982), 263-71.

14. For a good discussion, see R. Kysar, *John: The Maverick Gospel* (rev. ed.; Louisville, Ky.: Westminster John Knox, 1993), 97-127.

15. John has two types of "I Am" sayings: those followed by a predicate nominative (e.g., "I Am the bread of life": 6:35 and 51; 8:12 and 9:5; 10:7 and 9; 10:11 and 14; 11:25; 14:6; 15:1 and 5), and absolute statements (i.e., "I Am": 4:26; 6:20; 8:24, 28, 58; 13:19; 18:5-6). Notice that there are seven examples of each type.

16. It is also commonly argued that, in addition to Mark, Luke had his own independent passion source.

stories raise questions about its uniqueness. The contacts of this alleged signs source with the Synoptic Gospels are the formal and structural similarities (John 9:1-7 / Mark 2:2-12) and the parallels in thought and sequence (feeding and lake miracles in John 6 / Mark 6–8). As we stated earlier, Bultmann's alleged revelation discourse source is highly questionable. Our qualifications of Bultmann's signs source and so-called Johannine passion source also lessen their plausibility.

The Transpositions

There are also several breaks, or disjunctions, in John's gospel, which have stimulated many attempts to restore the text to its presumed original order. The most striking of these occurs at the end of chapter 14, where the words "rise, let us be on our way" (v. 31) are followed by three more chapters before Jesus and his disciples actually depart (18:1). A similar problem occurs at the beginning of chapter 6. Although John 5 leaves Jesus in Jerusalem (vv. 1-47), he crosses the sea in 6:1 as though he is still in Galilee (cf. 4:43, 54). And then in 7:21-23 Jesus refers to his healing of the impotent men on the Sabbath (5:2-9) as though he is still engaged in the debate that followed the incident (5:10-13). Also, in 18:13-24 the trial of Jesus under Annas (deposed in A.D. 15!) instead of Caiaphas the high priest (vv. 13, 24) is surprising.

R. Bultmann, J. Moffatt, and other scholars have attempted to reconstruct what they assume to be the original order. Difficulties arise, however, when such attempts are made. First, there is no textual evidence for a different order. Although there is some textual support (e.g., Sinaitic Syriac) for rearranging chapter 18, it may have been governed by the desire to correspond to the Synoptic account (which omits the role of Annas). Second, rearrangements do not completely solve the problem, and neither is it clear in which direction the material is to be transposed. For example, John 7:1 (Jesus went about in Galilee, but not Judea) still presents problems for those who would place John 6 (Jesus in Galilee) before John 5 (Jesus in Judea). Third, some of these alleged disjunctions are part of John's technique to have material from one section form the nucleus of the next. For example, the healing account in John 5 forms part of the discussion in 7:15-24, and the shepherd allegory in 10:1-18 is continued verses later in a different context (vv. 26-29).

Redactions

In the growth of the Fourth Gospel, there were also several later additions or redactions.

John 21. John 20:30-31 appears to have been the original ending of the book. The vocabulary and style of John 21 are different from the rest of the gospel. John 21:1 also makes an awkward transition from John 20:30-31. The gospel thus has two conclusions — the original, and a second added by an editor.

John 1:1-18. This prologue seems to replace or supplement the original opening, which began with John the Baptist, as in Mark. The Logos/Word never reappears in the remainder of the gospel, unlike other important christological titles that are developed throughout. Verses 6-8 and 15 probably belong to the original opening.

The Lazarus material. The stories about Jesus' friend Lazarus (11:1-46; 12:9-11) appear to have been included to prepare for the passion of Jesus. Many have suggested that this material breaks the connection between chapters 10 and 12.

Non-Johannine additions. The account of the angel who troubled the water (John 5:3b-4) and the story of the woman caught in adultery (John 7:53–8:11) are non-Johannine interpolations added after the final composition of the gospel. John 5:3b-4 is absent from the most ancient manuscripts (e.g., Alexandrian). John 7:53–8:11 interrupts the continuity of the narrative, is Synoptic in its content, absent from the earliest manuscripts, and found in later witnesses in different contexts (e.g., in John 7, at the end of John, and after Luke 21:38).

The Unity of John's Gospel

Narrative breaks and dislocations are noticeable in John because they disrupt its basic unity of thought and style. Throughout the Fourth Gospel, we find the use of specialized vocabulary (e.g., love, truth, life, know, world, belief), pervasive themes (e.g., God's only Son, man from heaven, Paraclete, light vs. darkness, life vs. death, eternal life), and long dialogues and monologues (chs. 4, 9, 10), all of which substantiate the basic unity of John.

The Process of Composition

John's gospel has been seen as the product of a close-knit community that sought to continue and develop the teachings of its founder (the "beloved disciple"), an explanation that seems to account for both the discontinuities and the underlying unity of the work.[17] The founder of the Johannine community, who is presented as an eyewitness (1:35-40; 19:26; 21:24), may have been responsible for passing on and probably composing an original framework for what would eventually become the gospel. He also may have helped to establish a community composed of both Hebrew and Hellenistic Jews (1:45-51; 4:39-42), formulated some of their distinctive beliefs (e.g., high Christology, 3:13; 6:62; realized eschatology, 3:17-19, 36), and faced both rejection and alienation from the Jewish synagogue (9:22; 12:42-43; 16:2-3).

After the founder's death, a disciple or representative of the community may have drawn upon the basic framework left to it, sifted, selected, and shaped the traditional material (e.g., 5:2-9a) into the dialogues (5:9b-18; 7:15-24) and discourses (5:19-47) of the Fourth Gospel. This editor-evangelist may even have been responsible for the dramatic techniques of storytelling (e.g., misunderstanding, 3:3-5; 4:10-15; irony, 8:22; 11:48), welding together the signs (e.g., 9:1-7) and their following discourses (9:8-41) into a three-year ministry scheme that alternates between Galilee and Jerusalem. He may also have been responsible for renaming the community's founder "the beloved disciple," given the apparent ego involved in any disciple calling himself the one Jesus loved best (see further discussion on this point below under "The Authorship of John"). The final product (John 1–20) seems to have been permeated with his style and thought (e.g., monologues, dialogues, moral dualism, and realized eschatology), with his be-

---

17. For various approaches to the hypothesis of a Johannine "community," see R. Culpepper, *The Johannine School: An Evaluation of the Johannine School Hypothesis, Based on an Investigation of the Nature of Ancient Schools* (Missoula, Mont.: Scholars Press, 1975); O. Cullmann, *The Johannine Circle* (trans. J. Bowden; Philadelphia: Westminster Press, 1976); R. Brown, *The Community of the Beloved Disciple: The Life, Loves, and Hates of an Individual Church in NT Times* (New York: Paulist Press, 1979); M. Hengel, *The Johannine Question* (trans. J. Bowden; Philadelphia: Trinity Press International, 1989), 74-135; J. Ashton, *Understanding the Fourth Gospel* (Oxford: Clarendon Press, 1991), 160-98; and C. G. Lingad, *The Problems of Jewish Christians in the Johannine Community* (Rome: Editrice Pontificia Università Gregoriana, 2001).

liefs reflecting those of his community, whose voice is echoed in the plural pronoun of 21:24, "*We* know that his [i.e., the beloved disciple's] testimony is true."

Literary Characteristics

The following sections highlight the literary character of the Fourth Gospel.

Vocabulary

Although the Fourth Gospel is profound in thought, its vocabulary is simple and limited. The author prefers abstract nouns such as "life" (*zōē*, 36 times), "truth" (*alētheia* and cognates, 55 times), "light" (*phōs*, 23 times), "sin" (*hamartia*, 17 times), and cognitive verbs like "know" (*ginōskō*, 56 times), "perceive" (*oida*, 84 times), "believe" (*pisteuō*, 98 times), and "love" (*agapaō*, 36 times; *phileō*, 13 times).[18] Such a preference for the abstract and perceptual gives the book a tone that is both dramatic and philosophical.

Style

The Koine Greek of John's gospel, like Mark's gospel, is colloquial. The author's use of connecting clauses with a simple conjunction (*kai, oun;* John 5:37-40; 9:18; 12:1-3; 13:1-4) or his listing of phrases and clauses with no conjunction (e.g., 1:40, 42, 45, 47; 2:17) is a characteristic of this conversational style.[19] The use of the historic present (1:15, 29, 39, 43), the preference for putting verb before subject (2:9; 6:3; 18:33; 19:38), and the preference for short weighty sentences (8:12; 11:32, 35; 13:20) all point to a colloquial style that is conducive to public reading. The so-called Semitic idioms in 3:29; 14:17; 15:14; 17:3, 12 also convey this simple conversational tone.

The Fourth Evangelist, more than the other gospel writers, makes selective but purposeful use of his narrative comments. They explain names

18. Statistics are from R. Morgenthaler, *Statistik des neutestamentlichen Wortschatzes* (Zurich: Gotthelf, 1958).

19. G. G. Bilezikian, *The Liberated Gospel: A Comparison of the Gospel of Mark and Greek Tragedy* (Grand Rapids: Baker, 1977), 113-17.

(1:38, 42) and symbols (2:21; 12:33), correct misapprehensions (4:2), remind readers of related events (3:24; 11:2), and identify characters of the plot (7:50; 21:20). The narrative comments also assist the audience in understanding the dialogues and discourses (e.g., 3–4; 9–10; 13–17).

Literary Techniques

The literary techniques used by the Fourth Evangelist include wordplay (esp. double entendre), the motif of misunderstanding, irony, paradox, and balance (i.e., parallelism, inclusion, and chiasm).[20]

Wordplay A double entendre, or double meaning, can be seen in the author's use of *pneuma* to denote both "wind" and "spirit" (3:8), *koimaomai* for both "sleep" and "death" (11:11-13), *katalambanō* in both the cognitive sense of "receive, understand" and the physical sense of "seize, overcome" (1:5), and *anōthen* as "from above" and "again" (3:3). Other words with a double meaning are *hypsoō*, meaning either "lifted up, raised up" (as on the cross) or "exalted, glorified" (as in ascended to heaven, 3:14); *zōn* as "living" or "flowing" water (4:10-11); and *anabainō*, "going up," in either a literal ("to Jerusalem") or figurative ("to the Father") sense (7:8).

The Misunderstanding Motif The motif of misunderstanding (e.g., 3:4, 9; 4:11-12, 15, 19-20; 6:41-43, 52; 7:35-36; 11:11-12, 24), an important structural element of the Johannine dialogues, joins with irony to provide the gospel with a dramatic plotline. Examples are usually preceded by some profound statement of Jesus (3:3, 8; 4:10, 14; 6:35-40, 51; 7:34; 11:11, 23) and provide the occasion for further exposition of the same or a similar theme (3:5-7, 11-12; 4:13-14, 21-26; 6:44-51, 53-58; 7:37-39; 11:25-26). In these discourses the characters function as foils in contrast to Jesus, who occupies the central spotlight. These repeated misunderstandings, which are reminiscent of the messianic secret found throughout Mark's gospel, are recognizable by the audience of the gospel, since they know more than the characters in the story (e.g., 20:30-31; 21:24-25).

---

20. For a good study of these Johannine literary techniques, see C. Koester, *Symbolism in the Fourth Gospel: Meaning, Mystery, Community* (2d ed.; Minneapolis: Fortress, 2003). See also Tate, *Interpreting the Bible*.

Irony Irony, a figure of contradiction found elsewhere in the NT (e.g., Mark 1:22; 6:3-4; 11:28; 14:30), occurs frequently in the Fourth Gospel. There is irony especially in sarcastic remarks or incredulous statements that are often true, in a sense not realized by the speakers (e.g., "Are you greater than our ancestor Jacob?" 4:12; see also 7:35, 46, 52; 8:22). There is even irony in statements of double meaning that denote one level of understanding for the speaker and another for the reader. For example, members of the Jewish council fear that "everyone will believe in him" (11:48), but this fear is exactly the missionary hope of John's community. Pilate mockingly says to the Jews, "Here is your King!" (19:14-15), although for John's readers, Jesus indeed is the true king of the Jews.

Paradox Paradox — an apparently contradictory situation that reveals some profound truth — is related to irony. The summary statement "he came to what was his own, and his own people did not accept him" (1:11) is the tragic paradox of a prophet without honor in his own country. Another is the question "Can anything good come out of Nazareth?" (1:46). For John and his readers, Jesus, who came from the obscure town of Nazareth, is the only Son of God (see also 9:29; 19:15).

Balance The author of John also employs three principles of literary balance: regular parallelism, inclusion, and chiasm. As in Hebrew poetry, the author uses several forms of regular parallelism. Synonymous parallelism is found, in which the second line repeats the idea of the first (speak/know, bear witness/seen, 3:11; see also 6:35, 55; 13:16). Antithetical parallelism also occurs, where the second line offers a contrast to the first (believes/not condemned, not believe/condemned, 3:18a; hates the light/comes to the light, 3:20-21; see also 8:35; 9:39). Finally, there is synthetic (or progressive) parallelism, where the second line amplifies and explains the first (8:44), and climactic parallelism, where successive lines are repeated and developed to form a climax (6:37; 8:32): "they who have my commandments and keep them are those who love me; and those who love me will be loved by my Father, and I will love them and reveal myself to them" (14:21).

The techniques of inclusion and chiasm involve enveloping or bracketing enclosed material. The framing device of inclusion is found in statements about the "signs" Jesus performed (2:11 with 4:46, 54), where John baptized (1:28 with 10:40), the explicit and implicit references to Jesus as the Passover lamb (1:29, 36 with 19:36 / Exod 12:46), and Jesus' insistence that he "can do nothing" on his own (5:19, 30). Chiasm, or introverted parallelism (A B C B′ A′ thematic pattern), can be detected in 6:36-40 and 18:28–19:16.

The Seven Signs

John's gospel is unique in referring to Jesus' miraculous acts as signs. In the gospel Jesus performs seven signs,[21] which serve as enacted parables — an observation that may help to explain John's neglect of the Synoptic parables. Each sign is a literary double entendre working on two levels simultaneously: the historical level, communicating a specific significance to the eyewitnesses or the original hearers of the oral tradition; and the literary level, constructing a symbolic significance available only to readers of the gospel. The climax occurs in the seventh sign (seven is often a symbolic number for completion), the resurrection of Lazarus.[22] (See table 7.2 on p. 168.)

These seven signs further highlight the role of John's literary devices considered above, especially wordplay, irony, and paradox, creating a gospel narrative that requires readers to attend to multiple levels of meaning throughout the entire storyline.

The Johannine Structure

Prologue

John's prologue (John 1:1-18) provides an introduction and background for the contemporary audience. In the prologue the divine identity and preexistence of the Logos (Word) sets the tone and informs the audience. Then John the Baptist announces the entrance of Jesus, the central character.

Plot Complication

The gospel of John conveniently breaks down into the plot structure of: complication (1:19–12:19), crisis (12:20-26), and denouement (12:27–

---

21. The eighth sign, in 21:1-6, was a later addition included with the epilogue.

22. For more insight into John's signs, see Nicol, *The Sēmeia in the Fourth Gospel;* Van Belle, *The Signs Source in the Fourth Gospel;* and D. M. Smith, *The Theology of the Gospel of John* (Cambridge: Cambridge University Press, 1995), 106-9.

TABLE 7.2. JOHN: THE SEVEN SIGNS

Sign	Historical significance	Literary/symbolic significance
1. Turning water into wine (2:1-11)	Revelation of power/ glory; disciples begin to believe	Jesus brings abundant life, replacing/fulfilling OT traditions
2. Healing the official's son (4:46-54)	Jesus has power to heal the sick	Critiques the quest for miracles and teaches about faith
3. Healing the lame man (5:1-15)	Power to heal and to work on the Sabbath	Sovereignly brings wholeness and confronts personal sin
4. Feeding the 5,000 (6:1-15)	Miraculous power to reproduce the works of Moses (e.g., manna)	The true manna/bread sent from heaven (see also 6:25-40)
5. Walking on water (6:16-21)	Divine power to control the elements	The Final Moses (Messiah),[23] who controls/parts the sea
6. Healing the blind man (9:1-12)	Power to heal those infirmed from birth	The True Light, who brings spiritual sight to the spiritually blind
7. Raising Lazarus (11:1-44)	Divine power to raise the dead	Previewing his own resurrection, Jesus brings eternal life for those who believe

20:31).[24] In the complication the audience is immediately drawn into the drama of the divine mission of Jesus the Son of God. The different characters (e.g., Nathanael, Nicodemus, the Samaritan woman, the Jews) typify the responses of belief or unbelief to Jesus' identity and mission. The "hours" (2:4; 7:30; 8:20) and the "time" (7:6, 8) unfold the story's plot by raising questions: when will the hour of Jesus arrive? Why could he not attend a certain feast or be arrested before his time had come? The statements that envelope the complication section (1:14 and 11:40) raise the question of how God's glory will be revealed. The "signs" that Jesus performed manifest God's glory (2:11), reaching a climax in "the hour" when the Son of Man would "be glorified" (12:23).

---

23. W. Meeks, *The Prophet-King: Moses Traditions and the Johannine Christology* (Leiden: Brill, 1967).

24. For an analysis of possible similarities between John's dramatic structure and Greek tragedy, see J. Brant, *Dialogue and Drama: Elements of Greek Tragedy in the Fourth Gospel* (Peabody, Mass.: Hendrickson, 2004). See also comparisons in C. Puskas, *An Introduction to the NT* (Peabody, Mass.: Hendrickson, 1989), 135-38.

Suspense is caused by the unbelief and hate of both the Jews and the world (5:16-18, 42-47; 8:37-59; 10:19-20, 31-33). The schemes and attempts to kill Jesus appear both to jeopardize (8:59; 10:31-33, 39; 11:8) and to expedite (11:47-53) the accomplishment of Jesus' mission.

Although his disciples are given clues before 12:20-26 about the "hour" of Jesus' glorification (11:40; 12:7), the audience has been informed throughout the drama (1:29; 3:14-15; 8:28; 10:11, 17; 11:50; 12:16).

Plot Crisis

The turning point occurs with the coming of the Greeks (John 12:20-26), with the ironic statements in 7:35 hinting at their entry. The many references to the "hour/time" (of glorification, 2:4; 5:25, 28; 7:6, 30; 8:20) make the statements in 12:23 a climactic discovery: "the hour has come for the Son of Man to be glorified!"

Plot Denouement

As a result of Jesus' disclosure, the plot moves to its resolution, or denouement (John 12:27–20:31). The denouement has two lines of development: (1) preparing the disciples for Jesus' glorification and departure (chs. 14–17) and (2) the success of the opposition in putting Jesus to death (chs. 18–19).

The chief antagonist who brings about Jesus' arrest is Judas, whom Satan has possessed (John 6:70-71; 13:2, 26-27). It is through Judas (and his Jewish collaborators) that "the ruler of this world," the "evil one," is revealed (14:30; 16:11; 17:15). The trial scenes provide the forensic debates, with the accusers and judges serving as foils for Jesus (18:12–19:16).

The "hour" of glorification (17:1, 4) is accomplished with Christ lifted up on the cross (19:18-27). The somber setting of the burial scene (19:38–20:11) is enlivened by the surprise appearance of the Lord (20:14-18; a kind of hyporcheme, or ancient Greek song in honor of the appearance of a god). He now affirms the faith of his disciples and bestows on them the Holy Spirit (20:19-22).

Epilogue

The epilogue, or closing narration (20:30-31), functions as a brief concluding summary.

Key Terms

Key terms that signify divisions in the book are (1) "signs" performed by Jesus (2:11; 4:54; 12:37; 20:30; see table 7.2), which concern his public ministry in the first twelve chapters; (2) "glory" (*doxa*, 2:11; 11:4, 40; 17:5, 24) and "glorify" (7:39; 11:4; 12:16; 13:31-32; 16:14; 17:1-5), which refer to Christ's crucifixion and exaltation and characterize the remainder of the book (chs. 13–20); and (3) "hour" (*hōra*, 2:4; 4:21, 23; 5:25, 28; 7:30; 8:20; 12:23, 27; 13:1; 16:25, 32; 17:1; 19:27) and "time" (*kairos*, 7:6, 8), which also concern his crucifixion and exaltation.

Outline

John 12:23 marks a crucial turning point for Jesus. It pinpoints the watershed separating Jesus' time *before* from the time *after* his "hour," to which the structure of the book conforms. The pericope of 12:20-26 describes the arrival of Jesus' hour to be glorified. An earthly dimension of glory is described in vv. 12-19, but in chapters 13–17, the Last Supper and farewell discourse, Jesus prepares his disciples for his ultimate "hour of glorification" (i.e., passion/resurrection narrative, chs. 18–20). Utilizing the above information and the author's dramatic techniques, we propose outline 7.1.[25]

OUTLINE 7.1. JOHN

1. Introduction   1
    Prologue   1:1-18
    Testimonies of John and his disciples   1:19-51

---

25. This outline has been derived from the insights of C. H. Dodd, *The Interpretation of the Fourth Gospel* (Cambridge: Cambridge University Press, 1968), 289-443; R. E. Brown, *The Gospel according to John* (2 vols.; 2d ed.; AB 29-29A; Garden City, N.Y.: Doubleday, 1966-70); and Smith, *The Theology of the Gospel of John*, 20-48.

The Purposes of Writing

As with the Synoptic Gospels, many reasons can be postulated for the composition of John, five of which we consider here.

Apologetic

First, from the author's own statement (John 20:31), an apologetic reason is present: "these are written so that you may come to believe that Jesus is the Messiah, the Son of God, and that through believing you may have life in his name." This theme of salvation and a call to deeper faith is evident throughout the work (3:15-16, 18, 36; 5:24; 6:35, 40, 47; 7:38; 11:25-26; 12:44, 46). Many scholars argue that John's gospel was directed to fellow Christians, presenting an appeal to Christian Jews within the synagogues (12:42-43) and Jewish Christians of inadequate faith (6:60-66; 7:3-5).[26] The exhortation to believe is usually in the present tense *(pisteuō);* it denotes the idea of continuous action: "continue to believe" or "keep on believing" (3:15; 5:24; 6:47; 7:38; 20:31). The evangelist's assertion that believers "may have" (present subjunctive of *echō,* 3:16; 20:31) or "have" (present indicative, 3:36; 5:24) "eternal life" also indicates that all believers now experience the future hope as a present reality (i.e., realized eschatology).

26. Brown, *An Introduction to the Gospel of John,* 182-88.

Some scholars, however, argue that John's purposes are largely evange-listic.[27] For instance, John's identification of the incarnate Christ with "the Logos" may be a brilliant example of cross-cultural communication. Given the currency of Logos/Word ideologies in the OT, Platonism, Stoicism, and Hellenistic Judaism,[28] Jesus' connection to the preexistent Word could cross numerous barriers, stirring interest among a broad audience.

Eschatological

A second purpose for the writing of John's gospel is related to the first. As we have seen, John's exhortations to continue believing are reinforced by his realized eschatology — the belief that future realities become available here and now. Although the author retains the traditional future hopes (e.g., 5:28-29; 6:39-40, 44; 12:48b), he reminds his readers that eternal life, resurrection, judgment, and the parousia can be experienced as present re-alities (3:17-19, 36; 5:24; 11:25-26; 12:31). The bestowal of the Holy Spirit is to ensure the continued presence of Christ among believers (14:15-17, 25-26; 15:26-27; 16:5-11, 12-15; 20:22). This emphasis on actualized eschatology may also be the evangelist's response to the delay of the parousia. That is, for long-suffering believers whose patience is faltering as they await the Lord's return, the experience of eternal life is not deferred entirely. It has already begun, and the Father can be counted upon to finish what he has started.

Christological

A third purpose is christological. John seems to consolidate the acceptable views of Christ within his community and to defend the Johannine view of Christ against opponents. There is some evidence, both in the NT (Acts 19:1-7) and elsewhere, that disciples of John the Baptist continued to form a

27. D. A. Carson, "The Purpose of the Fourth Gospel: John 20:31 Reconsidered," *JBL* 106 (1987): 639-51, and "Syntactical and Text-Critical Observations on John 20:30-31: One More Round on the Purpose of the Fourth Gospel," *JBL* 124 (2005): 693-714.

28. Brown, *The Gospel according to John*, 1:519-24; G. Beasley-Murray, *John* (2d ed.; Nashville: Thomas Nelson, 1999), 6-10; and M. Hengel, "The Prologue of the Gospel of John as the Gateway to Christological Truth," in *The Gospel of John and Christian Tradition*, ed. R. Bauckham and C. Mosser, 265-94 (Grand Rapids: Eerdmans, 2008).

"Baptist sect" after the ministry of Jesus,[29] with some even insisting that John was the true Messiah (see the *Clementine Recognitions* 1.60, early 3d cent.).[30] By denying to John the Baptist all messianic prerogatives (John 1:8, 19-23; 3:28, 29; 10:41), the evangelist appears to show followers of the Baptist that Jesus is greater than John.[31] With the Logos Christology (1:1-18), numerous christological titles (e.g., "Son of God" and "Son of Man"), and "descent from the Father" imagery (3:13-15; 6:62; 7:33; 8:14, 42; 16:28), the author argues for a high preexistent Christology possibly against Jewish and Jewish-Christian critics. The "I am" statements of Christ, in both their absolute (4:26; 6:20; 8:24, 28, 58; 13:19; 18:5-6) and predicate nominative forms (6:35, 51; 8:12; 9:5; 10:7, 9, 11, 14; 11:25; 14:6; 15:1, 5), identify Jesus with the God of Abraham, Isaac, and Jacob, underscoring the deity of Christ and thus (some argue) his superiority over Jewish law and tradition. Jesus' superiority to the tradition is because of his complete fulfillment of the tradition's significance.

The issue of fulfillment also lies at the center of a christological "replacement theme" in John's gospel. Jesus is consistently portrayed as the fulfillment of, and even the replacement for, certain OT traditions and promises. The feasts of the Jews were now superseded by Jesus' coming (5:1; 6:4; 7:2). Jesus' "better wine" replaces the OT traditions (2:1-11). Jesus is the "king of Israel," and believers are now "Israelites" (1:47, 49; 12:13). Entry into God's community is no longer by natural birth but by the will of God (1:12-13; 3:3-7). Jesus is the new temple, which has superseded the old one (2:19-21; 4:21-24). He ultimately dies as the final sacrifice, "the Lamb of God who takes away the sin of the world" (1:29; 13:1; 18:28; 19:36).[32]

Soteriological

Fourth, John's gospel offers a unique perspective on Christian salvation. The Fourth Gospel effectively replaces the Synoptic focus on the kingdom

29. Brown, *The Community of the Beloved Disciple*, 69-71.

30. C. Kraeling, *John the Baptist* (New York: Charles Scribner's Sons, 1951), 181-87.

31. W. Wink, *John the Baptist in the Gospel Tradition* (Cambridge: Cambridge University Press, 1968), 87-106; R. Webb, *John the Baptizer and Prophet: A Socio-historical Study* (Sheffield: JSOT Press, 1991), 70-77.

32. John's unique chronology places Jesus' crucifixion during the time at which the Passover lambs were sacrificed in Jerusalem; their last meal is thus not a Passover supper in John. It was also essential that the Passover sacrifice had no broken bones (Exod 12:46; Num 9:12).

of God with the promise of eternal, abundant life (John 1:4; 3:15-16, 36, et al., occurring fifty times). Eternal life begins with the believer's adoption into the divine family (1:12-13), effected by the Holy Spirit (3:3-8).[33] Disciples enjoy a spiritual "union" or "oneness" with the Father and the Son, participating in their eternal, divine life here and now. Jesus says, "On that day you will know that I am in my Father, and you in me, and I in you. . . . My Father will love [those who keep Jesus' word], and we will come to them and make our home with them" (14:20-23; also see 17:20-26).[34] This personal, mystical union of the believer within the life of the Father and the Son through the Spirit is what the Johannine Jesus refers to when promising his disciples abundant life (10:10). The principal means of demonstrating one's eternal, abundant life in this world is to obey Jesus' commands (13:34-35; 14:15, 21, 23-24; 15:10, 14, 17, 20; 17:6).

Polemical

A fifth purpose in writing the Gospel of John was polemical, possibly to address the community's conflicts with Judaism. At some point in the Johannine community's history, it seems that believers were "put out of the synagogue[s]" (John 9:22; 12:42; 16:2).[35] This expulsion of Jewish

33. M. Vellanickal, *The Divine Sonship of Christians in the Johannine Writings* (Rome: Biblical Institute Press, 1977); M. Appold, *The Oneness Motif in the Fourth Gospel* (Tübingen: Mohr Siebeck, 1976); J. Kanagaraj, *"Mysticism" in the Gospel of John* (Sheffield: Sheffield Academic Press, 1998).

34. For a more extensive discussion, see D. Crump, "Re-examining the Johannine Trinity: Perichoresis or Deification?" *SJT* 59 (2006): 395-412.

35. See the classic presentation of this view in Martyn, *History and Theology in the Fourth Gospel*. R. Kysar outlines the growing criticisms of this theory in "The Expulsion from the Synagogue: The Tale of a Theory," in *Voyages with John: Charting the Fourth Gospel* (Waco, Tex.: Baylor University Press, 2005), 237-45. The date and relevance of the Twelfth Benediction (the *birkat ha-minim/Nazarim*), expelling heretics, including Jewish Christians, from the synagogue continue to be debated; see D. Instone-Brewer, *Prayer and Agriculture* (vol. 1 of *Traditions of the Rabbis from the Era of the NT;* Grand Rapids: Eerdmans, 2004), 104, 108-17, who argues that "the curse of the *Nazarim* was added not long before 70 CE" (115). For a diversity of opinion, see R. Kimelman, "Birkat Ha-Minim and the Lack of Evidence for an Anti-Christian Jewish Prayer in Late Antiquity," in *Aspects of Judaism in the Graeco-Roman Period* (vol. 2 of *Jewish and Christian Self-Definition;* ed E. Sanders et al.; Philadelphia: Fortress, 1981), 226-44; W. Horbury, "The Benediction of the *Minim* and Early Jewish-Christian Controversy," *JTS,* n.s., 33 (1982): 19-61; S. Katz, "Issues in the Separation of Judaism and Christianity after 70 CE:

Christians from their own places of worship may have been the result of disputes over Jesus' divine status (5:16-18; 8:58-59) and violations of Jewish customs (5:16; 7:19, 22-24). Consequently, John gives an inordinate amount of attention to "the Jews" in his gospel (approximately seventy references, as compared with six in Mark and five each in Matthew and Luke), most of it negative. Since the majority of these references describe the Jews as enemies of Jesus (e.g., 5:16, 18; 6:41), some readers of the gospel have accused John of anti-Semitism.[36] Such a verdict, however, is unfair to the complexity of both John's gospel and the situation in which it arose.

First, as with many other Johannine terms, "the Jews" is used in several different ways: neutrally, to describe an ethnic/religious group (2:6); positively, to designate the actual and potential believers in Jesus (4:22; 8:31); and negatively, of Jesus' opponents (5:16, 18; 6:41), who are often identified with the Pharisees. These observations alone blunt the harsher charges of Johannine anti-Semitism.

Furthermore, it is crucial to remember that John's gospel was written to be read on multiple levels. In this case, there is (1) a historical level on which Pharisaic and priestly opponents conspired to eliminate Jesus and have him crucified, but there is also (2) a literary level directed at the Johannine community (and subsequent readers) enduring persistent opposition of their own. Jesus' Jewish followers may have faced expulsion from their synagogues.

John's gospel straddles the historic turning point when Jewish-Christians must begin to choose one religious identification or the other; it seems that they can no longer be both. The real issue is not that John is anti-Semitic but that, like the OT prophets before him, he is convinced that the Jewish *establishment* has once again missed out on the true work of God among them.

A Reconsideration," *JBL* 103 (1984): 43-76; and W. McCready, "Johannine Self-Understanding and the Synagogue Episode of John 9," in *Self-Definition and Self-Discovery in Early Christianity* (ed. D. Haudin and T. Robinson; Lewiston, N.Y.: E. Mellen Press, 1990), 147-66.

36. For a historical and theological discussion, see R. Bieringer et al., eds., *Anti-Judaism and the Fourth Gospel* (Louisville, Ky.: Westminster John Knox, 2001); and R. Kysar, "Anti-Semitism and the Gospel of John," in *Voyages with John*, 147-59.

The Authorship of John

Some of the evidence bearing on questions of authorship was touched on above in "The Process of Composition." Now that the contents of the gospel have been explored, we are in a better position to address the historical questions more directly.

Internal Evidence

In chapters 1–20 the author of the gospel is not identified, although it is implied that he is an eyewitness ("lived among us, . . . we have seen his glory," 1:14). In the second half of the gospel we are introduced to the disciple "whom Jesus loved" (13:23-25; 19:26-27; 20:2-8), but his identity is not stated. The beloved disciple is probably the "other disciple" who was known to the high priest (18:15-16), and possibly the unnamed disciple of John the Baptist who followed Jesus (1:35-40). The reference to the testimony of an eyewitness (19:35) probably refers also to the beloved disciple.

John 21, a later supplement, includes the beloved disciple in Jesus' postresurrection appearance in Galilee (vv. 7, 20-24). His death is presupposed in the discussion about the disciple's remaining alive until the Lord's return (vv. 22-23). In v. 24 there is explicit mention that the beloved disciple was an eyewitness of these things (narrated in the gospel) and that he either wrote or caused these things to be written (does 19:22 reflect also the author's convictions?). Since it is unlikely that any disciple would have had the audacity to call himself the one Jesus loved most, it is likely that this term of endearment is additional evidence of the community's hand in shaping John's final contours (as some scholars have argued).

External Evidence

The external evidence identifies the beloved disciple as John the son of Zebedee, who wrote the Fourth Gospel from Ephesus. The earliest tradition comes from Irenaeus, bishop of Lyons, in Gaul (ca. 180). He stated that John, the Lord's disciple, published the gospel in Ephesus and remained there until Trajan's time (98-117).[37] Irenaeus also specified that this

---

37. Irenaeus, *Against Heresies* 2.22.5; 3.3.4; also cited in Eusebius, *Hist. eccl.* 3.23.3-4.

disciple John was the one who reclined on the Lord's chest (13:24-25).[38] The source of Irenaeus's authority is attributed to Polycarp and Papias, both of whom claimed to have known John and learned from the apostles.[39] In Irenaeus's letter to his boyhood friend Florinus, he writes of their early acquaintance with Polycarp and of Florinus's remembrances of discussions with John and others who had seen the Lord.[40] Both contemporary and later traditions — including the *Acts of John* (ca. 150) and writings of Polycrates (ca. 190) and Clement of Alexandria (ca. 200) — support the position of Irenaeus.[41]

Arguments against Johannine/Apostolic Authorship

A number of problems arise, however, in ascribing the authorship of the Fourth Gospel to John the apostle in Ephesus. First, there is no corroborating evidence before the mid-second century of the apostle John's residence in Ephesus. Revelation was written by a person named John on Patmos near Miletus (Rev 1:4, 9), but he seems to distinguish himself from the apostles (e.g., 18:20; 21:14). Even though some similarities between Revelation and John may indicate ties between the Apocalypse and the Johannine community, their theological and eschatological differences argue against authorship by the same person.[42] In Paul's speech to the Ephesian elders at Miletus in Acts 20:18-35, no reference to John is made. In Ignatius's letter to

---

38. Irenaeus, *Against Heresies* 3.1.1; Eusebius, *Hist. eccl.* 5.8.4.

39. Irenaeus, *Against Heresies* 3.3.4; Eusebius, *Hist. eccl.* 3.39.1-4; 4.14.3-8. Two related ambiguities, however, surround Irenaeus's testimony. First, he seems to assume that Polycarp and Papias are always referring to the same individual, which is not self-evident. Second, it is not always clear, especially in the Papias material, whether the John under discussion is the apostle or another John called "the elder." See the section "Arguments against Johannine/Apostolic Authorship."

40. Eusebius, *Hist. eccl.* 5.20.4-8.

41. *Acts of John*, in E. Hennecke, *NT Apocrypha* (ed. W. Schneemelcher; 2 vols.; Philadelphia: Westminster Press, 1963-66), 2:215-58; Polycrates, in Eusebius, *Hist. eccl.* 3.31.3, 5.24.2-3; and Clement of Alexandria, in *Hist. eccl.* 3.23.6-19.

42. R. H. Charles, *A Critical and Exegetical Commentary on the Revelation of St. John* (2 vols.; ICC; Edinburgh: T&T Clark, 1920), 1:xxixff; L. Vos, *The Synoptic Traditions in the Apocalypse* (Kampen: J. H. Kok, 1965); D. Aune, *Revelation 1–5* (WBC 52A; Dallas: Word Books, 1997), xlviii-lvi. Eusebius suggested that the gospel was written by the apostle and Revelation was written by the elder (*Hist. eccl.* 3.39.6).

the Ephesians (ca. 110) there is no allusion to John's residence there. Neither does Polycarp say anything about John in his letter to the Philippians (ca. 135), despite their alleged association. It should be noted, however, that 1 Peter makes no reference to Paul, even though the letter addresses churches within Paul's mission field.

Second, to complicate further the identity of John, 2 and 3 John and Papias refer to John the elder, who appears to be distinct from John the apostle. In the Papias tradition, the apostle John is distinguished from the elder John, although both are called disciples of the Lord. Eusebius himself observes, "It is proper to notice that the name of John was mentioned twice, [one of whom] was not ranked among the apostles. . . . So it was here proved that there were two men of the same name in Asia."[43] Furthermore, Papias claims to have been a student of John the elder, not John the apostle.

Third, certain NT data raise doubts about ascribing the authorship of the Fourth Gospel to John, the son of Zebedee. All the events in which John of Zebedee had a decisive role are omitted (e.g., Mark 1:19-20, 29; 3:13-19; 5:37; 9:2-8; 10:35-41; 14:32-34), although this could say more about the author's self-restraint than about his identity. John's brother, James, is never mentioned. Even though the sons of Zebedee were Galileans, the Fourth Gospel displays no particular interest in Galilee. Finally, both sons of Zebedee may have been martyred around the same time in A.D. 62.[44]

Conclusions on Authorship Questions

Concerning the authorship of the Fourth Gospel. we conclude that (1) the final editor of the Fourth Gospel was an unknown member of the Johannine community; (2) this community was founded by the "beloved disciple," who the final editor believed was an eyewitness of Jesus; some of the Jesus-sayings and early material may also have been attributed to him; and (3) this beloved disciple was probably not one of the so-called twelve apostles.[45]

43. Papias is first quoted and then commented upon in Eusebius, *Hist. eccl.* 3.39.3-4. See discussion in Bauckham, *Jesus and the Eyewitnesses*, 15-21.

44. Note the prediction in Mark 10:39 and the death of James of Zebedee in Acts 12:2. The tradition of both Zebedees being martyred is ascribed to Papias by Philip of Side in A.D. 430; see C. K. Barrett, *The Gospel according to St. John* (2d ed.; London: SPCK, 1978), 103.

45. Brown, *The Community of the Beloved Disciple*, 22-24, 31-34. Bauckham argues that

The Place of Composition

As we have shown, the external evidence is late and questionable for maintaining that Ephesus was the place of writing the Fourth Gospel. However, parallels between John and Revelation (written from Patmos, in Asia), common antisynagogue motifs (John 9:22; 12:42; Rev 2:9; 3:9), and the presence of a baptist sect in Ephesus (John 1:35-51; Acts 19:1-7) are internal evidence for Ephesus as the place of writing.

Some have argued for Alexandria, Egypt, as John's setting, since our earliest Greek papyri of John are found there, and the Fourth Gospel shares *some* common conceptions with Philo, the Hermetic writings, and the Nag Hammadi codices.[46] Given the Hellenization process that followed Alexander the Great, however, similar conceptions could just as easily be found in Asia Minor.[47]

Finally, it has been argued that John originated in Syria near Palestine for the following reasons. First, Ignatius of Syrian Antioch (ca. 110) was acquainted with certain Johannine themes.[48] John's gospel shares over one dozen themes with the *Odes of Solomon,* which probably originated from Syria (ca. 200). The *Gospel of Thomas,* probably of Syrian origin (ca. 100), is also familiar with Johannine thought (*Gos. Thom.* 77 / John 8:12; *Gos. Thom.* 108 / John 7:38; *Gos. Thom.* 28). In addition, John's affinities with the Dead Sea Scrolls (modified dualism, unity and community, antitemple bias) argue for a setting in or near Palestine.[49]

John the Elder (not the son of Zebedee) is the beloved disciple and the author of the Fourth Gospel, *Jesus and the Eyewitnesses,* 420-37.

46. Dodd, *The Interpretation of the Fourth Gospel,* 10-73, 97-130; J. M. Robinson, ed., *The Nag Hammadi Library in English* (3d ed.; San Francisco: Harper & Row, 1988); Brown, *An Introduction to the Gospel of John,* 115-32. The Egyptian papyri are discussed in "The Date," the following section of this chapter.

47. See several important works by M. Hengel: *Judaism and Hellenism: Studies in Their Encounter in Palestine during the Early Hellenistic Period* (trans. J. Bowden; London: SCM Press, 1974); *Jews, Greeks, and Barbarians: Aspects of the Hellenization of Judaism in the Pre-Christian Period* (Philadelphia: Fortress, 1980); and *The "Hellenization" of Judea in the First Century after Christ* (Philadelphia: Trinity Press International, 1989).

48. Jesus came in the flesh (Ign. *Trall.* 10); Christianity has superseded Judaism (Ign. *Magn.* 8.1); Christ is the Word of God (Ign. *Magn.* 8.2).

49. See A. DuToit, ed., *Essays on the Jewish Background of the Fourth Gospel* (Neotestamentica 6; Pretoria, 1973); J. Charlesworth, ed., *John and the Dead Sea Scrolls* (New York: Crossroad, 1990).

Furthermore, the Fourth Gospel is acquainted with Palestinian customs (2:6; 5:10; 7:21-23, 27; 9:31-41) and geography (1:28; 2:1; 3:23; 4:5, 21, 46; 6:1; 9:7; 11:54), but the author seems outside the jurisdiction of the Jerusalem authorities (9:22; 12:42; 16:2-3). Also, Jesus' early concern for the Samaritan woman (4:4-30), the accusation that he is a Samaritan (8:48), and references to John the baptizer's activity "across the Jordan" (1:28; 3:26; 10:40-41) may indicate a setting in or near Palestine.[50] At this point, it is difficult to decide between a Palestinian or an Ephesian provenance; however, we favor a Syrian or Palestinian setting for John, although it is likely that members of the Johannine community (Rev 1:4, 9) had migrated to the province of Asia.

The Date

The date for John can be fixed within a definite time span. The latest possible date is the early second century because of two papyrus fragments: Papyrus 52 and Papyrus Egerton 2. Papyrus 52 (Rylands 457 of Manchester), the oldest fragment of the NT (early second century), contains parts of John 18:31-33, 37-38. Papyrus Egerton 2 ("unknown gospel"), which contains many Johannine themes, is also dated around the early second century. Both fragments were discovered in Egypt.

Certain considerations favor a dating for John in the late first century. First, it has been shown that the author was probably acquainted with Mark and possibly Luke, although he did not follow them closely.[51] Second, the Fourth Gospel may imply a situation after A.D. 70, since reference appears to be made to the temple's destruction (may imply "destroy," 2:19-20; esp. 11:48). Third, the gospel responds to the delay of the parousia by reemphasizing many of the future hopes as present realities (3:17-19, 36; 5:24; 6:40; 11:25-26; 12:31). Finally, the Fourth Evangelist's attitude toward "the Jews" and "their feasts" (e.g., 5:1; 6:4; 7:2; 8:44; 12:37-40), combined with the leaders' threats of excluding disciples from the synagogue (9:22; 12:42; 16:2), seems to presuppose a separation between the church and synagogue characteristic of the late first century.

50. O. Cullmann mounts a compelling argument for John's Samaritan connections in *The Johannine Circle: Its Place in Judaism, among the Disciples of Jesus, and in Early Christianity; A Study in the Origin of the Gospel of John* (trans. J. Bowden; London: SCM Press, 1976).

51. See "John and the Synoptics" at the beginning of this chapter, as well as the relevant sections on chs. 3 and 6 on dating Mark and Luke.

Summary

Our responses to the opening questions about John's gospel can be summarized by the following statements. First, the author of John has some acquaintance with Synoptic traditions and probably used Mark or pre-Markan traditions; he may even have used Luke or traditions similar to those used in Luke's gospel. Second, the sources of John's gospel may have consisted of Synoptic-type Jesus-sayings (e.g., 3:6, 8, 11), sayings parallel to the Synoptic tradition (1:51; 12:25; 13:20), and Synoptic stories (e.g., cleansing of the temple, anointing of Jesus, feeding and sea miracles, Peter's denial). Third, the gospel contains a number of disjunctions, or breaks in the narrative sequence (4:43; 5:1; 6:1), which may often reflect the author's own literary techniques and redactions but which seem to signify a process of development in its composition (John 21; much of 1:1-18).

Fourth, the author has a limited vocabulary, but his preference for the abstract and perceptual (e.g., truth, light, life, love, belief) gives his book a dramatic and philosophical tone. Fifth, the author's use of misunderstanding (e.g., 3:4, 9; 4:11-12, 15; 11:11-12) and irony (4:12; 7:35; 8:37; 11:48, 50) serves a dramatic function in the gospel. Sixth, the gospel's use of Hebrew symbols and parallelism gives it a strong Semitic flavor.

Seventh, the structure of John can be outlined as "Introduction" (ch. 1); "Revelation to the World" (chs. 2–12), with a turning point at 12:20-26; and "Revelation to Disciples of Jesus' Glory" (chs. 13–20), with an epilogue (ch. 21). Eighth, affirming Jesus Christ as the preexistent Son of God, encouraging Christians to continue in the faith, reminding them of the present benefits of their future hopes, and addressing the problem of Jewish rejection are at least four reasons for the writing of John's gospel. Ninth, the departed community founder had been an eyewitness of Jesus (but probably was not John, the son of Zebedee). Chapter 21 was probably added after the founder's death by other members of the Johannine community, who then renamed him "the beloved disciple."

Tenth, the Fourth Gospel may have been written in the late first century ($\mathfrak{p}$52) in the Syria-Palestine area. This conclusion rests upon the gospel's familiarity with that locale and its affinities with the literature of that region (e.g., Qumran, *Gospel of Thomas, Odes of Solomon,* and the writings of Ignatius of Antioch).

Name Index

Meltzer, E. S., 57
Mendenhall, G. E., 25
Menzies, R. P., 136
Merlan, P., 13
Metzger, B. M., 86
Meye, R. P., 86
Meyer, M., 9
Meyer, R., 33
Meyers, E., 29
Miesner, D. R., 113, 115
Millar, F., 14
Miller, J., 17
Miller, J. M., 17
Miller, R. J., 141
Moessner, D. P., 117, 119, 139, 141
Moffatt, J., 161
Mohrlang, R., 98
Moore, S. D., 68
Morgenthaler, R., 164
Mosser, C., 172
Moule, C. F. D., 86
Mounce, R. H., 104

Navone, J. J., 121
Neirynck, F., 54, 92
Neufeld, V. H., 63
Neusner, J., 24, 28, 32, 33
Neville, D. J., 50
Neyrey, J., 26, 106, 138
Nickelsburg, G. W. E., 32
Nicol, W., 158, 167
Niebuhr, B. G., 44
Nineham, D. E., 85, 87
Nock, A. N., 12
Nolland, J., 104, 151
Nordern, E., 58

Oegema, G., 30
Olrik, K., 111
O'Neill, J. C., 123, 142
Orton, D. E., 54
Osborne, G. R., 43
O'Toole, R. F., 111, 116, 117, 118, 130, 134, 135, 142

Overman, J. A., 103

Parsons, M. C., 122
Patte, D., 68
Pearson, B., 10
Penney, J. M., 136
Perkins, P., 10, 91
Perowne, S., 21, 22
Perrin, N., 61, 64, 73, 75, 78, 83, 85, 156
Perro, R. I., 149
Petersen, N. R., 68
Peterson, D., 130
Pilch, J., 60
Plümacher, E., 119
Plummer, A., 104
Pomykala, K., 30
Porter, S. E., 25, 43, 68, 108
Powell, M. A., 68
Praeder, S. M., 112
Prickett, S., 68
Przyblyski, B., 98
Puskas, C. B., 131, 134, 168

Rackham, R. B., 113
Rahlfs, A., 47
Räisänen, H., 80
Rajak, T., 17
Ramsay, W. M., 108
Ravens, D., 130, 139
Reicke, B., 50, 82, 89, 106
Reid, B. E., 138
Rhoads, D. M., 22
Richards, K. H., 26
Richardson, P., 21
Riches, J., 99, 100, 103
Riesenfeld, H., 58, 61
Rist, J. M., 13
Robinson, J. A. T., 82, 85, 86
Robinson, J. M., 10, 52, 179
Robinson, T., 175
Robinson, W. C., 121
Roetzel, C. J., 63
Rohde, J., 64, 76
Rohrbaugh, R., 26, 99

Subject Index

Albinus of Smyrna, 13
Alexander Jannaeus, 20-21
Alexander the Great, 1-2, 3, 179
Antigonus, 3
Antioch of Syria, 102-3
Antiochus IV Epiphanes, 18-19, 26, 82
Antoninus Pius, 6
Apocalyptic eschatology, 30-31
Apollonius of Tyana, 12, 40-41
Archelaus (son of Herod), 22
Arrian of Bithynia, 2
Astrology, 8
Augustus Caesar, 4, 8, 21

Babylonian Exile, 16-18

Caligula, Gaius, 5, 6, 22
Cassander, 3
Chiasms: in John, 166-67; in Luke-Acts, 113-15
Claudius, 5, 144
Clement of Alexandria, 13, 100, 177
Constantine, 6
Conversion experience and Hellenistic philosophy, 12

Dead Sea Scrolls, 20, 28, 31, 34-35, 46, 179
Decius, 6

Diaspora Judaism: after Second Jewish Revolt, 24; and Hellenistic Judaism, 14, 17
Dio Cassius, 3, 5, 24, 144
Diodorus of Sicily, 2
Domitian, 5, 6

Eschatology: apocalyptic, 30-31; and John's gospel, 172; and Josephus, 82; Mark's theme, 82-83
Essenes, 20, 34-35; and apocalyptic eschatology, 30-31; and study of the law, 28. *See also* Dead Sea Scrolls
Eusebius: and authorship of John, 177, 178; and authorship of Matthew, 100; on Mark, 60; and oral traditions, 40
Ezra, 18

Felix, 22
Festus, 22
First Jewish Revolt (66-70), 22-24, 143; and Flavian dynasty, 5; and Matthew, 102; and the Zealots, 35
Flavian dynasty, 5
Florinus, 177
Florus, Gessius, 22
Form criticism, 55-63; basic features of literary forms (five characteristics), 56-58; Mark's miracle story of heal-

Scripture Index

195